Celebrate!
West Hartford

An Illustrated History

Miriam Butterworth, Ellsworth Grant and Richard Woodworth

Published by Celebrate West Hartford, LLC., West Hartford, Connecticut, 06117
Christopher Larsen, Managing Partner

The partners of Celebrate West Hartford, LLC, are Miriam Butterworth, John E.Davison, Ellsworth S. Grant, and Richard M. Woodworth.

The publishers wish to acknowledge the Noah Webster House/Historical Society of West Hartford for the support made possible through the generosity of the Gordon Bennett Trust.

The publishers also acknowledge the support of the Town of West Hartford.

Cover photo by Gregory Kriss
Cover design by Christopher Larsen

Book design by Richard M. Woodworth

Printed by Wolf Printing Co., Inc., West Hartford, Connecticut 06110

ISBN 0-9711-962-0-6

CELEBRATE! WEST HARTFORD
An Illustrated History
Miriam Butterworth, Ellsworth S. Grant, and Richard M. Woodworth
192 pp., includes index

First printing September 2001

Contents

I am pleased and very proud to introduce the reader to this important, informative book about the West Hartford community. This pictorial history is the story of our town from its beginning days to modern times, with an emphasis on the last 50 years.

There are many individuals who share in the credit of its production. To list all who have contributed would be a daunting task, but special credit must be given to former mayor Nan Glass who had the foresight to commission this history. Also special recognition must be given to Chris Larsen who provided that extra ounce of help when it was most needed, and Dick Woodworth, Mims Butterworth, and Ellsworth Grant, who by their intellect and special love and devotion to West Hartford have made this book possible.

Happy reading!

Robert Bouvier
Mayor
Autumn 2001

TOWN OF WEST HARTFORD

TOWN OF WEST HARTFORD   50 SOUTH MAIN STREET
WEST HARTFORD, CONNECTICUT   06107-2431
(860) 523-3142   FAX: (860) 523-3522
www.west-hartford.com

Authors' Foreword

In anticipation of the town's Sesquicentennial in 2004, then-mayor Nan Lewis Glass "commissioned" the authors to produce a pictorial history of West Hartford. This book is the result.

It is an illustrated history, a retrospective of the 150 years since the West Division separated from Hartford in 1854. The emphasis is on the last 100 years, particularly the last 50 years – a period not covered by any other history.

In fact, this history has only three predecessors: William H. Hall's definitive *West Hartford,* published in 1930; *The West Hartford Story,* published by Richard N. Boulton and Bice Clemow for the town's Centennial in 1954, and Nelson R. Burr's *From Colonial Parish to Modern Suburb: A Brief Appreciation of West Hartford,* published in 1976 for the U.S. Bicentennial.

More than the others, this is a popular, even populist, history. We have given short shrift to some of the historic icons of old in favor of illustrating more recent trends and personages. This book is not for the scholar but rather for the layman, the citizen who lives in West Hartford or has ties to the town and wants to know how it came to be. It is a broad-brush history embellished with specifics and nuances to make West Hartford and its story come alive.

Although the authors share a common bond – our town of residence – we come at this task from different perspectives. Mims Butterworth moved by marriage from Windsor to West Hartford, where she became a Democratic activist, served on the Town Council and on state commissions, and is town historian. Ellsworth Grant is a town native and former Republican mayor, past president of the Connecticut Historical Society, and has written 20 histories of Connecticut places and institutions. Dick Woodworth moved to West Hartford to become editor of the West Hartford News and stayed to make it the base for his travel book publishing business. All three are current or past trustees of the Noah Webster Foundation and Historical Society of West Hartford.

The authors also share a common cause: to celebrate the history and the people, the attributes and the variety that make up this great, multi-faceted town of 61,000 people. We know of no other town quite like it – so large, diverse and blessed a suburb of a state capital and financial center. It is a bedroom suburb for some, a self-contained small city for many, and a home for all.

Although we have tried to detail people, groups, and institutions of historic significance and interest throughout West Hartford, it is inevitable in a town of so many facets and so many people that some will be slighted. We trust any lapses are of omission rather than commission.

We have relied on input from many people and groups, but none more than Nan Glass. Her perspective as town native, journalist, mayor, and town clerk is evident throughout this work. Special mention is also due Christopher Larsen for spearheading the partnership that funded this effort.

As the book evolved, we were struck by how recent West Hartford's history really is. We date officially to 1854 as a town, and go back to 1636 as a settlement. Yet West Hartford was still essentially a farming community of 3,000 hardy souls at the start of the 20th century, the threshold of its development.

The new century saw a spurt of residential and commercial construction that would change forever the old farmlands on the East and South sides. Two world wars and the Great Depression barely slowed the growth.

Fifty years ago, when the town celebrated its Centennial, development was at its height. Yet fully half the schools, churches, and synagogues were still to come. The West and North ends were no longer to be farmlands. The Center was becoming a true center. Bishops Corner, Corbins Corner, and Westfarms Mall were barely dreams in developers' eyes. Hall High (the elder) was only three decades old. Conard High, Northwest Catholic, and the University of Hartford had not been started. Telephones were in the ADams and JAckson exchanges, and the postal code was West Hartford 7, Conn. Black and white television was showing test patterns and cartoons, and broadcaster Bob Steele soothed talk with music, "real" music.

At the turn of the 21st century, a mere 50 years later, West Hartford – like life and the world – is very different. The biggest building boom yet left the town almost fully developed by 1970. Like the population, the town has matured. The Computer Age drives us. We work and live by technology. Still, this is a community of neighborhoods in the town that cares. We preserve our heritage, while we prepare for the future.

As the town's sesquicentennial approaches, we pause to celebrate. This town has a short but spirited history. We the people have helped make that history, and we are still making it. As West Hartford's history continues to unfold, it becomes increasingly clear just how wonderful a town this is. We have much to celebrate.

Miriam Butterworth, Ellsworth Grant,
and Richard Woodworth

West Hartford began as a community of farms, and this photo probably conveys more flavor of life here in the 1870s than any still existing. View is of the Ellsworth house and farm at South Main Street and Pelham Road looking northwest toward Talcott Mountain. South Main runs across the foreground. In the center is the old West Hartford Omnibus, which ran back and forth to the city from about 1850 to the 1890s, when it was supplanted by the horse-drawn railway and then trolleys.

I. Prologue: The West Division

How We Got Here

At the start of Connecticut's colonial history, the town we know as West Hartford was not a part of the plan laid out by Hartford's early English settlers.

The original boundaries of Hartford, the colony founded along the Connecticut River in 1636 by the Congregational minister Thomas Hooker, extended "from the Great River on the east, the whole breadth to run into the wilderness towards the west full six miles, which is to the place where the Hartford and Farmington bounds meet."

In 1675, the 97 proprietors who had acquired all the land between Quaker Lane and Mountain Road – 5,154 acres – divided it into 72 "long lots." The proprietors included many who would become settlers and leaders of a new community.

For some years nobody had dared move very far from fortified settlements because of the danger of Indian attacks. The final and most serious Indian uprising in New England was led by the Wampanoag sachem, Metacomet, called King Philip by the English settlers. He rallied his tribal allies in 1675 for a last desperate stand against the steady advance of the colonists. King

Philip's War took place mainly in Massachusetts, but ranged as far north as Maine and south into Connecticut. Even the nearby town of Simsbury was raided and burned. The war ended in 1676, a little over a year after it started, when King Philip was killed in an ambush. The way was now clear for the proprietors of the 72 long lots to make use of their western land.

Stephen Hosmer was the first to venture west from the original Connecticut River settlement. His father, Thomas, a follower of Hooker and a large landowner along the river, acquired some 300 acres near what is now West Hartford Center. In 1679, he built the first commercial enterprise in the western section of Hartford, a dam and sawmill for his son Stephen, near where North Main Street crosses Trout Brook.

Other pioneers, finding the land fertile, built homes about midway in their long lots on the ridge west of Trout Brook and the seeds of a community were planted. By 1709, when they petitioned the General Assembly of Connecticut for a separate Congregational parish, 34 houses and 164 people occupied the area. Their petition claimed that "a good part of God's time is spent traveling backwards and forwards, which if otherwise we might spend in his service to our comfort." They were granted their wish a year later, and the "Fourth Church of Hartford" was organized in 1713. Its first meetinghouse was located on North Main Street just north of Farmington Avenue. For more than a century, Hartford's Fourth Church parish was the center of vital communal activities, dominating the religious, educational, and political life of what was then called the West Division of Hartford.

West Hartford Historical Society Photo

Hartford Times Photo

Founding settler Thomas Hosmer built the first dam on Trout Brook in 1678, just west of North Main Street in the midst of his family's 1,200 acres in the area that is now known as Wyndwood Road. Beside it rose his son Stephen's sawmill, the first commercial enterprise in the West Division. Photo at left shows houses fronting on Millwood Pond in 1954.

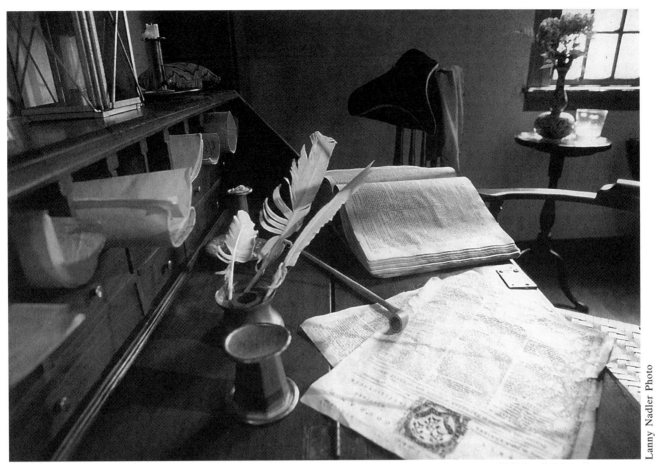

Noah Webster's desk is the only original furnishing from his boyhood home, now a museum at 227 South Main St.

Lanny Nadler Photo

Noah Webster: Shaper of Language and of the Republic

The town's most famous native son began life in a small saltbox-style house on South Main Street. He was tutored by the Rev. Nathan Perkins of the Fourth Church parish and went on to Yale. Known as the man who Americanized the English language, he wrote two of the most influential books in American history.

His *Blue-Backed Speller,* published in 1783, was not only a speller but also a grammar text and a reader that settlers carried across the continent, standardizing the language and helping to create a sense of cultural unity throughout the developing country.

Income from the best-seller helped support his decades of work writing entirely by hand the monumental, 20,000-page *American Dictionary of the English Language.* When he finished the last of 70,000 words in 1825 at age 67, he was

"seized with a trembling" – he did not know whether it was because he might not live to finish or because he was so near the end of his labors.

He also wrote numerous textbooks and treatises, some of which helped set up the Federalist republic. He was a confidante of George Washington, Alexander Hamilton, and other Founding Fathers, and many of his ideas helped shape the early nation. He was largely responsible for the country's first copyright laws and was instrumental in the founding of Amherst College.

He lived in the West Division until he was 16 and frequently returned to the West Division to visit his parents, Mercy Steele and Noah Webster Sr. For a time he even settled here to practice law. His birthplace is now the Noah Webster House and Museum of West Hartford History.

Lemuel Haynes was born in the West Division in 1753. His father was African and his mother a member of a prominent white family. His white grandfather sent the mulatto infant to Granville, Mass., where he was raised by a pious deacon and his wife in their family of five children. He received a good education and proved to be an outstanding scholar. He eventually became a widely respected Congregational minister and was the first black in New England to preach regularly to white congregations.

Where We Live

Mountain Road was originally the West Division's western boundary. But because the farmers on the east side of Talcott Mountain found it convenient to attend church in the West Division, the state legislature in 1830 took from Farmington and added to the West Division all the territory west of Mountain Road to the top of Talcott Mountain.

A boundary dispute long raged between Farmington and the West Division. Noah Webster Sr., then a West Division justice of the peace, added to the arguments when he affixed his signature to a deed conveying to Joseph Selden a home on Great Hill near what became Farmington Avenue, property that was not inside the West Division's territory. Selden had come from East Haddam to the West Division around 1793. As he acquired more land and prospered as a farmer, he and his descendants fought to have their property, then called Selden Hill, included in the Fourth Church parish. Finally, in 1859, the newly formed town of West Hartford annexed from Farmington the Selden Hill area and at

the same time acquired the West Hartford Common, pasture land between Quaker Lane and Prospect Avenue that had been set aside in 1674 "for the use of all the people."

By the Civil War, West Hartford had reached its present size of 22.4 square miles. Townspeople finally appeared satisfied that the town had reached its appropriate boundaries.

Who We Were

The community grew slowly. The first U.S. Census of 1790 showed only 124 families and fewer than 1,000 inhabitants in the West Division. Most shared not only a common Puritan faith but also an Anglo-Saxon ancestry. Other than native Americans, the only other sizable group was African slaves, who made up about 2 percent of Hartford's population in colonial days. The colonies had legalized slavery in the 1640s and at least 20 West Division families owned slaves.

The first pastor of the Fourth Church, the Rev. Benjamin Colton, who presided over the parish and settlement for 46 years from 1713 to 1759, owned a slave, Chris, who did much of his master's farming while the minister wrote his sermons and took care of his parishioners. Several of the wealthiest men in the West Division, such as John Whiting, Stephen Hosmer, Thomas Hart Hooker, and Samuel Whitman, owned as many as eight or nine slaves. The rest of the owners had one or two men, skilled or semi-skilled, to help with the kind of diversified agriculture and small business enterprises indigenous to the area.

Our town, like the rest of Connecticut, was governed as a theocracy until 1818. Church and state were practically synonymous – and that church was Congregational. It controlled the government, everyone was taxed to support the church, and its teachings prevailed in the schools. No other religions were allowed. Only "freemen," landowners who had been formally accepted by the General Court and were usually leaders in the church, could vote or be magistrates of the Commonwealth of Connecticut. Another rank, called "inhabitants," men of some property who were approved by a majority of their peers, could vote on local matters. Everyone else – women, children, non-Congregationalists, and slaves – were "residents" and non-participants. These political

The Sarah Whitman Hooker House billeted British prisoners during the Revolution. The arrangement proved satisfactory for the young widow, whose husband was killed in the siege of Boston. She became the town's first recorded innkeeper, maintaining her house as the Sheaf of Wheat Tavern, one of what was eventually many taverns and inns in the West Division. Restored by the West Hartford Bicentennial Trust and the Daughters of the American Revolution under the leadership of Frances Fransson of Dodge Drive, the historic homestead is now a house museum on New Britain Avenue just east of South Main Street. The property at right now houses an Asian restaurant.

and social systems prevailed for nearly two centuries before the town was officially established.

Another early pastor of the Fourth Church parish, the Rev. Nathan Perkins, was even more durable and influential than Colton. His pastorate spanned 66 years from 1772 through the turmoil of the Revolution until 1838. During the war, he drilled the militia on the church-owned green and fed the colonial troops from his own crops. A remarkable man, with a rare sense of humor and great physical strength, he was reputed to have preached more than 7,000 sermons. He also educated 150 West Division boys for college and 50 for the ministry. He helped establish the American Board of Foreign Missions and laid the cornerstone for the Hartford Theological Seminary. One of his first pupils was Noah Webster Jr.

What We Did

Agriculture and raising livestock were the West Division's chief occupations during the 18th and 19th centuries. By the time of the Revolution, the "wilderness" had become a prosperous farming and grazing community with many orchards, 1,920 plowed acres, 2,560 acres in meadow, and 3,200 in pasture. Cattle, Merino sheep, and horses were the main sources of wealth. Horses, cows, pigs, and oxen numbered in the hundreds and sheep in the thousands. Capt. Samuel Whitman, Col. Charles Wadsworth, and Timothy Seymour were early breeders of horses and mules, which attracted blacksmith and wheelwright shops. On Selden Hill, Edward Stanley and his son bred fine Devonshire cattle and pedigreed horses. Large harvests of apples and grain supported a surprising number of distilleries – five on Mountain Road and Still Road and two more on Fern Street and Gin Still Hill. In 1796, Timothy Dwight, the well-traveled president of Yale College, praised "the fertility of (the West Division's) soil, the pleasantness of its situation, the sobriety, industry, good order, and religious deportment of its inhabitants not, so far as I know, excelled in the state."

In the colonial period, the community's sawmills, gristmills, and blacksmith shops served mainly local needs. Taking advantage of the fine clay deposits in the southern section of the West Division, Ebenezer Faxon in 1770 started producing pottery, the first real industry. The pottery of the Goodwin family, also in the southern section, achieved regional fame. Beginning in 1798, Seth Goodwin and later his son, Thomas O'Hara Goodwin, made everything from flower pots to tableware and advertised their products as "Earthen Ware Manufactured in West Hartford, Conn." Clay also spawned a number of brickyards.

Schooling began soon after the West Division became a parish. The parish established school districts, and by 1780 the West Division had eight one-room schoolhouses, five of them spread along the length of Main Street. Total enrollment was about 200. The original model of a one-room, wood-heated frame schoolhouse lasted far into the 1800s. It had a "shelf-like desk around three sides, some backless benches, papered walls, window shades, a few pictures, a pair of small flags and scattered books," according to William Hall's *West Hartford*. Teachers "boarded around." Older boys, needed on the farms, attended only in winter. The eight school districts, which lasted into the 1860s, give an idea of the early residential clusters: Middle, South, South Middle, Northwest, North, West, Prospect Hill, and Commons (Flatbush Avenue).

We Catch the Spirit of Liberty

When the American Revolution began in 1775, the West Division responded with patriotic fervor. Like Connecticut as a whole, the parish did its part in

A Revolutionary War Campsite

West Hartford has a rare Revolutionary War treasure within its borders. The remains of about 200 horseshoe-shaped stone fireplaces can still be found in the woods on Talcott Mountain off Albany Avenue, where 1,000 of Gen. George Washington's troops under Gen. Israel Putnam camped for a week in 1778. The campground, once thought to have been built by the revolutionary French General Rochambeau, has been preserved because it is hidden in deep woods and is covered with leaves. Interested groups are working with the town to find the best way to protect this historic landmark while making it accessible to the public.

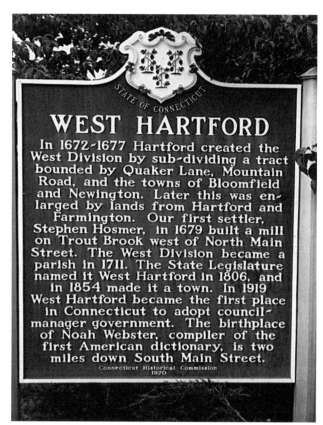

The town's start is detailed on an historic marker on Memorial Green at northwest corner of Farmington Avenue and North Main Street.

supplying the Continental forces with manpower as well as other resources. The new pastor, the Rev. Nathan Perkins, inspired many of his parishioners to enlist by preaching a rousing sermon that attacked the "British imperial policy as a threat to the New England way of life" and civil liberties.

One episode during the Revolution nearly resulted in bringing the armed conflict into the West Division. When Col. Philip Skene, considered a particularly dangerous Tory leader, was taken prisoner in 1775, Connecticut Governor Trumbull ordered Skene and his son to be billeted under house arrest with "suitable Lodgings & Entertainment in some remote Part of the City of Hartford." Sarah Whitman Hooker's comfortable home, an early tavern still standing on New Britain Avenue, was where the prisoners were held during most of 1775 and the winter of 1776. Their presence created unease among Mrs. Hooker's West Division neighbors. Colonel Skene liked to entertain and gave a party for Tory friends one January night shortly after the American army had been defeated in the attempt to

Early milk deliveries to residents of the West Division were by horse and buggy.

capture Quebec. Thinking the Tory prisoners were celebrating the defeat, about 20 armed men gathered at the Stanley house across the road, intending to attack the revelers. Capt. Abraham Sedgwick of the militia tried to persuade the patriots to desist, but Sarah Hooker, a 28-year-old widow with two young children, decided to talk to them, too. One of the Tory partygoers wrote in his diary, "the Woman of the House (who was greatly frighten'd) went over & at her return told us they were dispersed, thus ended this affair, happily without Blood Shed."

The spirit of freedom was in the air. The state legislature in Hartford abolished slave trading in 1774, and most West Division slaves were freed by the beginning of the Revolution. The 1790 census listed only three African American "servants" living in the West Division. There were also six free African Americans living with white families and eight free African American households. Sarah Hooker's husband, Thomas Hart Hooker, had allowed his slaves to buy their freedom before he fought and died in the seige of Boston. He is reputed to have said "he would not fight for liberty and leave a slave at home." But these sentiments did not cause him to turn down the 60 pounds his slave Bristol, 44 years old at the time, paid to be free. The freed servant gained such fame as an agricultural expert that he was consulted by farmers from miles around until his death in 1811 at age 83.

After the Revolution, Noah Webster began writing anti-slavery articles and in 1791 he helped found an early abolitionist group, the Connecticut Society for the Promotion of Freedom and the Relief of Persons Holden in Bondage. The change in attitudes toward slavery during and after the Revolution can be seen in the Sedgwick family. In 1774, The Hartford Courant published the following ad: "Run away from the subscriber of Hartford West-Division....a Molatto servant named Jude, about 21 years old....Twenty dollars reward...will be paid to any person who shall return such fellow to Stephen Sedgwick." Seven years later, Stephen Sedgwick's nephew, Theodore, served as lawyer for a Massachusetts woman, the first slave to sue her master for freedom. And in 1839, another Theodore Sedgwick was on the defense team representing the Mendes "mutineers" from the Amistad slave ship. The Amistad trial began in Hartford's State House, followed by the harboring of the freed Mendes by abolitionists in neighboring Farmington.

The Emerging Town and Nation

For more than half a century after the war ended, many West Division residents sought to become an independent township.

Fueled by the Revolution's fervor for liberty and equality, dissent grew as Europeans flocked to the new nation and its territory expanded. In Connecticut, a reform General Assembly in 1818 – responding to pressures from Jeffersonian Republicans as well as Baptists, Methodists, and Episcopalians – called for a constitutional convention.

The new constitution set most religions on an equal footing, although Jews were not granted equal privileges until 1843. It also extended the right to vote to all white Christian males. Blacks would not get the vote until after the Civil War, and women would wait another 100 years for full suffrage. But the widening of democracy had begun.

Immigrants were settling in Hartford and to a lesser extent in the West Division, and locally by 1860 the census counted Irish, German, French, Swedish, and other nationalities, who were generally Roman Catholic or Lutheran. The monopoly of the Congregational church over the town's religious and secular affairs slowly gave way.

Along with the desire to run their own show, political differences impelled residents of western Hartford to separate from Hartford, which was becoming a Democratic stronghold in a state of Federalist leanings. The ferment over state's rights, slavery, equal rights, common education and the like in a young but rapidly growing country led to the growth of the new Republican party. Many West Division residents who would become leaders of the independent town of West Hartford supported the new party and its candidates for president, John Fremont in 1856 and Abraham Lincoln in 1860. They, too, opposed the expansion of slavery and favored "freehold homesteads, free speech and free labor."

"View of West Hartford" looks toward the Center from West Hill in 1907. Famous oil painting by artist William J. Glackens shows Unionville trolley and ice skaters near his in-laws' home. Original is part of the Wadsworth Atheneum collection.

Farmington Avenue hill from Trout Brook area looks west toward Main Street. At left is the fourth greystone edifice of First Congregational Church, erected in 1882. Visible in center is the steeple of Baptist Church and, to its right, the old Town Hall housed in the third Congregational church building. The Andrews family lived in the house on the corner (center).

II. The Beginning (1854-1899)

If you happened to be ballooning westward from Hartford on a pleasant May afternoon in 1854, you would gaze down on a green expanse that stretched as far as Talcott Mountain, on top of which rose Daniel Wadsworth's lookout tower built in 1810. In the foreground snuggled a tidy village. The demarcations of original land grants that crossed the West Division east to west would be visible. Two streams nourished the area, snaking down from the mountain. Wooden bridges crossed them. The fancier homesteads had appendages of barns, carriage houses, and woodsheds. Several thousand acres were under cultivation or dotted with herds of cows and sheep. Trees were everywhere: great stands of elm, oak, maple, evergreens, and more.

Certain landmarks would stand out: the third parish church (built only 20 years earlier and soon to be renamed the First Church of Christ, Congregational) and the gravestones in the old cemetery nearby. Others were Noah Webster's birthplace on South Main Street, Philip Corbin's farm in the southwest corner, the home of Sarah Whitman Hooker on New Britain Avenue,

Chester Faxon's wheelwright shop and Wales L. Andrews' market garden in Elmwood, Alfred Whiting's nursery, and Thomas O. Goodwin's home and pottery, the village's biggest industry. A sharp eye would pick out the eight one-room schoolhouses.

This was still Hartford's wilderness, an area of 22 square miles, nearly 25 percent bigger than the mother city. Connecticut's first historian, John Warner Barber, had chronicled some years earlier that "West Hartford...is a fine tract of land. The inhabitants are mostly substantial farmers, and the general appearance of the place denotes an unusual share of equalized wealth and prosperity."

Peering closely at the ground, some movement catches your eye, and you let the balloon descend to see what's going on. Many of the 1,200 residents are marching through the unpaved streets with banners, to the sound of fife and drum, toward Goodman Green. They are waving a petition and shouting, "We've got it! We've got it!" Victory had been won in a struggle that began in 1792. The General Assembly, meeting in New

Haven, had granted the petition of 153 West Division citizens to become an independent town.

A Disputed Victory

It was not a foregone conclusion, since about a hundred residents had opposed separation, including Sidney Wadsworth, keeper of the inn on Albany Turnpike; the blacksmith Timothy Sedgwick; Philip Corbin, a prosperous farmer; nurseryman Alfred Whiting, and Harvey Goodwin, owner of the pottery in Elmwood. But they were outnumbered by others such as John and Samuel Whitman, who would become town clerk and treasurer respectively; Nathan Burr, storekeeper and postmaster; Jonathan Butler, farmer; Joseph Bishop, tobacco merchant and manufacturer; Chester Faxon, the Elmwood wheelwright; and Myron N. Morris, pastor of the Congregational Church.

Solomon Flagg, whose name was first on the petition for independence, issued a call for the first town meeting, which was convened at the church on June 19, 1854. Five selectmen were chosen. So were officials, according to ancient custom, to act as poundkeepers in charge of stray animals, haywards to care for fences and hedges, justices of the peace, a sealer of weights and measures – nearly 40 in all. Edward Stanley, a descendant of an original settler on Selden Hill, was the town's first representative in the Legislature. The Whitman family set a record for public service: Samuel was treasurer for 13 years, and his son Henry followed him for 35 years (until 1925) and also was town clerk from 1894 to 1929.

Until well into the 20th century West Hartford would be "town meetin'" country. A fine for not attending town meetings insured a good turnout.

It had taken a long time for West Hartford to become a town, so strong were its ties to Hartford. In seniority it ranks 152nd among Connecticut's 169 municipalities, and it was the next to last parish in Greater Hartford to be incorporated.

Even then, two attempts were made to retie the knot to Hartford. In 1895 a group of wealthy residents on the East Side failed in an effort to secede. In 1924 the Hartford Chamber of Commerce proposed a "Greater Hartford Plan" that included the annexation of West Hartford. Its logic was that the town had grown beyond

The Beach Farm

Five years after the town's beginning in 1854, Charles M. Beach of Hartford purchased a few acres in Elmwood that he developed into a large, model dairy farm. Originally, there had been a gristmill on the property powered by nearby Trout Brook. Soon Vine Hill Farm extended from South Main Street east to South Quaker Lane. A herd of cows supplied milk, cream and butter not only for West Hartford but also for surrounding towns. The creamery occupied the site of today's Beachland Park Clubhouse.

Beach's youngest son, Charles Edward, took over the general management of the farm. A civil engineer, he also had charge of the town's surveying and served for several terms as a selectman. Remarkably, in those Republican days locally, he was elected a state representative on the Democratic ticket. In World War I he headed both the state's War Bureau and the Red Cross.

The genius of Vine Hill was Frank H. Stadtmueller, a Yale graduate who became general manager in 1885. He perfected a process for preserving milk and was the originator and promoter of the certified milk business in Connecticut. Widely known as a lecturer, at different times he headed such organizations as the Hartford County League & Farm Bureau, the Connecticut Dairymen's Association, and the Connecticut Sheep Breeders' Association. In 1907, he was named state dairy commissioner. Stadtmueller did not neglect the town's interests, serving as a selectman, a trial justice and, for more than 20 years, health officer.

its ability to provide the improvements the residents had a right to expect. The pivotal figures against the proposal were West Hartford's Huntington Phelps Meech, a retired insurance executive, and Thomas W. Russell of Connecticut General. A referendum defeated the annexation question, 2,119 to 631. By this time the town was so jealous of its autonomy that it refused in 1930 to join the Metropolitan District, a regional entity formed for water and sewer purposes. It finally joined in 1981.

We Fight for the Union

Soon after West Hartford won its independence, it became embroiled – along with the rest of the country – in the tumult leading to the Civil War.

Charles M. Beach built Vine Hill Farm into a leading dairy farm. Lower part of farm later became Beachland Park. The wraparound veranda of the house (above) was a favorite gathering and entertainment place for the Beach sisters (below).

Civil War veterans gather for Memorial Day ceremonies on Goodman Green early in the 20th century.

The first of more than 100 men from West Hartford who answered President Lincoln's call for volunteers to save the union were Buell Root and John C. Sternberg. Sternberg was one of eight brothers who joined the Union Army, sons of a German lawyer who had fled his native country in 1848 and settled on a farm later called Buena Vista. At least fifteen West Hartford residents gave their lives, including four at Antietam, the heaviest casualties for any town of West Hartford's size.

Those who survived brought back stories of horror and heroism. Hiram Elmer had promised his wife and two small sons he would not enlist, but one day in 1861 he took a wagonload of apples to the Hartford market and was so excited by the war atmosphere that he volunteered to join the First Cavalry. With his friend Hiram Hurlbut he served under the colorful Gen. George Custer in several engagements. Writing home, Elmer told his family a shot had torn off his hat and another time his horse was killed under him. "You need to be proud, my sons, to think that your Papa was permitted to contribute in some small degree in the restoration of our glorious Union." Both Elmer and Hurlbut came through the war unscathed.

Civil War records of West Hartford list First Lt. Joseph Talcott, John Day, William Gaines, and "several Irish draftees" in the First Regiment, reputed to be the best artillery in the army. The Second Regiment of Artillery was not as fortunate; it suffered heavy losses, among whom were James Stanley and Thomas Foster. Six local men were in the famed Seventh Connecticut, the first to plant Union colors in South Carolina. When African Americans were allowed to enlist in the Union Army in 1863, five from West Hartford responded. William Green, William Clinton, William Gardiner, Jesse Cowles, and John Wilson served in the 29th Regiment, which was one of the first to enter Richmond.

After the Civil War

The Civil War veterans returned to a West Hartford full of optimism and a new entrepreneurial spirit. Most long-time residents were moderately prosperous farmers, who continued to benefit from the large market provided by Hartford, a bustling river port and rapidly growing city. Early industry was growing and changing. The east side of town was on the verge of losing its rural character, as Hartford burst out of its narrow limits and spilled into West Hartford. The rest of the town was still mostly farmland. Most farms were small and grew corn and other vegetables or bred horses and cattle. One of the leading institutions to develop was the West Hartford Grange, which promoted scientific agriculture from its landmark building still standing on South Main Street facing Goodman Green. It became

THE TROUT BROOK ICE & FEED CO.
W. HARTFORD, CONN.

Trout Brook Ice & Feed Co. was the biggest business in the Center in the late 1800s. This rendering looks north along the frozen brook toward the ice-cutting operation. The trolley car is on Farmington Avenue.

a powerful influence for civic welfare, led the opposition against annexation to Hartford, promoted better roads and mail delivery, and gave $100 for the first Noah Webster Memorial Library.

As crop farming shifted from this state to Connecticut's Western Reserve in Ohio and other fertile territories to the west, West Hartford became one of the nation's top dairy towns. Notable were such farms as that of E.A. Whiting, Frederick Duffy's Meadowbrook, D.D. Monroe's Sunset and, especially, Charles Beach's Vine Hill.

The Beginning of Industry

The southeast section was the locus for what little industry existed in town. Trout Brook had provided early waterpower for both the Center and the southeast section. But the Center was destined to become the focus for retail and business. The South End's rich clay deposits prompted the development of potteries such as the Goodwin Brothers, by this time the largest employer. Some of its products were shipped by the New York, New Haven & Hartford Railroad that by the late 19th century ran along the southeastern section

of town. The launching of the Whitlock Coil Pipe Co. in 1891 heralded the future concentration of factories in the South End. Elmwood grew into a self-contained community with its own school, church, post office, railroad station, and stores. It took its name from elm trees dating back to the Burgoyne Elms planted by patriots celebrating the defeat of British General John Burgoyne at Saratoga in the Revolutionary War.

Early merchandising was centered along Farmington Avenue and Main Street. The biggest business was the Trout Brook Ice & Feed Co., founded by Edwin Arnold in 1879 on Farmington Avenue. Ice from Trout Brook was cut into blocks with long saws, hoisted into the icehouse by an escalator and packed in sawdust. Huge red wagons delivered the blocks to homes in the area and carloads were shipped as far as New York.

Residential Development

For years, travelers passing through from Hartford en route to Farmington, New Britain, or Avon on the South, Middle, or Albany turnpikes and perhaps stopping overnight at one of the eight taverns, complained about the clay mud roads, virtually impassable in winter.

"There's no mud like West Hartford mud" was the lament of delivery men as well as residents in the late 1800s. The Village Improvement Society was formed in 1878 partly to start paving with gravel the roads and walkways in the center of town.

Crushed stone and later black asphalt improved travel significantly between the 1850s and 1870, and horses and stagecoaches gave way to newer modes of transportation.

Fred Brace had started a horse-drawn omnibus service from his home at Farmington Avenue and Dale Street to Hartford around 1845. The Hartford & Wethersfield Horse Railway Co. extended its original line out Farmington Avenue past Prospect Avenue to reach the Center in 1889. Five years later it was replaced by an electric trolley line that ran through the Center to Farmington and Unionville – a service that

From Clay to Pottery: Earthenware from West Hartford

At the age of 21, Ebenezer Faxon of Massachusetts decided he would seek his fortune in the West Division. Having heard of the excellent clay deposits in the South End, he set up a thriving pottery business on the South Road in 1770. In 1777, he built an elegant colonial house for his bride, Abigail Pantry Whitman, on the northeast corner of South Quaker Lane and New Britain Avenue. He was the town's first successful industrialist, and his son carried on the business until at least 1806.

Perhaps Faxon's pioneering attracted Seth and Thomas O. Goodwin, members of a family that played a prominent role in the growth of Hartford since its founding. Seth's pottery enterprise, started around 1798, burned down, but his son Thomas rebuilt it in 1822 and he and his three sons

continued the business. In the days before the Civil War the Goodwins would make up a load of earthenware and peddle it by horse and wagon from town to town. Sometimes they traveled as far as Vermont. The pottery of the Goodwins achieved regional fame. Among items manufactured were jugs for the gin manufactured in West Hartford's distilleries.

After a second conflagration leveled the factory in 1867, the sons bought more land south of New Britain Avenue and erected a three-story pottery with three kilns and steam-powered potters' wheels. They employed more than 75 people. Besides ordinary pottery, they added terra cotta designs and fine china. Henry Goodwin enhanced the reputation of the Goodwin Brothers Pottery Company until another fire terminated its existence in 1908.

The Village Improvement Society

The secretary of the state Board of Education came to West Hartford one day to conduct a teachers' institute at the Congregational Church. The muddy walkways and streets distressed him, and he inspired Paul Thomson, the Scotsman who ran a market garden on Park Road, to form the Village Improvement Society in 1878. Operating with volunteers, the society started to build gravel walks and to install street lamps along Main Street and Farmington Avenue. The men worked on summer evenings, while the women sponsored strawberry festivals, debates, lectures, and other entertainments to raise money for the materials used. When the walks were finished, the society started semi-annual cleanup drives and promoted the idea of a townwide refuse collection. Hundreds came to sidewalk rallies and fencing bees, signing up to keep the sidewalks clear of snow and light the lamps. By 1914, the town had grown from 1,700 in 1878 to more than 6,000 and the municipal government began to take over the society's duties.

Yung Wing

The first of his nationality to graduate from Yale College (1854), Chinese mandarin Yung Wing returned to the United States in 1871 to set up an educational mission. He chose Hartford for its headquarters and brought with him 30 long-gowned Chinese boys to be educated in Hartford's public schools. In the mission's nine-year life 120 young men received their education for government service and returned to China. They were often referred to as "the fathers of the Chinese Republic." In 1876 Yung Wing was appointed associate minister to the U.S. He married Mary Kellogg, the daughter of a prominent Hartford physician, and they reared two sons in their home on Prospect Avenue. To the end of his life he worked devotedly for the welfare of his native country, to which he never returned.

West Hartford Historical Society Photo

Yung Wing's tall brick castle was part of "Rich Man's Row" along Prospect Avenue at northwest corner of Fern Street. Built in the Victorian era, the house has since been replaced by condominiums.

lasted 40 years. By 1900, West Hartford had 20 miles of hard-surfaced roadways.

These improvements stimulated the town's first housing developments. One of the earliest, begun in the late 1880s, was the dream of Bernard Caya, a French-Canadian carpenter who had been lured to Hartford during the Civil War by the high wages being paid by the arms plants. The father of 14 children, Caya started building homes on farmland in the area of New Park and Oakwood avenues near Charter Oak Park. As he boasted to friends of the open air and scenery of his property, other French-Canadians came to look and bought. He subdivided his acreage into small lots and sold them for as little as $5 down and $5 a month. For years, Caya Avenue and the adjoining streets were known as "Frenchtown."

"Own Your Own Home," advertised a real-estate developer promoting the former Stanley Farm on Selden Hill as Buena Vista, which "fronts on the Farmington and Unionville Electric Line." The West End Land Co. held an auction in Elmwood of "Choice Suburban House Sites" by offering $1,500 worth of "beautiful and useful presents." Its "Elmhurst" included Yale, Harvard, and Florence streets. The New England Development and Improvement Co. offered home sites in "West Hartford Heights" on the west side of North Main Street, including Sylvan, Grennan, Brunswick, Clifton, Hilltop, Argyle, Whitman, and Keeney avenues.

Already, starting about 1870, some of Hartford's more affluent people had settled in West Hartford's then developing East Side. The west side of Prospect Avenue

Twain's Reports Exaggerated

No less a lionized figure than humorist Mark Twain (Samuel Clemens) used to stride through West Hartford in the 1880s from his Victorian home on Farmington Avenue in Hartford with his friend, the Rev. Joseph Twitchell. Autograph seekers would stop him – he carried a supply of autographs, which he generally sold upon request – as they made their way to their favorite rendezvous, Monte Video, off Albany Turnpike atop Talcott Mountain.

His observations often influenced Twitchell, pastor of Hartford's Asylum Hill Congregational Church. The writer called it the "Church of the Holy Speculator." West Hartford was mentioned in Twain's autobiography because the Asylum Hill church deacons wanted to fire their pastor for voting for Democrat Grover Cleveland in 1884. At the congregation's annual meeting, Twitchell would have been removed had not a cooler head appealed: "Reflect before you vote. The church in West Hartford is waiting upon this vote with deep solicitude. That congregation's real estate stands at a very low figure. What they are anxious to have now above everything else under God is a price-raiser. Dismiss Mr. Twitchell tonight and they will hire him tomorrow. Prices there will go up; prices here will go down." The speaker was a bit premature in his prophecy about real estate values, but his argument won the day.

Mark Twain was just as happy. Exhibiting the financial acumen that was to leave his own affairs in disarray, he took a dim view of West Hartford's real estate prospects.

That Joseph Twitchell, "or any other expert, could have raised the prices in West Hartford, is, to my mind, exceedingly doubtful," the author wrote.

Bishops Corner in the 1890s

Because of the heavily traveled Hartford to Albany Turnpike (now Route 44), its intersection at North Main Street now known as Bishops Corner became an early business center and stopover for stagecoaches. Aaron Goodman ran a tavern, store, and post office there from 1803 to 1832. The area was named for Joseph Bishop, who came here in 1842 and raised tobacco. Immediately to the east of the tobacco warehouse was the Eliza Mansfield strawberry farm. At strawberry time word went out for pickers to appear at daylight the next morning; the pay was 3 cents per quart basket. At the Flagg Road corner were the Frank Strong blacksmith shop, wheelwright, and wagon factory.

Near the northwest corner was the North School, a small building 40 feet long and 20 feet wide holding 30 desks. A huge, pot-bellied iron stove, fired with wood, furnished heat. Outside on opposite corners of the schoolyard were small outbuildings, one for boys and one for girls – really cold places in winter. When the Rutherford School in the Center was opened, the North School was closed (as were the schools on Mountain Road and Prospect Hill). Pupils who attended these three schools were picked up by one of the first school buses in the country, drawn by two horses driven by Charles Fulton.

*The Electric Trolley promoted suburban home sites
in West Hartford with gifts and free transportation.*

West Hartford Historical Society Photo

*Charter Oak Race Track, established in 1873, drew thousands to West Hartford for almost daily summer trotting races into
the 20th century. When the state legislature passed anti-betting legislation, racing lost its popularity. The property was
turned into Luna Park with a carnival midway and became the home of the Connecticut State Fair.*

Celebrate!West Hartford   17

Eccentric's Gift to Neighborhood: Elizabeth Park

West Hartford was among the beneficiaries of Charles M. Pond's gift of 101 acres to the city of Hartford for a park. Eighty-one acres of the park lie in West Hartford, and Pond lived on the town side of Prospect Avenue. His family had made a fortune in the New York, New Haven & Hartford Railroad and he had been state treasurer as well as an officer of the Hartford Trust Co. and a founder of the Hartford Club.

Pond, an eccentric who kept horse-racing stables, often drank heavily and terrorized his neighbors by using his living room fireplace as a shooting gallery. A morose man who fancied spiritualism as well as spirits, he brooded over the notion that he would die at the same age as his father – and he eventually did, in 1894. Since he was a widower with no children, he had planned to leave his estate as a refuge for inebriates. But the Rev. Francis Goodwin, who envisioned a ring of parks around the city and headed the Hartford Park Commission, persuaded him instead to donate it in memory of Pond's wife Elizabeth, whose maiden name happened to be Park.

The park was designed and laid out by Theodore Wirth. The rose garden – the oldest municipal garden of its kind in the United States – contains 900 varieties and more than 14,000 bushes. Pond's residence was demolished in the 1960s, and the caretaker's cottage now houses the office of the Knox Parks Foundation. The deterioration of the park prompted a proposal in 1970 that the town help the city with maintenance by cleaning the pond and repairing the tennis courts, but the idea was rejected. Instead, an anonymous gift enabled the town to donate $10,000 for the tennis courts. Formation of the Friends of Elizabeth Park saved the rose garden and restored the adjacent rock, perennial, and sunken gardens. The will of Ethel Donaghue, a wealthy recluse who lived near the park's north side, provided a bequest for much-needed drainage and other improvements. In 1997 the Pond House was renovated at a cost of $760,000 and became a restaurant.

and parts of Fern and Highland streets became known as "Rich Men's Row" because of the elaborate homes. Most notable were those of Charles M. Pond, who soon donated all of his property for a park named after his wife Elizabeth, W.C. Russell, and the Chinese scholar and diplomat Yung Wing.

Another resident of that area was Frederick Rockwell, a promoter of the early trolley line, who bought up most of the land between Farmington Avenue and Park Road in 1895. He planned to have trolleys run south along Main Street and then east on a parkway he would call the Boulevard. The line was never completed, but the Boulevard between Main Street and Trout Brook stands today just as he laid it out.

On Vanderbilt Hill, now West Hill, silk manufacturer Ira Dimock lived in an elaborate mansion built but never occupied by Cornelius J. Vanderbilt.

On Park Road stood the estate of James M. Thomson, founder of Hartford's Brown-Thomson department store. Across the street, Paul Thomson ran a popular nursery and market garden. In Elmwood, Charles E. Beach's "Vine Hill" overlooked his flourishing dairy farm.

Education and Culture

West Hartford has long valued good education. According to the 1860 census, only seven people over 20 years of age were illiterate and "six of those were immigrants." Farmers followed scientific developments by attending agricultural fairs and cattle shows and applied their knowledge to the dairy business and to cattle breeding.

Townspeople indulged in cultural activities. They attended oratorical contests, joined societies for peace, anti-slavery, and temperance, and flocked to lyceum lectures.

In 1753, Noah Webster Sr. and others started a book society, and 84 years later his son gave to the Congregational church a collection of books that formed the nucleus of a Free Library Association, housed in the church vestry. In 1897, the town took charge of the library. That same year the Woman's Literary Club was organized, holding weekly meetings for more than 20 years. The West Hartford Grange and the Sarah Whitman Hooker Chapter, Daughters of the American Revolution, later took the lead in raising funds for a library building on the west side of North Main Street

Students and their elders pose for graduation photo outside old Northwest School on Albany Avenue, circa 1880.

near the center. They named it, appropriately, the Noah Webster Memorial Library.

Awareness of the need for reform of the common schools gradually gathered momentum. More than half of the schoolhouses were in wretched shape; 200 varieties of school books made "confusion worse confounded." Male teachers were paid $15 a month during the winter. The growing number of female teachers received about $6 a month teaching mainly girls in summer while the older boys worked.

In West Hartford, educational reform efforts were led by William Hutchins Hall. Born on a farm near Mountain Road

William H. Hall, a school dropout, returned in 1872 to the town in which he grew up to become a teacher, principal, and superintendent. His career spanned the spectrum from the one-room schoolhouse to the beginning of today's prized school system with a comprehensive high school.

South School, built in 1852, was the first in West Hartford to have two outside doors, a basement, and a furnace.

Watering trough helped horses cool off opposite old Town Hall (third Congregational Church) in West Hartford Center.

and Fern Street, he had attended one of the district schools and, upon returning to the same school as a teacher in 1872, was outraged by the inequities between districts. Some were able to pay higher salaries and provide better facilities. Others lagged.

Hall began a lengthy battle against backward-looking officials.

Finally, in 1877 a town meeting accepted consolidation of the districts, and seven years later the state legislature approved West Hartford's plan to place the schools

The Reservoirs After Flood: 'You Might Have Run Steamboats from Town to Sea'

At the outbreak of the Civil War, the burgeoning city of Hartford was running out of water. Pollution of the Connecticut River was fast destroying its potability. The city fathers looked west to the Trout Brook watershed. Granted the right by the Legislature to take water from Trout Brook, they acquired 80 acres of woodland along the east side of Talcott Mountain north of Farmington Avenue. By the turn of the century they would own nearly 3,000 acres all the way to Bloomfield for an eventual complex of six reservoirs.

In 1866, the Water Board began building Reservoir No. 1, covering 32 acres, and a pipeline was laid along Farmington Avenue to conduct water downtown. Just eight months after the water started flowing, in September 1867, a torrential rain filled the new reservoir to capacity. At 10 o'clock the next morning, with the sound of an earthquake, the base of the 53-foot-high dam gave way. A gigantic wall of water – 200 million gallons – swept down

the hillside. Great elms and maples, centuries old, disappeared. The gristmill and sawmill of Stanley & Thompson in what is now Sunset Farm was nearly destroyed.

The flood rushed across Mountain Road, carrying away its bridge, then on to Fern and North Main streets – snapping the spans in both places and finally undermining the central pier of a new bridge being built on Farmington Avenue. For several days, as one reporter wrote, "you might have run steamboats from West Hartford to the sea."

Hartford had to pay the town $11,370 for damages to bridges and roads and $17,000 to property owners for deposits of stone and gravel on their fields. It took nearly three years to put Reservoir No. 1 back into service.

Reservoir No. 2 was added in 1868, No. 3 in 1875, No. 4 in 1880, and No. 5 in 1884. The final and largest reservoir, No. 6, was completed in 1896 on the north side of Albany Avenue.

Trees stood in middle of the town's major intersection in late 19th century. This view looks west on Farmington Avenue at Main Street. The original First Baptist Church is in the center.

under central control of a school board. Salaries were equalized, a uniform calendar was adopted and new schools were constructed of brick.

All the grades having been mixed together, the town had no high school as such until December 1872, when 40 students climbed the stairs to the second floor of the new Center School at 14 North Main St., successor to the original one-room Center schoolhouse built in 1745. They were greeted by William H. Hall, the newly promoted principal and only teacher, who later became school superintendent. His salary was $430.60 annually. He dreamed of seeing the high school permanently established in its own quarters. Finally, at the town meeting in 1895, West Hartford's durable "first citizen" persuaded the reluctant selectmen to buy property at the corner of Memorial and Raymond roads and build a larger Center School. The new Center School was shared by the elementary and high school grades until 1910, when the high school occupied the entire North Center Building, eventually known as the Rutherford Building. The lower grades moved into a new South Center Building, later to be renamed Whitman School.

There were three other elementary schools late in the century. The Commons District School at Flatbush and New Park avenues burned to the ground in 1878 and was rebuilt, the precursor of what became Charter Oak

School. Elmwood School began at New Britain Avenue and Woodlawn Street as a two-room wood structure in 1888, with a four-room brick addition in 1900. The East School was a seven-room wood structure built in 1888 on the site of the current Whiting Lane School.

The End of the Century

Except for the residential facade of the Prospect Avenue area, West Hartford was still made up mostly of farms as the century ended. The early West Hartford Common, a strip along the East Side reserved for grazing and common use, was giving way to Elizabeth and Charter Oak parks and residential development. The town was divided into three fairly distinct areas: the residential East Side, the primarily rural west and north, and industrial Elmwood.

A board of three selectmen governed the town, the majority of voters were Republican, and the Town Hall was located in what had been the third meeting house of the Congregational Church. There were three other churches, nine common schools, a few general stores, and a new cemetery. The sale of liquor was illegal, but that didn't mean a lack of hard cider, wine, and other spirits on special occasions like the Fourth of July and Thanksgiving. Only four telephones were in use. The automobile was yet to be manufactured.

The Ladies' Glee Club serenades passengers on horse-drawn Hartford & West Hartford Omnibus.

First horse-drawn trolley prepares for return trip to Hartford at side of old Town Hall, northwest corner of Farmington Avenue and Main Street, in 1889.

West Hartford Center is expanding to the west in this photo of intersection at Farmington Avenue and Main Street in the early 1930s. Marquee of Central Theater can be seen beyond First Baptist Church at right.

III. Growing Up, 1900-2000

At the beginning of the 20th century, there were approximately as many cows as people in West Hartford. Its population of 3,186 was far surpassed by Hartford with 79,850. How would the town deal with a population that would grow 20 times larger in the next 75 years?

The State Register & Manual for 1907 listed the principal industries as agriculture, flowers under glass, bricks, pottery, water heaters, and ice. The Register defined the town as "to a considerable extent a residence town for Hartford businessmen" and their families.

The town's population swelled as people continued to move out of Hartford into the town's East Side, where streets sliced through farms and fields between Fern Street and Park Road, south along Quaker Lane and north to envelop Elizabeth Park. The population increased more than 50 percent in the first decade to 4,898, and again during the World War I decade to 8,894 in 1920. It increased nearly three-fold to 24,941 by 1930.

During that time the automobile had opened up the entire state. Roads were built and the suburbs around Hartford exploded. While the city grew by a modest 19 percent, Bloomfield rose 36 percent, Windsor 47 percent and Wethersfield 73 percent. Newington nearly doubled its population. West Hartford virtually tripled.

A Major Change in Form of Government

From its beginning, as was typical of the times, decisions about West Hartford had been made by the influential men of the church and the community. By the time of World War I, the descendants of early families had been joined by business leaders from Hartford. They believed in professional management, assumed that running things was their responsibility, and thought government could and should provide solutions to the problems of a rapidly growing community in which business and industry were vying for space and resources with the expanding residential population.

Out of these changes came a new West Hartford

Firemen take break (above) after fighting fire in 1923. At right, West Hartford's finest pose at Police Headquarters in a house on Raymond Road in 1936. Below, Officer Ernie Hitchcock was a Center landmark in the 1930s, directing traffic at Farmington and Main.

charter at the end of 1919. The charter abolished the town-meeting system in favor of a council-manager form of government, the first in Connecticut and one of the first in New England. It replaced the decision-making selectmen with a 15-member town council elected by districts to set policy for implementation by a town manager. The new charter established a variety of citizen-based boards and commissions to advise on specific aspects of town affairs. Soon a town court was established, with a judge taking over most functions of the justices of the peace. A comprehensive zoning plan, among the earliest in New England, was adopted.

Since 1898, the town has had a police force. At first it consisted of a part-time constable, James Livingston, who rode a "penny-farthing" bicycle on the job. He was upgraded to fulltime policeman and, in 1923, to police chief with two assistants. Fire control continued under the almost autonomous, club-like fire districts manned by volunteers until 1937. Since then, the town has run a professionally staffed fire department.

The Great Depression

The Depression era did not stop the town from growing. While per-capita personal income fell and unemployment rose statewide to more than 25 percent, the trend toward suburban living accelerated. West Hartford's population increased 35 percent to 33,776 by 1940.

West Hartford Center began to take on its modern-day look in the 1930s with the arrival of stores like Hartford's Sage-Allen & Co. (among the earliest branches of a city department store anywhere), Pfau's Hardware, Plimpton's, Carlson's Footwear, and the Shoe Box as well as the Central Theater.

The Depression era provided the first major test for the new town government. With remarkable foresight, the first town manager, Benjamin I. Miller, had started innovative "make work" programs. When Rodney L. Loomis took over in 1933, the town was ready to take advantage of the federal government's New Deal programs, such as the Civilian Conservation Corps,

Corner Might Have Become Welch's Instead of Bishop's

Bishops Corner could have been called Welch's Corner in the 1920s when Welch's Inn – where a police chief was appointed and where many of the town's official decisions informally came to a head – stood at the southeast corner of Albany Avenue and North Main Street.

Katharine and David Welch operated the inn, with a gas station beside it, from 1919 to 1931. In its 12 years, it became a storied place. Mr. Welch, a former Hartford policeman who had opened the Knickerbocker Bar, found himself out of business and with many cases of liquor on his hands when Prohibition was legislated. In moving to Bishops Corner where he expected to sell ice cream in the inn, he stored the accumulated liquor in the cellar in the hope the government would eventually buy it. It wasn't long before casual wayfarers prompted him to operate a restaurant, where five waiters served about 300 chicken dinners on Sundays. It became a gathering mecca, and at one dinner the decision was made to appoint Joseph F. Grogan the town's police chief.

The worst evening of Katharine Welch's career came shortly after a policeman friend warned that businesses known to be storing liquor were to be raided. Friends from the state and city police helped them move the liquor. When they were nearly

finished, in walked two men in blue uniforms. "Is Mr. Welch in?" Terrified, she told them he was out of town. "That's too bad," the man answered. "I'm Jim Livingston, the constable, and I wanted to see him. I wanted to sell him some tickets to the Volunteer Fireman's Ball."

During the 1920s, North Main Street was small and narrow and Town Manager Benjamin I. Miller, looking forward even then to a business expansion at Welch's Corners, tried to have the road widened. Seth Griswold, who owned the southwest corner, got a court injunction halting the project. After the injunction, the town manager paid a visit to Welch's small gas station. "Dave," he said, "how much do you want for the little park on the other side of your road?" Answered Welch: "I won't sell it, Ben. But because I believe this corner holds the key to part of West Hartford's future, I will give it to you, in the name of the town."

In 1931 the Welches sold the corner to Standard Oil Co and moved their inn 50 feet back from the corner on North Main. That made it harder for Albany Avenue traffic to reach and it never regained its popularity. Two years later, David died and Welch's Inn was finished, becoming home for the Bon and Bill Grocery Store. The corner kept the name of tobacco farmer Joseph Bishop.

A policeman awaits disposition of an early fender-bender, which draws spectators to the accident scene, believed to be Farmington Avenue near the Center.

Federal Emergency Relief Act, National Recovery Act, Public Works Administration, and Works Projects Administration. Unemployment reached a high of 572, about 10 percent of the local work force. Government programs funded such projects as the Beachland Park baseball field and pool, two community centers, a new library, most of the cost of a new Town Hall at 28 South Main St., and the commissioning of local artist Walter O.R. Kordor's famed murals in Hall High School and Charter Oak School.

The Flood and the Hurricane

Two memorable storms affected West Hartford in the late 1930s.

In March 1936, the melting of an unusually heavy snow accumulation combined with heavy spring rains to raise the Connecticut River a record 37.6 feet above the river base level in Hartford. On LaSalle Road, then home of the American Radio Relay League, amateurs worked for 50 hours to provide communication throughout Southern New England for the Army, Red Cross, and government officials. The Hayes-Velhage Post, American Legion, organized a 100-man rescue crew, under the leadership of Albert Powell, Eugene Welles, and Everett D. (Brub) Dow, to man the dikes against the river's raging waters on Front Street in Hartford.

On Sept. 21, 1938, most of West Hartford was in the dark as a result of the Great Hurricane, the first in 100 years to hit Connecticut. Hundreds of massive trees had fallen, dragging phone and power lines with them and caving in the roofs of homes and stores. Most of the trees on Goodman Green were gone. Two weeks later, the town was back to normal, and the Board of Finance had approved clean-up costs of $10,000.

The Circus Fire

During the most critical year of World War II, the Ringling Bros. and Barnum & Bailey circus came to Hartford, and families starved for entertainment looked forward to seeing the animals and the acts. On the warm afternoon of July 6, 1944, more than 6,000 people filled the main circus tent. Then, just as the lions were herded back into the runway cages and the Flying Wallendas ascended to the high wire, fire broke out, possibly as the result of a carelessly thrown cigarette. A total of 168 men, women, and children perished. Twenty were West Hartford residents, eight of them children. Scores more were injured. Some 25 policemen from the town rushed to the Barbour Street circus grounds and aided in rescue and traffic work.

And, through the foresight of Dr. Ralph Kendall, a town resident who was chief of pathology at Hartford Hospital, blood plasma – stored in A.C. Petersen Farms freezers here in the event of possible wartime civilian crises – was immediately available to save the lives of many of those critically burned in the fire.

Municipal center in early 20th century was along North Main Street at northwest corner of Farmington Avenue. Town Hall is at left (above), facing Farmington Avenue, with Congregational Church in middle and library at right. By 1936 (below), the library was planning to move to a new site beside the new Town Hall on South Main Street across from Goodman Green.

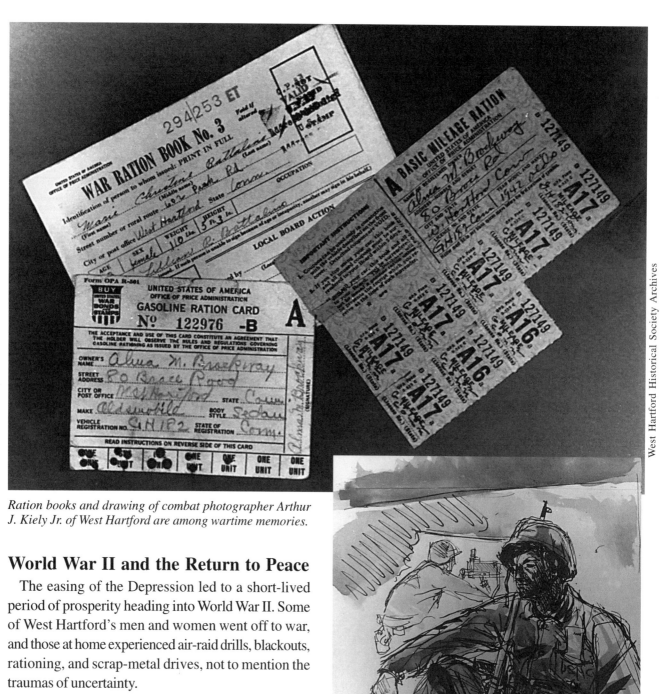

West Hartford Historical Society Archives

Ration books and drawing of combat photographer Arthur J. Kiely Jr. of West Hartford are among wartime memories.

World War II and the Return to Peace

The easing of the Depression led to a short-lived period of prosperity heading into World War II. Some of West Hartford's men and women went off to war, and those at home experienced air-raid drills, blackouts, rationing, and scrap-metal drives, not to mention the traumas of uncertainty.

Local defense plants expanded exponentially and employment soared. Coils, turbines, set screws, ball bearings, steel tumblers, chucks, flexible wiring, and electrical outlets all played an important part in preserving freedom and democracy. Pratt & Whitney Machine Tool Co., by this time the town's largest industry, employed 7,000 people making precision parts and refrigeration equipment for army camps, Liberty ships, and planes.

After the war's end in August 1945, the people of West Hartford resumed more or less normal lives, though

New Britain Avenue railroad underpass was widened in 1937, allowing trolleys and cars better access. In 1959, Elmwood celebrated 75 years of progress for the underpass, issuing souvenir wooden nickels in honor of the occasion.

initially there were food and material shortages. More than 4,000 veterans returned home. Their main concerns were a place to live, new clothes, and a hard-to-find automobile. Gas rationing had ended a year earlier. Center merchants did a brisk business and pressed the town to provide more parking spaces.

West Hartford again experienced strong growth during the 1940s, adding nearly 11,000 residents for a total population of 44,000. In 1946, the first year of the Baby Boom generated by peacetime and the return of war veterans, the town recorded 857 births – a record that would be exceeded every year until 1965. Also by 1946, school enrollment had climbed to 6,500 – half of its eventual peak.

The war was over, and the age of television and technology was about to dawn. The boom was on.

The Fabulous Fifties

The post-war era saw the largest population shift from city to suburb. Highways were built, shopping plazas emerged, and urban sprawl accelerated. Single-family housing developments proliferated in the Greater Hartford area. So many people moved into the suburbs that the Roman Catholic Archdiocese set up the first of three new parishes in West Hartford. When Hartford deputy mayor Nicholas R. Carbone attended his 20th reunion at Bulkeley High School in 1975, he noted wistfully that only ten percent of his classmates still lived in Hartford, while 74 percent had moved to the suburbs.

Overcrowding in the schools was a hot topic of the 1950s. Births exceeded 1,000 annually and enrollments reached more than 12,000. Nine new schools were built

Wartime Miracle

The story of a miracle of modern wartime industry – a seven-fold expansion over two years – was emblazoned on the records of the Pratt & Whitney Machine Tool Co. here in 1942

Clayton R. Burt, president, accepted the joint Army-Navy "E" flag won by his company for excellence in war production. "Tough problems have been met and solved," he told thousands of workers gathered at the West Hartford plant. "We can all feel proud that today we have increased our production to eight times our normal output, with an increase in our working force in three years from 1,800 to approximately 7,000."

Hardly had he finished speaking than chairman Edward A. Deeds conducted dedication ceremonies for two more additions to the company's plants. "Soon several thousand more men and women will join our ranks in these new quarters to help swell the stream of machine tools, small tools, and gauges that are so vital to American production."

The flag was presented by Gen. William S. Knudsen, who said the planes, tanks, guns and ships used by the fighting forces "depend on the skill of your hand and brain."

Gov. Robert E. Hurley said the award "is a renewal of America's warning to Hitler and to the Japanese that the workers and producers of America will not cease until victory is won."

Town's 1954 centennial banner is overhead backdrop for waiting school children.

The Centennial Extravaganza

No previous event in the town's history had been more carefully planned, staged, and attended than the Centennial. A week-long celebration, from June 6 to 12, its slogan was "1854 Priceless Heritage – Challenging Future 1954." Chairman of the Centennial Commission was Clarence A. Boyce, president of the West Hartford Trust Co., who doubled as the town's treasurer. The celebration opened on Sunday at the First Church of Christ, Congregational, where Gov. John Lodge and historian Nelson R. Burr spoke. For two nights, before crowds of 8,000 on the grounds behind Hall High School, 1,000 children in period costumes performed in a pageant depicting key episodes in West Hartford history. It was written by Marjorie S. Rice, a Sedgwick School teacher.

The Exposition Committee, headed by Edward M. Flannery, mounted a display of "civic progress" by business and industry at the West Hartford Armory. On Friday there was a mammoth parade with 21 floats, and on Saturday the celebration climaxed with spectacular fireworks at Sterling Field.

Two previous observances had set a precedent. In 1932 the bicentennial anniversary of George Washington's birth was celebrated with a pageant and parade. At Hall High School, with Gov. Wilbur Cross in attendance, Rabbi Abraham. J. Feldman spoke eloquently on patriotism, religious tolerance, and his vision of democracy. Two years later, in September 1934, 20,000 jammed the Center in the Town's first "mardi gras" to celebrate the widening and repairing of Farmington Avenue.

Hartford Times Photo

In flowing robe, the Rev. Dr. Elden H. Mills plays role of Noah Webster in town's 1954 Centennial pageant.

in the 1950s alone: Bugbee, Duffy, King Philip, Whiting Lane, Braeburn, Norfeldt, Wolcott, Bridlepath, and Conard High School. A total of 18,000 new residents found homes here, establishing the residential development patterns that exist today.

As the town reached a population of 56,000 (a rise of nearly 12,000 in six years), officials paused to talk about its future. Fewer than 3,000 of the town's 13,866 acres remained for residential development. "West Hartford won't be the outer fringe of the suburbs," predicted Town Manager Donald H. Blatt in 1956. "We will become inter-urbanized." Building Inspector Arthur N. Rutherford looked into his crystal ball and envisioned 75,000 people in another decade. Up alongside Talcott

Mountain, beneath the Metropolitan District reservoirs, a stringent Triple A zone with the town's largest lots was adopted. It extended from Farmington Avenue to the Bloomfield line, and gave rise to the realtors' code for prime residential area: "West of Mountain Road."

The municipal budget more than tripled since 1946 to $8.6 million, 54 percent of which went to education. Town services were strained to the limit. More police and firemen were needed, as was more space to accommodate them. Because of the $150 million industrial economy, taxes were lower than if the town had been entirely residential. However, of the 525 acres zoned for industry, only 120 were vacant – a severe limitation that encouraged other suburbs with ample amounts of open space, including neighboring Bloomfield and Farmington, to establish industrial and office parks.

Another problem was traffic and parking. West Hartford was fast becoming a two-car-per-family town, and the planners were proposing to widen such cross-town thoroughfares as Mountain Road, North Main Street, and Trout Brook Drive and to install parking meters in the Center. The Trout Brook flood-control project was extended south from Farmington Avenue to prevent flooding for the new housing in the South End. The Town Plan & Zoning Commission labored to keep the Center business zone both suburbanly compatible and healthily dynamic, with appropriate buffers to prevent businesses from infringing on surrounding residential areas.

The Prosperous Sixties

By 1960, when the population had risen 44 percent in the previous decade to 62,382, West Hartford had become a mature suburb, considered by many the most desirable place to live in the metropolitan area. It attracted people who wanted to be close to their Hartford workplaces and yet enjoy the suburban lifestyle. They liked the well-tended houses and lawns, the nicely paved streets, the choice public and private schools, the variety of churches and synagogues, and the fine municipal services – the town-maintained sidewalks, the weekly garbage collection, the top-notch fire and police departments, and the extensive public recreation system.

Candidates for town office, regardless of political affiliation, invariably vowed to protect "the quality of life." Other sensitive issues were education, property taxes, zoning, traffic, affordable housing, and recreation facilities. There was concern over the construction of the East-West highway (now Interstate 84), which

The Enders Family

When John Ostrom Enders, chairman and CEO of Hartford National Bank, died in 1958, he was eulogized in a West Hartford News editorial:

"His death takes from the scene one of the last stalwart figures who helped make the colorful history of West Hartford's East Side. His baronial home on Highland Street symbolized a day that is past. The social and economic leaders of Hartford who came across the town line early in the century to build their estates on the 'high land' profoundly changed the rural character of West Hartford. The growth brought problems which they solved by creating their own fire protection and water districts.

"Men like John Enders added greatly to the stature of the town, taking active participation in its government and development."

Enders, who served a term in the General Assembly, was a board member of Aetna Life & Casualty for 60 years. He was the oldest member of the Hartford Club and the last survivor of the group that founded the Hartford Golf Club in 1894. His family gave the land for St. John's Episcopal Church.

His son, Ostrom Enders, took over the presidency of Hartford National in 1947.

Another son, Dr. John F. Enders, a scientist, won the 1954 Nobel Prize for research that led to the polio vaccine. When he returned home to accept the first honorary membership in the Hartford County Medical Society's 162-year history, he was ranked one of the 100 most important people in the world at the time.

Aging Observation

For nearly half a century starting in 1910, John C. Willian of 175 N. Main St. lived in the home at the cradle site of town history, beside the mill dam on Trout Brook where Thomas Hosmer built the first structure in town, a sawmill for his son Stephen. One of the millstones served as a front doorstep for the Willian house, and the grounds blooming with the fruits of his cultivation were known in the neighborhood as Willian Park. Through his efforts alone, the area was converted from a bare pasture into a cool and shady garden with Whitman Falls as a backdrop and a parade of swans floating on the pond beyond.

On the eve of his 90th birthday in 1955, he still strolled to the Center daily, to the amazement of people who saw him walking all over town. "Some people think it strange to see a man walking," he told the West Hartford News, tongue in cheek, "but it's only because you don't see people walking anymore. It's the same thing with horses. At one time, there were many of them on the streets, but now they are a rare sight. So are people walking."

Friedman brothers built the six-story Hampshire House, the town's tallest buildings, during the apartment boom of the early 1960s.

bisected the town, and its traffic noise that disturbed nearby homes.

In 1963, the Hartford Times in a three-part series took a look at where West Hartford was headed. One new trend was apartment construction. In 1961 and 1962, 23 permits were issued for apartment houses that would be filled mostly by older people, some of whom were down-sizing from larger homes and wanted to remain in town.

The aging of the population and the inevitable beginning of a decline in the number of school-age children posed concerns. "This community is losing its youth and vitality," bemoaned a president of the Chamber of Commerce. "Grandmothers, not parents, are buying children's clothes. There is hardly anyone left to sell Girl Scout cookies or deliver newspapers." In fact, the largest of the Capital Region suburbs had become a quasi-city, one of the ten largest in the state. Increasingly, thoughtful leaders were realizing that suburban West Hartford's fate was inextricably linked with that of the core city.

Reaching its population peak of 68,301 in 1970, the town had a budget of nearly $32.5 million, an expense of $464 per resident – nine times the amount a half

century earlier. Unused land and open space were at a premium. More people were driving every day to work in West Hartford than were leaving to work downtown.

Bachelor Builders

Attorneys Bernard I. and Joseph X. Friedman were among the town's busiest residential developers in the 1950s and 1960s. They built almost all the houses north of Albany Avenue on streets with Indian names in the 1950s. The bachelor brothers referred to the area as "the reservation" and lived separately in a low-slung, contemporary house at Norwood Road and Mohawk Drive. Neighbors likened it to two motel units with a meeting place in the middle.

The Friedmans also built the town's largest and tallest apartment buildings, the Hampshire House, as multi-family buildings spread out Farmington Avenue. They acquired the key corner property along Farmington Avenue east of Trout Brook Drive at a bank's sealed-bid auction, winning against three other bidders by a mere $50. They built two high-rise buildings that later were among the first in town to be condominiumized. They also built and owned other apartment properties on Farmington Avenue and Quaker Lane South.

East-West Highway, here heading north-south at S-curves near Park Road exit, is ready for Interstate 84 traffic in 1969. Ramps lead to Park Road and Center at top. Trout Brook has been relocated in culvert beside the highway, and new houses are evidence of a building boom on streets off Trout Brook Drive at lower right.

Bulldozers Slice Through Town for East-West Highway

No project has been more disruptive in the life of the town than the controversial East-West Highway.

Now part of Interstate 84, the highway was planned as early as 1945 to move commuters and shoppers quickly from the suburbs to downtown Hartford. Some claim it was an idea backed by Beatrice Fox Auerbach to insure the dominance of her G. Fox & Co. as the city's leading department store. Others claimed that local east-west arteries were overburdened because of a sharp increase in West Hartford's population in the 1930s and 1940s.

The first plan for the highway, which would have split the town in half, sparked outrage and rejection. By 1956, Department of Transportation planners had put forth eight possible routes. Many townspeople still insisted the traffic problems could be eased by widening the main arteries like Farmington Avenue, staggering work hours and making some streets one-way. A leading highway opponent was former Mayor Harold F. Keith.

By 1960, however, the majority was convinced the $25 million project could not be stopped. Construction began in 1962 and was finished seven years later. The dangerous S-curves in the vicinity of the West Hartford Center/Park Road intersection were being widened in 2000.

Traffic counts show that the West Hartford section of the six-lane highway is the area's busiest.

Trout Brook used to flood regularly during thaws, and nearby residents bore the brunt. Some even kept score.

Trout Brook has been contained, thanks to long-term flood control projects. Here the brook is being tamed between Quaker Lane South and New Park Avenue in 1974. The former Brixton Street incinerator stack is in the background.

Consolidations of the 1970s and 1980s

Why did West Hartford stop growing in 1970 and begin a gradual decline in population to barely 61,000 at the beginning of the 21st century? The answers lie in the statistics on aging population and smaller families, births, deaths, school enrollments, out-migration, and the exhaustion of land for further residential development, as well as on economic changes in Greater Hartford. One reason was the sharp drop in the annual birth rate by the end of the decade. Wags called the trend "the birth dearth." The population aged and many retirees remained in town, prompting some to dub West Hartford "the St. Petersburg of the North."

The growing recognition that no city or town could remain an island unto itself spurred the issues of regionalism and city-suburb interdependence in the 1970s. To forge a better deal for Hartford, the city's activist deputy mayor, Nicholas R. Carbone, brought suit against seven surrounding towns, including West Hartford, to block federal funding under the Community Development Act. The dispute pointed up the disparity in demographic and economic growth. The seven towns then had a combined population and a grand list half again greater than Hartford's.

There had been accomplishments in regional cooperation, albeit modest in nature: establishment of the Capital Region Council of Governments, a regional crime squad, a mass transit district, education and library councils, and a CRCOG policy to construct in

Detective Saw His Share

In his 22 years as a detective with the West Hartford Police Department Kenneth O'Brien encountered some of the most notorious figures in town crime annals. He was involved in the investigation of the $7.1 million Wells Fargo robbery in 1983, the Steven Woods/Sunset Farm and Dr. Russell Manfredi murder cases, and the series of arsons at two synagogues, a rabbi's house, and a state representative's house in the early 1980s. Interviewed upon his retirement in 1995, he said, "This is supposedly beautiful, quiet West Hartford. But we certainly have our share of crime, and it's often spectacular."

the suburbs 6,000 units of low and moderate income housing before 1981, of which West Hartford pledged to build 600 units.

In the 1970s, the West Hartford Housing Authority began providing public housing for senior citizens at Elm Grove and later at the former Plant School, plus 16 units at scattered sites for families. It has managed a federal subsidy program for another 398 units and over the years has rehabilitated about 1,000 rundown homes that owners could not afford to repair.

Westfarms Mall, at the time Connecticut's largest, opened in 1974 on the West Hartford-Farmington town line and changed shopping patterns in the metropolitan area. Although the mall has continued to upscale and expand its mix of businesses and attracted a flurry of big-box retailers nearby, its long-term impact was felt more by downtown Hartford than by stores in West Hartford.

Another trend was the attraction of "country living" in the still rural, outlying towns, as West Hartford ran out of space. In the 1980s West Hartford "lost" 1,191 more residents despite a rise in the birth rate. In the same decade the census figures showed a substantial increase in the African American, Hispanic, and Asian population, a trend that continues.

Lower school enrollments forced the closing of eight schools, some of which had been built or renovated only a few years earlier. The closings prompted heated debates between financially pressed school boards seeking cost savings and parent groups wanting to save their neighborhood schools.

West Hartford Senior Center

The Senior Center opened to considerable fanfare in January 1960 – the first municipally sponsored program of its kind in Central Connecticut and only the third in the state. In 1957, the town had been urged to set up an education and recreation program for the growing constituency of older residents. The former library at 7 North Main St. was reserved for the purpose after it was vacated by the YMCA, which moved to a new building up the street in 1958.

The drive was spearheaded by chairman Harry Silverstone of Mountain Road, assistant attorney general for Connecticut. The town provided a $7,500 operating budget. The refurbished building was furnished by public donations and a grant from the Hartford Foundation for Public Giving.

Hundreds of townspeople braved icy weather for the open house dedication. Director Charlotte Ford advised that many older folks already had dropped by to offer their services. "At this rate," said Ruth Wessels, vice chairman of the Senior Citizens Advisory Board, "there will be no one left to serve."

The Senior Center was utilized more than its backers expected. Its operations eventually moved into larger quarters in the Town Hall and Elmwood Community Center.

West Hartford's Population Makeup, 1860-2000

Year	Population	Caucasian	Foreign Born	African-American	Hispanic	Am. Indian & Asian	Mixed & Other
1860	1,296	1,287	13				
1870	1,533	1,489	240	44			
1910	4,808	4,725	1,319	83			
1930	24,941	19,912	4,900	126		3	
1940	33,776	33,617	NA	151		7	
1950	44,402	44,220	5,951	173		9	
1960	62,382	62,109		229		46	
1970	68,031	67,573		263		195	
1980	61,301	59,458		683	799	1,160	
1990	60,110	56,493		1,310	1,891	2,307	
2000	61,046*	50,528		2,702	3,883	3,034	889

* The original 2000 census tally included in the West Hartford totals 2,543 University of Hartford students whose dormitories are in Hartford. The town notified the Census Bureau of the error, and a new official count was to be issued The racial breakdowns are adjusted here according to pro-rated estimates.

The 1990s

The last decade of the 20th century began with Connecticut in a recession, the longest and deepest since the Great Depression. The Hartford area was severely hit, losing more than 70,000 jobs (mainly in aerospace, banking, and insurance). United Technologies Corp. alone laid off 30,000 workers. In downtown Hartford, the last of the large department stores, G.Fox & Co. and Sage-Allen, shut their doors, resulting in the takeover of branch stores in Westfarms Mall and West Hartford Center. Hartford National Bank and the Connecticut Bank & Trust Co., successor to the old West Hartford Trust Co., were merged into Fleet Bank. Society for Savings, the sixth oldest mutual savings bank in New England, was taken over in 1992 by the Bank of Boston, which in turn was merged into Fleet in 2000. The construction boom of the previous decades that had produced the Hartford Civic Center and office high-rises like CityPlace ended abruptly. The vacancy rate in downtown Hartford office buildings and retail stores soared.

West Hartford did not escape the impact. It was felt mainly in the real-estate market, as residential values declined as much as 30 percent. For-sale signs appeared in front of hundreds of homes at one point. Added to the distress of owners was the property revaluation of 1989, which resulted in an increase in assessed values of triple the previous level a decade earlier, just as sales prices began to fall. Corporate mergers and downsizing caused countless executives and managers to be transferred or lose their jobs. The total number of residents employed declined from 33,118 in 1986 to 27,212 in 1997. The rising birth rate and influx of younger people pushed school enrollments up by nearly 2,000 to 9,354 in 2001. Portable classrooms were added and closed schools were reopened.

By the mid-1990s and into the new millennium, there was a renewed sense of prosperity. The new economy was booming, real-estate values were rising, job openings were going begging, school test scores were on the increase, and there was an overall sense of optimism.

One of West Hartford's early residential neighborhoods: Washington Circle under construction off Park Road in 1919.

Original stone milepost marker stands at Four Mile Road and Farmington Avenue, four miles from the old state house in Hartford.

Elm Grove Apartments for the elderly and disabled are at 11 Grove St. in Elmwood.

One of West Hartford's recent residential neighborhoods: Governor's Square at Asylum Avenue and Steele Road in 1996.

IV. Living Together

West Hartford grew from a small town of mostly farms in the 19th century into a mature residential suburb in the 20th century. Except for West Hartford Center (its original business, government, and community center that made it indeed "The Center"), the industrial area in the southeast corner, and ultimately retail districts in Elmwood, Bishops Corner, and Corbins Corner, the town retained a residential identity.

The residential pattern started on the East Side in the late 19th century, when Hartford residents spilled across the city line. The residential movement moved west, out Farmington, Albany, and New Britain avenues, initially to Main Street and ultimately west to Ridgewood and Mountain roads and the east side of Talcott Mountain. West Hill, Elmhurst, Webster Hill, "Back of the Center," Buena Vista, Duffy-Sedgwick, King Philip, Astronaut Village, Golf Club Acres, "West of Mountain Road" – these became the neighborhood identities in a larger, rapidly growing town.

Today, West Hartford is a community of neighborhoods. Some were created by enlightened developers. Some have formalized as associations registered with the town. Others have more casual connections based on proximity, their neighborhood school, and the occasional block party. A sampling of those with formally established associations:

West Hill

West Hill was conceived in the 1920s by Horace R. Grant, a Hartford manufacturer, and Stanley K. Dimock. Originally a 75-acre farm belonging to the Hamilton family, West Hill was purchased in 1857 by the financier and transportation magnate Cornelius J. Vanderbilt. Two years after his death in 1879, his son built a colossal mansion, chocolate-colored with a veranda on three sides and a great cupola on top. Young Vanderbilt, who took his own life in 1882, never moved into the house. Instead, Ira Dimock, a silk manufacturer

Cornelius J. Vanderbilt's mansion on West Hill, largest early house in town, required a ton of coal a day to heat in winter.

and inventor, raised his family there. It was a grand setting for at least one memorable affair, the wedding of their artist daughter Edith to a fellow artist, William Glackens. Glackens's oil painting, "View of West Hartford," which shows the Unionville trolley car and ice skaters looking toward the Center from West Hill around the turn of the century, is part of the collection at Hartford's Wadsworth Atheneum. After Dimock's death, the mansion was torn down, to be replaced by a cul-de-sac of substantial homes. Today, West Hill is an official historic district.

Ellsworth S. Grant's memories of his childhood there give a vivid picture:

"The 1920s were West Hartford's heyday of home building. When I was about 6, we moved to West Hill, where my father and Stanley Dimock had started to build a number of fine homes and buried the utilities underground. Our residence at the north end backed up to St. Joseph's Academy for girls. I was rather frightened by the nuns in their black habits and didn't dare to trespass on the grounds. In wintertime, however, the hill west of the school teemed with kids sliding. No house or street broke the terrain, and a good sled could carry you all the way to North Quaker Lane.

"I can recall few homes between West Hill and Steele Road. Bainbridge and Birch roads were almost one entire marsh and woodlot.

"For children, West Hill was an island-like kingdom of their very own. There were endless fascinations: the foundations and frames of rising homes, the open lots for games and huts, and the lanes over which we could ride our bikes. The West Hill gang, armed with wooden swords and one BB gun, mostly boys in knickers and long socks but also open to girls who could fight, struck terror into would-be invaders from the Swedish enclave on the Boulevard."

Sunny Reach

One early community off Bloomfield Avenue started as an experiment of a New York businessman, Carl Sturhahn, who moved to Hartford as a partner in the Rossia Insurance Co. Around the time of World War I, he bought the farmland now occupied by Sunnydale and Sunny Reach roads, built a substantial barn for cows and a prize bull, hired a farmer, and planted a garden with some hope of creating a self-sufficient utopia. He

Carl Sturhahn's barn on Sunnydale Road was remodeled in the 1940s into an architecturally intriguing home by the Wallace Browns.

and his wife Maie lived for almost 20 years on the Sunny Reach estate.

By the 1930s they had stopped farming and had begun to transform their acreage into a residential development. Their two married sons had already built homes on some of the property and Sunny Reach was ready for additional elegant houses. New homeowners joined the association to acquire and maintain the roads and utility services and to mount a legal battle to prevent the town from turning Sunny Reach Road into a thoroughfare.

Sunset Farm

In 1917, Paul Butterworth and his wife Clare Smith Butterworth built the first year-round residence on William Brown Smith's dairy and horse breeding farm, 200 acres of meadows and woods snuggling up to the reservoirs at the foot of Talcott Mountain. Until then,

Sunset Farm's best-known achievement was when Smith's thoroughbred Thomas Jefferson won a $10,000 purse at Buffalo. Another was due to his wife's work as Hartford's city missionary. Virginia Thrall Smith used

Paul Butterworth kept neighborhood children entranced into the 1970s with stories of Sunset Farm and of "Thomas Jefferson, the handsomest horse in the world," who was pastured there in the late 19th century. In 1937, when Niles-Bement-Pond bought Charter Oak Park where Tom was buried, his tombstone was moved to Sunset Farm.

Sunset Farm sugar maples were tapped in the 1920s as they still are today. To a child of the Francis Fenn family, spring sap was tempting even before it was boiled down into syrup.

the property as a summer haven for impoverished mothers and children.

In 1935, the 13 families on the farm agreed to incorporate to provide a vehicle for joint ownership of ponds, roads, recreation facilities, and open space. Paul sold 60 lots for attractive, well-spaced homes and added such amenities as a swimming pool, tennis court, and upper pond. Paul wrote: "The sunny slopes, the woodlands, the brooks and ponds, all within striking distance of the schools and downtown offices, seemed to make this a preeminent place in which to live and to raise children." The early residents banded together to promote "a tolerant friendliness toward each other and toward the world," and signed a resolution to "pledge ourselves to the inculcation of this principle in the generation springing up around us."

One friend said of this tall, spare, and modest benefactor: "He was the kind of person who warms the world." Another added, "I find it hard to think of anyone who contributed more in the volunteer field than Paul." During his 92 years he gave time and money to many charities: as a founder of Child & Family Services, chairman of Hartford College for Women and the Ethel Walker School in Simsbury, and a director of the Newington Children's Hospital and American School for the Deaf. During World War II he helped Japanese and European refugees come to America. He paid most of the cost of building the Friends Meeting House on Quaker Lane South in 1950 and for years supplied it with wood he chopped himself.

There are now 75 families in the association. The last sheep were gone by 1960, but a few horses and chickens are reminders today of the farm tradition at Sunset Farm.

Woodridge Lake

When in 1912 the iceman Fred Arnold purchased land along what used to be the Middle Road to Farmington to build another ice pond for his Trout Brook Ice & Feed Co., he could not have foreseen that someday it would, as Woodridge Lake, become the centerpiece for a subdivision that got under way a few years before World War II. After dredging, he erected ice barns for storage and laid trolley tracks to carry the ice to Farmington Avenue for shipment. In 1927 he sold this

Woodridge Association Photos

Aerial photograph shows the start of the Woodridge Association around Woodridge Lake and Wood Pond, looking southeast in the early 1940s. New Britain Avenue is at top, intersecting with South Main Street at upper left. Ridgewood Road runs diagonally at left and Tunxis Road hugs lake at center. Conard High School, Corbins Corner, and the Buena Vista recreation complex were yet to be developed.

operation to the Southern New England Ice Co., which discontinued it nine years later.

Along came Wallace B. Goodwin of the Goodwin Pottery family, who found real-estate development more promising than making clay conduits. In 1936, he began acquiring the land west of Ridgewood Road and visualized the creation of what he called "the country development of seclusion – not isolation."

A descendant of the Goodwin potters, as a youngster Wallace had watched the old family enterprise burn to the ground. Elmwood had only one piece of fire equipment – a hose on a pair of wheels. The next year he opened the town's first insurance and real estate office on New Britain Avenue. There were only two dozen houses on the avenue from the railroad tracks to South Main Street; he reached his clients by bicycle and the more affluent ones by horse and buggy.

The Sunfish "fleet" competes during weekend races on Woodridge Lake. In the 1960s, some of the Woodridge Sailing Club fleet entered regattas with regional and national champions on Harrington Sound in Bermuda and at Hardings Beach on Cape Cod. They brought home trophies.

Goodwin was responsible for the location of Abbott Ball, Bennett Metal Treating and Wiremold Co. on the pottery site, and he built houses for New Departure workers on Woodlawn Street and developed Burgoyne Gardens.

Goodwin had trouble getting mortgage money from local banks and insurance companies for his Woodridge project. Their feeling was that people weren't going to go out there and live in the woods. There were also problems with zoning and building officials who felt houses should be lined up like soldiers and not set down in staggered formations according to the demand of the land.

Goodwin eventually acquired all of the land bordering Wood Pond and the larger Woodridge Lake, which stretches for more than a mile between Wood Pond and Tunxis roads. Norris Prentice was Goodwin's architect and Charles Robinson the builder. The first Woodridge house was built in 1937 for Charles Derrick, head of the Hartford Electric Light Co. The lakes and the house plans were so attractive that 44 families bought homes there even before the start of World War II. In 1944, the property owners banded together to form the Woodridge Association and three years later took over the water rights for recreational use.

The uniqueness of Goodwin's vision was captured in a newspaper article from the mid-1940s: "Few Hartfordites are aware that there is a winter-summer resort just a stone's throw from West Hartford Center – Woodridge Lake, just back of Ridgewood Road, formerly the old Arnold ice pond. Now this mile and a half long lake is a sight on Sundays – you see skaters, ice boats, toboggan slides, and 19 cabins dotting the edge of the water with smoke curling up from fireplaces. In the summer each owner dives off his own private wharf. The lake is stocked with fish. Last year over 10 sailboats were visible at a time."

By 1958 the racing of small Sailfish and Sunfish on the lake, the town's only recreational body of water, had become fully organized with a commodore, race committee, and trophies.

Today the lake and its beach are private, owned by 160 member families whose property deeds give them "lake privileges by invitation." A few of the early lakeside "cabins" remain beside the water, but the waterside homes are among the most desirable in town.

Elmwood Acres

In 1996, 25 members of the Women's Club of Elmwood Acres gathered for a reunion at Elmwood Community Center. Kay Beach, Polly Cunningham, and Alice Francis, who still live in the area, made many of the arrangements. The neighborhood organization they had started 52 years before meant so much to them in their young married lives, it was worth travelling a long way to talk over old times. Marge Boss LeBorgne came all the way from California.

Elmwood Acres was a federally subsidized housing project of 300 units, one of three projects built in West Hartford to house war workers and their families. Some of the wives labored in the industries. Others stayed home and found ways to help each other and the community. They formed a club that met for monthly programs and holiday parties, and sponsored scout troops, a summer church school and a nursery school.

Marge LeBorgne worked at Pratt & Whitney while her husband worked at Colt's. Years later she wrote: "We were like one big family. Many of us felt displaced and had no relatives in Connecticut. At first we looked forward to the war being over so we could go home. However, by 1945 Connecticut was home to most of us and we didn't want to leave. Elmwood was a great place to live and raise our children."

In 1956 the government decided to sell the three housing projects in town to returning veterans. Neighbors persuaded the town to turn one into Kennedy Park and another into single-family homes instead of apartment housing. Occupants of Elmwood Acres were given the opportunity to buy the houses in which they had been living. Some took up the offer, becoming first-time homeowners and staying in West Hartford. One group from Elmwood Acres, calling themselves the Tuesday Nighters, still meets. The rest depend on occasional reunions to talk about their wartime memories.

Wolcott Neighborhood Organization

The Board of Education had a plan in the late 1970s to organize a community school system. The schools would double as health centers and places where older people could come for a hot, nutritious lunch and where issues affecting neighbors could be discussed and where needs could be noticed and met. The town hired a

Former residents of Elmwood Acres, a federally subsidized housing project for World War II industry workers, organized a 50-year reunion in 1996 for members of their wartime women's club. From left are Marge LeBorgne of Laguna Beach, Calif., Alice Frances of Simsbury, and Kay Beach and Polly Cunningham, both of West Hartford.

facilitator, appropriated funds, and helped the communities organize and distribute newsletters. Most of the neighborhood groups organized by the town are no longer active, although some, Morley and Charter Oak in particular, were strong for years.

The experiment is still alive and well in the Wolcott School neighborhood. The Wolcott Neighborhood Association incorporated in 1982. A 13-member board meets regularly and hosts an annual meeting with a guest speaker at Faxon Library. For a while a volunteer nurse spent several days a week at the school, testing people's blood pressure and consulting about health problems. When that program stopped, the association sponsored Health Fairs where neighbors could check up on their well being.

The association sponsors special events – a plant sale before Mothers' Day, a September Back-to-School picnic, a Harvest Craft Fair. Several of these raise money to be donated to families through West Hartford's The Town That Cares Fund or through the school. The association also has a Welcome New Neighbors program and, to keep members informed, continues to publish a newsletter and holds a Meet the Candidates Night before elections.

The togetherness of the neighborhood has produced a community that knows how to work together – to participate, for instance, in an ongoing town-sponsored planning program to rehabilitate Elmwood Center. For several years, Wolcott Neighborhood Association members and other Elmwood residents have met regularly at Faxon Library to help shape their community.

Two members of the Wolcott Neighborhood board, Lynn Rossi and Rosemary Sliva with her daughter Katie, present a contribution to the Police Department's Canine Patrol Fund to Ed Sanady, representing the town. With them in front of Wolcott School are police officers Andrew Niederdorfer, Marc Bassos, and Dawn DiMauro and the patrol dog, Luke.

One of the town's newest neighborhoods is at The Reservoir, where two private developers are building single-family homes and condominiums on a hilltop off Farmington Avenue. Reservoir No. 1 is visible at left.

Celebrate!West Hartford **45**

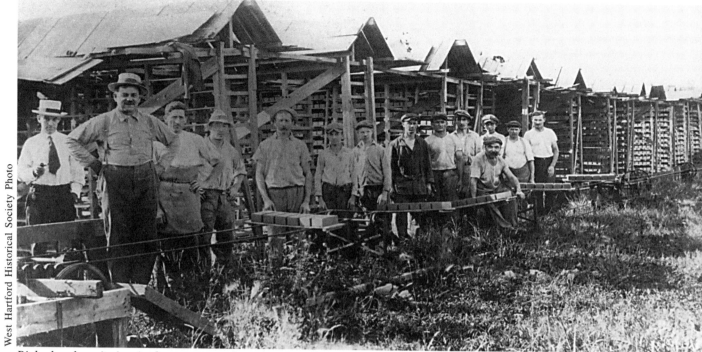

Rich clay deposits inspired pottery manufacturing as well as this early brickyard in Elmwood.

Workers cut ice from pond in Trout Brook to be hauled up a conveyor into ice house and packed in sawdust for shipment by railroad car – up to 50 carloads daily – to New York City. Hundreds of workers came by trolley from Hartford during ice harvesting. Trout Brook Ice & Feed Co. prospered in West Hartford Center and at Woodridge Lake from 1879 to 1927.

One of the busiest workplaces and nerve centers in the early 20th century was the office at Burnham's grocery store in West Hartford Center. Here, switchboard operators take orders for delivery across town. Prices are posted on blackboard at left.

V. Working

Business and industry grew gradually in what was essentially a farming community – an adjunct to the commercial center of Hartford. But West Hartford has always been more self-sufficient than the typical bedroom suburb.

Grist mills, blacksmith shops, sawmills, brickyards, ice manufacturing, and even distilleries helped sustain the early community and provide exports to Hartford in the 17th and 18th centuries.

From the earliest days, the town's industry located along Trout Brook, the source of waterpower. It became concentrated in Elmwood because of its rich clay deposits essential to early pottery-making. The arrival of the railroad in the late 19th century cemented Elmwood's position as the place for businesses to locate.

Modern manufacturing officially began in 1891 when the Whitlock Manufacturing Co. was persuaded by Elmwood's Walter E. Goodwin to locate on South Street along the railroad tracks. Goodwin served as president until 1894. Its business was bending pipe, pre-heated by steam, for automobile radiators, water heaters, and giant water turbines for the Gatun Dam in Panama. Later, the company concentrated on making storage heaters and tubular heat exchangers for laundries, textile plants, hotels, and other large users of hot water. During World War II, Whitlock was involved in the Manhattan (Atomic Bomb) Project and afterward supplied specially designed systems for nuclear submarines and aircraft carriers. In the 1960s its research laboratory developed equipment for producing ammonium nitrate and urea fertilizers. The company was then sold and relocated to Texas.

In 1912, machinist and inventor George Edward Abbott purchased the Goodwin Brothers pottery works on the south side of New Britain Avenue, just west of the railroad tracks, which had burned in 1908. He

Workers take break at Frank Strong's carriage, woodworking, and blacksmith shop at Bishops Corner in late 1800s. Buildings at fork of Albany Avenue and Flagg Road burned in 1904.

The Albany Avenue Ornamental Iron Shop at 2575 Albany Ave., near the site of Frank Strong's blacksmith shop, is owned and operated by Graham T. Jones. He is the third generation of the Jones family to run the more than 100-year-old business there.

brought his 10 employees from Hartford to produce steel ball bearings in an enterprise called Abbott Ball Co., which survives to this day.

Two years later, two brothers from Bristol set up the New Departure Co., which also manufactured ball bearings for the burgeoning auto industry. It also forged an unusual paternal approach to employee benefits that made a substantial contribution to the life of Elmwood. During World War I, its work force zoomed from 200 to 1,200. To lure workers living in Hartford, New Departure paid their carfare to and from work. Then it bought a huge tract of land between Woodlawn Street and Newington Road, and sold 100 lots at rock-bottom prices to employees for home sites. A cafeteria, medical department, intramural sports, and outings were other benefits provided. After the war, New Departure became a division of General Motors and during the Depression was merged into GM's Meriden plant. The factory here remained idle until 1946 when Royal Typewriter acquired it to produce ribbons.

The first factory to appear on New Park Avenue traced its beginning to a West Hartford church. As a young man, Ira Hobart Spencer worked part-time at St. James's Episcopal Church, pumping the organ. He invented a small water turbine that did the job better than he could. He founded Spencer Turbine Co., which produced more than 50,000 blowers that power nearly every organ in America. He also introduced the turbine vacuum cleaner system, and in 1919 moved his factory to West Hartford. Before his death in 1928 he had taken out about 100 patents and was nationally recognized as a leading authority on low-pressure air engineering. At

The Fuller Brush Man

Alfred C. Fuller of Colony Road, the first Fuller Brush Man, started in 1906 peddling brushes out of a suitcase in the Boston area. He made them himself, manufacturing at night and selling door-to-door by day. He soon left Boston and got off the train in Hartford. He liked what he saw, made it his headquarters and West Hartford his home. He and his wife Mary Primrose (both Nova Scotia natives, who met at a sales meeting in Toronto) had two sons in the business. In 1958, when he was 72 and chairman of board of the closely held company, the Fuller Brush Co. had three factories, 23 distributing stations, 109 branch offices, and 7,400 dealers who sold $1.6 million worth of brushes, cleaning chemicals, cosmetics, and vitamins a week.

Fuller recognized in Hartt School of Music co-founder Moshe Paranov something of his own up-by-the-bootstraps spirit and became the Hartt School's principal benefactor until his death in 1971. The three-building Hartt complex was named the Alfred C. Fuller Music Center in 1963, with the main classroom building called Paranov Hall. Prim Fuller, also a benefactor of Hartt as well as the Hartford Symphony and the Bushnell Memorial, died here in 1997 at age 94.

The Fuller Brush Co. moved in 1973 to Great Bend, Kan., where the business continues.

its height in the 1950s, the company bearing his name employed 250 persons. It later relocated to Windsor.

The progressive, formerly family-owned Wiremold Co. has been a fixture in Elmwood since 1929. D. Hayes Murphy, son of the founder, moved the company from Hartford, where it produced flexible conduit for wiring

Elmwood railroad station on New Park Avenue, just north of New Britain Avenue, made Elmwood the place for businesses to locate. It provided easy access for employees and for shipping.

West Hartford Historical Society Photo

Celebrate!West Hartford   **49**

and electrical outlets known as "wiremold" and "plugmold." Murphy introduced employee profit sharing long before its general acceptance and served his community on the Town Council. On West Hill he built a large residence for his family of two sons and three daughters. He trained his sons, John and Robert, to run

P&W: 'Best Plant Anywhere'

West Hartford's biggest factory, Pratt & Whitney Machine Tool Co., opened in record time in 1940. The first excavations began in March on the site of the old Charter Oak race track. Two thousand men worked three million man-hours to ready the site for employees and 23,000 tons of machinery moved from the Capitol Avenue complex in Hartford. The one-story plant was 1,000 feet long and 550 feet wide, with 110,000 panes of glass for natural light. The Hartford Times described it as "the newest and probably the best equipped plant of its kind anywhere." And Fortune magazine called West Hartford the world headquarters for the strategic industry.

A company history published in 1940 was effusive. "Never before has an old-time company occupied a gradually increasing group of buildings for 79 years and then deliberately abandoned them for a new plant in a new location designed specifically for its own use. To build and move a plant of this size in such a brief time is an achievement and a record! It could not have been done even a few years ago. Modern methods and materials made it possible.

"Working conditions for the men are tremendously improved. There is ample light and ventilation. All the newest conveniences are available so that a man can do his work and yet retain his physical comfort at a high level. Jobs are no longer backbreaking, because electrical and mechanical lifting devices have taken the 'tough' part out of a machinist's life forever. He is well fed at a company cafeteria at noon, where hot meals are served to him at cost. All day food trucks are available throughout the plant to give those who require it "in-between" snacks. An excellent first-aid station is maintained. Masks and goggles are provided to guard against eye and lung injuries. Pratt & Whitney craftsmen now work under modern, safe, healthy conditions, in a plant that is absolutely fireproof."

The P&W Men's Club even got a sparkling new clubhouse – the former 4-H Building from the old State Fair on the property.

the business, but at the same time devised a special plan to forestall family feuding after his death by distributing two classes of stock – voting and non-voting. Only the daughters had voting rights.

Holo-Krome's birth here was anything but auspicious. On the very day of the stock market crash in 1929, its three founders – William A. Purtell, William C. Stauble, and Russell E. Gregory – produced their first cold-forged socket screw to compete with the fasteners pioneered by Hartford's Allen Manufacturing Co. in 1910. They did not have enough money to meet the payroll for their 20 employees, but the infant company was saved by West Hartford's Graham H. Anthony, head of Veeder-Root Co. It was hand-to-mouth financing even after Purtell had secured a patent. Thanks to the salesmanship of Stauble, who cultivated Detroit's auto manufacturers, Holo-Krome was able to move into a new facility on Newington Road in 1936 with a staff of 40. In 1946 the company became a wholly-owned subsidiary of Veeder-Root, and Purtell quit as president to enter politics. In 1952, he was elected a U.S. Senator, the first from West Hartford.

Five years after the founding of Holo-Krome, Jacobs Manufacturing, the leader in drill chucks, built a plant almost next door on Newington Road. Engineer Arthur I. Jacobs had received a patent for a new type of chuck, which was a phenomenal success, accepted by the trade within weeks after its introduction. Two young bankers, Hubert M. Toppin and Louis E. Stoner (Jacobs's son-in-law), soon joined him and both eventually served terms as president. In 1941, the growing company purchased nine acres on Newington Road and constructed a 60,000-square-foot plant and office. After the retirement of Stoner and Toppin, Louis B. Stoner took over the family-owned business. In 1953 it was sold.

The manufacture of Pope-Hartford automobiles in Hartford inspired the founding of the Dunham-Bush Co. Philip Bush began making radiators for automobiles in 1907 and the next year, strapped for capital, he turned to Col. Richard J. Goodman, who agreed to become president and served for 30 years. Goodman's family had lived in West Hartford for five generations; he was chairman for a time of the Board of Finance. By 1927 the company entered the air-conditioning and refrigeration business. In 1947, Bush moved from Hartford into a new 100,000-square-foot plant on South

Pratt & Whitney plant, built in 1940, was razed to make way for Home Depot development near Charter Oak School.

Street and soon became the Dunham-Bush Co. The local factory is now called Hartford Compressors.

The largest and most famous enterprise to make West Hartford its home was a division of Pratt & Whitney Machine Tool Co., which established Hartford's reputation as a major machine tool center and made enormous contributions to the metal technology of the world. The Chandler-Evans Division of Pratt & Whitney moved from Hartford to the abandoned Charter Oak Park here in 1940. Some 2,600 employees transferred into a well-lighted and ventilated one-story plant that covered 20 acres, just in time to meet the production demands of World War II. More than 7,000 were employed at war's height.

A latecomer to West Hartford, yet the oldest manufacturer of all, is Colt's Manufacturing, founded in 1847 to produce guns under the landmark blue-onion dome of Hartford's Colt Armory. Starting in 1965, its offices and manufacturing operations were moved by

degrees to the former P&W complex in West Hartford. By the 1990s, the company, in serious financial trouble, filed for bankruptcy. A New York merchant banking firm took control and reorganized the management.

In the post-war era, the area of New Park and Oakwood avenues became the home of such companies as Carling Electric, Walton, Curtis 1000, and Connecticut Manifold Forms.

General Cigar created the town's first and only industrial park in 1972 on a 12-acre site off Oakwood Avenue that formerly was the last location of the Jewell Belting Co. For 30 years General Cigar had used the property for tobacco warehouses and dormitories for tobacco pickers. Bernard Kohn of Westwood Road, chairman of Culbro Tobacco, a division of General Cigar, described the extensive renovation: "We took a group of old buildings, tore most of them down, converted an ugly factory into an office building, and turned the area into something quite special." When completed, the park included eleven handsome brown and tan buildings, nine of them new, with 150,000 square feet of interior space and parking for 600 cars.

The $12 million federally-funded Piper Brook urban renewal project, Elmwood's last industrial redevelopment, was completed in 1973. It is filled with more than a hundred small commercial and light industrial establishments, among which are a new U.S. Post Office on Shield Street.

The local Greenberg family built a leather-goods company into a major but short-lived player in the toy industry. Coleco Industries transformed the old Talcott Junior High School in Elmwood into a state-of-the-art administrative headquarters. Later, Ames Department Stores, also started by a local family, the Gilmans, made the former school its corporate headquarters for a time.

The Rise in Service Businesses

With the decline in manufacturing, West Hartford turned to other forms of business and commerce. Some of the original farmland was converted to nurseries and landscaping services: Whiting Greenhouses dates to 1852. Others included W.W. Thomson, Peter Cascio, P.A. Torizzo, Albert Gledhill, Richard F. Patrissi, and William Butler.

A.C. Petersen Farms, a dairy business begun in 1914, established its main retail outlet and plant at 240 Park Road. At its height, it had ice cream parlors and

H. Joseph Gerber

One industrialist was a Holocaust survivor who came here empty-handed and without command of the English langue in 1940 from Vienna. H. Joseph Gerber, who founded a new company in East Windsor as a college junior, moved to West Hartford when he was married and lived here the rest of his life.

His discovery of a graphic computer called the Gerber Variable Scale and a $3,000 investment launched the Gerber Scientific Instrument Co. The feat also inspired a Broadway play called "A Young Man in a Hurry." With more than 600 patents in his name, he was awarded the National Medal of Technology in 1994. A General Electric vice chairman who served on the Gerber board called him "the most creative and innovative individual" he had ever known. He is also called the "father of the automated apparel industry."

Coleco Industries

Who would have thought that an old leather-goods company – Connecticut Leather Co. – would soar in 1983 with two of the hottest products in all consumerdom, the Cabbage Patch Kids dolls and the Adam home computer system? They made brothers Arnold and Leonard Greenberg two of the area's greatest fortunes in the post-war period and vaulted Coleco into an impressive new headquarters in the old Talcott Junior High School in Elmwood Center.

At its height in the mid-1980s, Coleco employed 800 people in West Hartford and 6,000 internationally, most of them in manufacturing in upstate New York.

The much-ballyhooed Adam computer helped drive the stock price to $65 a share before Adam was abandoned as a failure, swamping the company in red ink. With gallows humor, an office wit suggested a new name for the company that abruptly went bankrupt in 1988 after 57 years: Toys Were Us.

luncheonettes in 14 towns. When Allen C. Petersen, president and grandson of the founder, sold the family-owned chain's last four outlets in 2000, three partners took over the ice cream plant and continued using original recipes that made the ice cream a local favorite. Petersen's was a celebratory place for life's milestones. Parents would take their children there after report cards were issued. "It was the place where everyone seemed to go as a reward, and it had the best ice cream around," said new partner Elliott Tertes.

French Cleaners opened in 1911 and has continued through four generations.

Viking Bakery started in 1928, moved to 68 Park Road and eventually to 500 Oakwood Ave., where Arvid Marcuson did a thriving business – especially in doughnuts. Its Swedish limpa bread was thick, dense, dark, and so good that if you made it home and inside the door you probably ate it before it got to the table.

The Roaring 20s ended with W.D.Clark Co. erecting the "first modern office and retail building" in the Center – "out in the country" on the north side of Farmington Avenue, west of Main Street. Offices and stores quickly followed. Thirty years later, 4,000 people would go to work in nearly 500 offices and stores in town. When more people commuted into town than out, the West Hartford News called the suburb "The Working City."

Bishops Corner in 1960 exemplifies rise of service business sector. This aerial view looks southeast. North Main Street slices horizontally through developing shopping area. At right center is regional office of Allstate Insurance Cos.

Largest Industries in 1960

Company	Total Tax Assessment
Pratt & Whitney	$6,279,670*
Dunham-Bush	1,755,430*
Holo-Krome	1,572,840
Jacobs Manufacturing	1,402,050*
Chandler-Evans	1,372,010
Wiremold	1,371,880
General Cigar	1,262,860
Royal McBee	971,330*
Spencer Turbine	832,390*
United Tool & Die	654,760
Hartford Steel Ball	494,930
Abbott Ball	394,490
Curtiss 1000	286,450*
Carling Electric	284,570*
Connecticut Manifold Forms	181,250*
Walton Company	136,880

*As of 2000 no longer in operation here

Major Employers in 2000

		(Approximate number employed)
Town of West Hartford	municipal	484
	education	1,133
University of Hartford	education	960
Colt's Manufacturing	firearms	657
Wiremold	electrical controls	637
Hebrew Home for the Aged	nursing home	540
Filene's	department store	400
Chandler-Evans	control systems	390
Sears, Roebuck	department store	330
St. Mary Home	nursing home	328
Holo-Krome	fasteners	300
Community Outreach for Elderly	social services	162
Konover & Associates	real estate	150
Blum Shapiro	accounting	120
Abbott Ball	ball bearings	113

Family homestead of Myron Allen Andrews and Suzie Butler Andrews faces Farmington Avenue at prime northeast corner of North Main Street. In 1926 the house was razed to make way for new West Hartford Trust Co., the town's first bank. Myron Andrews and his sons, Morris and George, had raised cows on their property, which stretched down to Trout Brook. The Andrews family owned other residential properties along Farmington Avenue and Brace Road and developed other buildings that they leased to retail and commercial tenants.

The Doctors Root

There was only one other physician's office here in 1923 when Dr. Maurice T. (Tim) Root hung out his shingle at 51 North Main St. He took over the practice of another general practitioner who accepted a fulltime position with an insurance company. "It was a middle-class practice made up of the type of people I knew and understood," he said.

After raising their four children, Dr. Sophie Root, an endocrynologist, set up her own practice in her husband's home-office. Dr. Tim, the first physician appointed to the Hartford Hospital staff who didn't maintain a Hartford office, later became chief of medicine there. He continued to make house calls and visit convalescent homes even after increasing deafness compelled him to close his office practice in 1963. Dr. Sophie cut down her office practice to four days a week at that time. When the couple officially retired, they had 89 years of private medical practice here between them.

This was still the era when most local telephone exchanges were ADams and JAckson and addresses were West Hartford 7, Conn., and West Hartford 10.

Phoenix Mutual Life planned in the 1950s to move its home office to 60 acres on Asylum Avenue west of St. Joseph College. The Hartford Chamber of Commerce squelched the idea, however, and the landmark "boat" building was born in downtown Hartford.

As the town matured and its population aged, stores, offices, dry cleaning, house renovations, day care, auto repair garages, landscaping, and financial services were among the needs. In a 1976 Bicentennial message, Mayor Anne P. Streeter noted that in many instances both parents must work in order to afford a home in West Hartford. She predicted that by 2000, most women would be part of the workforce.

Banking began when a group of community leaders founded the West Hartford Trust Co. in 1926. One of the early principals was Norman G. Fricke, who joined the bank in 1929 and managed what became the Center office of Connecticut Bank & Trust Co. until 1963, when he became first manager of its Elmwood office. At one time there were 27 banks and branches in West Hartford, although continuing consolidations reduced the numbers.

The growth in homes produced an increase in real estate agents. Some contended that more people worked in real estate than any other single occupation in town (although that could be disputed by educators and those in the medical and legal professions). When Tom Faulkner started the T.D. Faulkner Co. here in 1910, he sold real estate from a horse and buggy. An average eight-room house could be purchased for $4,500. The 1920s were boom years, when most of what he called "the large gracious homes which now exist" were built. A standard eight-room house sold then for $6,500. In the late 1940s, another housing boom got under way in West Hartford. Mortgage rates dropped to 4 percent in 1945. An eight-room house sold for $20,000. During the 1950s and 60s, median prices increased to $45,000. A generation later, the median house value in West Hartford was $172,000.

Barrows & Wallace, T.R. Preston, Heritage, and Hurwit & Simons were realtors who left their imprint if not their names on the local landscape. Some were absorbed into Prudential Connecticut Realty, the largest in town, headquartered in the former Senior Center on North Main Street. Others became part of DeWolfe New England, the second largest, which turned a few heads when it located its offices in the former Lucy Baltzell shop on LaSalle Road.

Construction became a major industry. At the time of the 1954 Centennial, West Hartford home builders advertised that since 1940 they had built 5,880 homes valued at more than $80 million in town. Forty builders were listed, from individuals and the Liljedahl Brothers to I.R. Stich Associates and F.P. Carabillo Construction Co.

Developers and management companies emerged. West Hartford Center has been dominated by three "landlords," the Sinatro brothers (who launched their insurance agency and management company there in 1936), W.D. Clark Co., and the Andrews family properties, managed since 1965 by Richard L. Mahoney Co. Samuel and Robert Lavery, Seymour Sard, and Leonard Udolf also played major roles in the Center.

Postman Followed Golden Rule

A West Hartford postman became so widely known an authority on dogs that he once was asked to psychoanalyze a neurotic cocker owned by a woman psychologist.

James B. Smith of 1232 Farmington Ave. retired in 1952 after 31 years as one of the town's first postmen. His route included the area from Prospect Avenue to West Hill between the Boulevard and Fern Street. He saw many changes, but he found the toughest to take was "watching the old families break up and their beautiful homes turned into convalescent hospitals and boarding houses."

Smith, who raised and showed dogs in his off hours, only got bitten once on his rounds – by "a mean old dog. I thought I had his confidence. I'd been feeding him chocolate and crackers for weeks and we had become good friends. One day, though, I approached him a little too fast and he jumped and nipped me in the instep."

A reporter asked what he had learned after all those years on the route. "Just this. If you treat people and dogs the way you'd want them to treat you, you'll get along all right. You get just what you give out of both. Be a decent guy and you'll enjoy every minute you work."

Gerald M. Steinberg developed Corporate Center West on South Main Street. David T. Chase, Simon Konover, Stanley D. Fisher, Allan Hutensky, Richard F. Mulready, and Philip A. Schonberger were among those who went bigtime, but whose roots remained here. And, alas, in the 1990s there was Colonial Realty, a West Hartford-based real-estate investment company that made and lost fortunes.

When it opened at Bishops Corner in the mid-1950s, Allstate Insurance Cos. was the largest office employer. Other insurance and travel agencies blossomed, from Andrews Associates to Singer Travel Service and, sign of the times, Walsh Brothers and Sisters. So did funeral homes: Molloy, Sheehan-Hilborn-Breen, Newkirk & Whitney, and Taylor & Modeen.

Household names in interior design were Jeanette S. Ward, Irene Sorokin, Harrald de Groff, and John LaFalce. Bernard Vinick started an interior design firm that became one of the largest in the country. His work is evident in area restaurants, banks, offices, and stores.

Personal service is trademark of local service businesses like Thierfeld Tailors at Sunset Triangle. Here in 1978 photo are (from left) Morris Kurebart, Gisela Mueller, Vasilios Tsikrikis, founder Gunther Thierfeld, and Stilianos Tsombanos, current owner of the custom tailoring shop.

He was "knighted" by the French government in 1985 for his work as the first American president of the International Federation of Interior Designers and Architects. Harvey & Lewis opticians and Battiston Cleaners served other needs. William G. Marholin and William Lane were ahead of their times when they built the free-standing Marholin-Lane furniture store on Farmington Avenue in 1965.

Suburbanites needed cars, and there was an early Studebaker dealership (with a gasoline station beside) on Farmington Avenue next to Sage-Allen. Israel Grody

Shorty the Clown

Harold C. Horton of Rockledge Drive was an engineer by training but a clown by heart. Also known as Shorty the Clown, during retirement he became the Connecticut Leukemia Society's clown. When he was named clown of the year in 1992 by the 5,500-member Clowns of America International, he was honored at the Elmwood Community Center because much of his work was local. Known for his kooky and colorful props, he touched a lot of people, volunteering hundreds of hours to a wide range of groups, PTOs, scouts, churches, and the like. Countless parents, children, and senior citizens knew him on a first-name basis.

opened Grody Chevrolet on Raymond Road in the lower Center in 1934. Clayton Gengras's Ford dealership went in across the street, later to be renamed Williams Ford by owner Robert Newman. The Auto Club of Hartford (AAA), which dates to 1902, has been headquartered since 1967 at 815 Farmington Ave. in one of the town's larger owner-occupied office buildings. When service stations and garages sprouted, names like Guthrie, Cormier, Troy, Matties, and Steben followed.

Restaurants came and went, no fewer than a dozen in the Manga Reva/House of Zodiac building at Farmington and Trout Brook. Standbys were the Maple Hill, Edelweiss, and West Hartford Diner in the Center, Scoler's and La Scala at Bishops Corner, and the Fernwood in Elmwood, the only one still in business.

Because it was built up earlier than others, West Hartford did not participate to the same extent in what became known late in the century as the "exit ramp economy." Kane Street office buildings, Corporate Center West, and the Westfarms area were exceptions.

Although there were inns and taverns putting up overnight guests in early times, West Hartford at the end of the 20th century had no commercial place to stay other than the West Hartford Motor Inn-turned-Inn. That could change. Town officials anticipated renovations and growth in the Raymond Road area,

Town of West Hartford Photo

Executive director Linda I. French (left) of the West Hartford Chamber of Commerce and Mila Limson, the town's senior planner, visit Alex S. Toback (second from left) and Robert G. Nystrom of Metcalfe Corp. Inc. as part of the community outreach plan to retain businesses in West Hartford.

including office and retail development and possibly a boutique hotel. Newpaper reports said the Center had become "the region's hottest commercial center," and with neighborhood constraints on all sides, there was nowhere else to grow.

At the end of the 20th century, 27,290 people worked in West Hartford. Manufacturing employment had declined to 3,370, while jobs in "service producing" establishments, including government and non-profits, had increased to 23,120. One-quarter of those employed in the town were residents. A new development was the increase in computer-driven, home-based enterprises, which the Chamber of Commerce estimated to number about 2,000. Approximately 21,000 residents work elsewhere in the region or beyond.

Their World of Work

West Hartford is not only home to business and industry, but residents have been in the vanguard beyond town limits – and not just in Hartford insurance companies.

Some typical and notable examples:

Marjorie Anderson, who served on the Town Council, became president of the state League of Women Voters, head of the World Affairs Council, and president of the 1892 Club (formerly Hartford's Twentieth Century Club).

Curtis L. Blake of Sunset Farm opened the first

Friendly Ice Cream store in Springfield in 1935 at age 18 with his brother, S. Prestley Blake. They borrowed $500 from their father to get started, and paid themselves $2 a week for two years. When they sold in 1978 to Hershey Foods, they had 625 Friendly stores throughout the Northeast.

Dr. Francis J. Braceland was an international leader in psychiatry and psychiatrist-in-chief at Hartford's Institute of Living. A longtime trustee and a scholar in residence at St. Joseph College, he transformed the institute from a haven for wealthy eccentrics and celebrities into the largest private psychiatric hospital in the nation.

Joseph B. Burns, former chairman of Fuller Brush Co., chaired the state Gaming Commission, the state GOP, and the state Chamber of Commerce, and served as state transportation Commissioner.

Dr. Kevin V. Dowling, chairman of orthopedic surgery at St. Francis Hospital and Medical Center and former president of Hartford County Medical Association, was instrumental in developing the University of Connecticut Health Center. A longtime UConn trustee, he was the first person to receive both an honorary degree and the University Medal, UConn's highest honor.

John F. Droney Jr., attorney, former town councilman, and former state Democratic chairman, chaired

President Clinton's campaign in Connecticut in 1992. Not since John Bailey has a Democratic chairman left such an indelible mark on the political scene, wrote the Hartford Courant.

Wilson H. Faude, executive director of the Old State House, became a leader of Hartford's cultural scene with fellow residents John Boyer, executive director of the Mark Twain Memorial, and Douglas Evans, executive director of the Bushnell Memorial.

Brendan Fox Jr., former legal counsel and deputy chief of staff to Gov. John Rowland, in his early 30s became executive director of the Capital City Economic Development Authority.

Isadore Gold became foreign policy advisor to Israeli Prime Minister Benjamin Netanyahu in 1996. He took leave from his foreign policy post with the University of Tel Aviv to lead peace talks with the Arabs.

R. Bartley Halloran, attorney and former school board member, became head of the Connecticut Economic Development Authority. Past president of the Connecticut Trial Lawyers Association, he helped win a $90 million settlement from the Arthur Andersen accounting firm for investors in Colonial Realty.

Burton C. Hoffman started as a salesman in his father's car dealership, took it over upon his death, and bought the East Hartford site for Hoffman Enterprises. He also opened an auto park straddling the Avon-

Working Retiree

John K. Springer of Albany Avenue retired in 1997 as president and CEO of the parent company of Hartford Hospital and the Connecticut Children's Medical Center. Like many others, he was a working retiree, continuing as chairman of MedSpan Inc., the state's first provider-sponsored health plan, which he helped found in 1990 and ranked as the fastest growing company in Connecticut and one of the fastest growing private companies in the nation. He started it in part because hospitals and doctors were growing more and more frustrated with what they saw as insurance companies' interference in medical decision-making. Also active as a board member of the American Hospital Association, he was the one to whom other members listened when talk turned to managed care, largely because he worked in the middle of Insurance City.

Modern Worker

Ronald F. Van Winkle of Wood Pond Road, director of community services for the town, is one of the state's prescient and most-quoted economists. Known among colleagues as "Dr. Doom," in 1990 following the boom years he was among the few to predict Connecticut's "Great Recession." He also was among the first to predict the revival in 1995. In charge of the town's zoning enforcement, building inspection, and oversight of construction and street repair projects, he started as an economist for Pratt & Whitney in the 1970s and later was an economic planner for the state Department of Economic Development.

Simsbury line and became a defining figure in the region's automobile business. He loved to sell cars, the more exotic the better. His sons, Brad and Jeffrey, continue the tradition.

Charles H. Kaman founded the Kaman Corp. in his parents' West Hartford garage in 1945 after United Aircraft Corp. dismissed his ideas for helicopter design. The aviation pioneer built his Bloomfield-based venture into a miniconglomerate that makes aircraft parts and musical instruments and is one of the largest distributors of industrial parts in North America.

Andrea Miller Keller was nationally known in art circles as curator of the Wadsworth Atheneum's Matrix Gallery. Husband Anthony S. Keller was executive director of the Connecticut Commission on the Arts.

Herbert J. Kramer, publicist (originator of the Travelers' red umbrella logo), Board of Education member, and author whose writings included the motto for Special Olympics International, became director of communications and assistant to the chairman of the Joseph P. Kennedy Jr. Foundation and Special Olympics International, an organization he helped found. During the Johnson administration he was director of public affairs for the U.S. Office of Economic Opportunity.

Roland H. Lange, who joined the Hartford Insurance Group as a mailboy, rose to president and vice chairman. He retired in 1970 to work as a volunteer with the American Red Cross, for whom he helped raise more than $100 million as national vice chairman.

Morris Lipman went from pumping gasoline at

Seymour Sard's Town Centre, a four-story retail and office complex, gives a contemporary look to South Main Street.

16 to become founder and chairman of Lipman Motors, the world's largest American Motors dealership.

Elaine Title Lowengard, mascot to her mother's Girl Scout troop at age 3, left a vice presidency of Connecticut Bank & Trust Co. in 1989 to become executive director of the Connecticut Valley Girl Scout Council. She served as secretary of the town's charter revision commission in 1970 and as a member of the human rights commission and state Board of Higher Education.

Nancy Lublin founded Dress for Success, a chain of shops that dresses needy women trying to seek jobs and get off welfare. She founded the organization while attending New York University Law School and launched 20 fledgling shops across the country.

Robert E. Patricelli served in Washington as deputy undersecretary of Health, Education, and Welfare and head of the Urban Mass Transportation Administration in 1975. He later became chairman and CEO of Avon-based Value Health Inc.

Louis B. Rogow, chairman of Birken Manufacturing Co. of Bloomfield and philanthropist, served on the boards of Mount Sinai and St. Francis hospitals, St. Mary Home, and the Newington Children's Home. He received the Albert Einstein Award from Israel's Technion University, where the aeronautical research center bears his name.

Silicon Valley Star Starts Here

Steve Perlman graduated from Hall in 1979 and now heads Web TV Networks in Palo Alto, Calif. He returned in 1997 to Talcott Mountain Academy of Science and Mathematics with a $1 million donation for the school. School president Donald LaSalle announced the naming of the school's library and technology conference center after the benefactor.

The science center was founded in 1967, six years after Perlman was born. The youngster began attending Talcott Mountain classes on weekends and in the summer when he was 10. He said school officials realized he had talent that would not be tapped if he did not have another creative outlet such as the advanced science and math courses offered at Talcott Mountain.

"If I had grown up anywhere else in the world," Perlman said, "I couldn't possibly have gotten where I am today." He said there isn't another place in the country like Talcott Mountain Science Center.

His years at the school and subsequent career as a technology guru at Apple Computer helped to mold the school into what it is today. "Most of the computers we have here, we have because of Steve," LaSalle said. "There are three types of people in the world – those that make things happen, those that watch things happen and those that say, 'What the hell happened?' Steve is definitely the epitome of the first."

Milton P. Rosenberg is head of Bernie's Audio Video TV and Appliances, taking over from his father who started selling TVs and radios out of his small gas station and garage in Hartford. Now with 12 stores and more than 450 employees in Southern New England, Bernie's is growing in a field in which big players like Sound Playground, The Wiz, and Lechmere failed.

Dr. Frank E. Roth was the first chief of staff in 1951 at Mount Sinai Hospital, where he also was chief of pediatrics. A pediatrician for six decades, he started in the pre-antibiotics era, made house calls, and was the first doctor to use sulfa drugs when they became available. When he died in 1999 at age 99, he was the oldest member of Congregation Beth Israel.

Theodore S. Sergi is the longtime state education commissioner.

Samuel J. Silberman, former CEO and chairman of Consolidated Cigar Corp., helped fund the construction of Hunter College School of Social Work in New York, was on the national board of the Conference of Christians and Jews, and chairman of the Association of Governing Boards of Universities and Colleges.

Roger Wolcott Sperry, Elmwood native and 1931 Hall High grad, won a Nobel Prize for Medicine in 1981 for his pioneering brain research. He was honored as California Scientist of the Year in 1972 while a professor of psychobiology at California Institute of Technology.

Harleigh Trecker, professor and dean for 26 years at the UConn School of Social Work, was author and editor of 21 books and a national leader in the field. The school's library is named for him.

Frank O.H. Williams, retired senior vice president of CIGNA, became one of state's leading charitable, educational, and political fund-raisers. He served as national chairman of the Yale University Alumni Board.

West Hartford Chamber of Commerce

The West Hartford Chamber of Commerce dates to 1903. It is one of the only area chambers to remain independent and not to be absorbed by the Greater Hartford Chamber of Commerce.

It grew out of the West Hartford Businessmen's Association, which voted in 1917 to change its name. Gustave Fischer, president at the time, advocated the posting of signs at approaches to the town "informing passers that they are approaching the best town in New England."

A 1920 report said, "We had hoped to bring the membership up to 350, counting on bringing many new members from Elmwood and the so-called Oakwood Avenue Section. The majority of our members come from the thickly settled section bounded by Prospect Avenue, Mountain Road, Park Street, and Asylum Avenue."

Since then, membership has grown to 700 businesses and three retail affiliates, representing all sections of town.

Past Presidents / Chairmen

Because early records of the Chamber are lacking in detail, this list begins with 1957:

James E. Kelley, Kelley Frozen Foods, 1957

Norman G. Fricke, Connecticut Bank & Trust Co., 1958

John Robinson, Robinson School, 1962-1964

Paul N. Stanton, 1965

James E. Heffernan Jr., Heffernan & Heffernan, 1966-1967

Hugh G. Collins, 1967

Normand Allen, Sage-Allen & Co., 1969-1970

Dr. Albert H. Kleiman, dentist, 1971

Paul O. Roedel Jr., Wiremold Co., 1973-1974

Louis M. Salzburg, Young Set, 1975-1976

Walter B. Schatz, Schatz & Schatz, 1977-1978

Davild Gilchrist, Dunham-Bush Co., 1978-1980

John E. O'Keefe, Sears, Roebuck & Co., 1980-1982

Howard D. Nitchke, Nitchke Associates, 1983-1984

Robert B. Shea, SNET Co., 1985-1986

Douglas Thomas, Thomas Cadillac, 1987-1988

Elizabeth Basil, DeConti-Basil Associates, 1989-1990

Thomas Filomeno, Filomeno & Co., P.C., 1990-1991

Robert P. Powell, Gledhill Nursery, 1992-1994

Stephen Guest, Blum Shapiro & Co., 1994-1996

Scott Conover, Connecticut Natural Gas, 1997-1999

Kevin Galvin, Colonial Handyman, 2000-

Executive Directors

J. William Burns, 1964-1969

Robert E. Bellevance, 1969-1973

Robert W. Simmons, 1974-1988

Carol Way, 1988-1991

Linda I. French, 1991-

Interior of M.J. Burnham's grocery store in the Center was a busy place and a community institution from 1898 to 1959.

VI. Shopping

Even more than four decades after its closing, the memory of West Hartford's best-loved "country" grocery store in the wood frame building at 19 South Main St. lingers. In 1898 a young Vermonter, Myron J. Burnham, moved here and bought out the Center branch of the Guilfoil Grocery Co., in a building that had once been a school. It was tough going for the first ten years. "We started business," he said, "with $500 and a lot of courage." When he celebrated the store's 50th anniversary in 1948, M.J. Burnham's was valued at more than $500,000, had 60 employees and was treasured as a community center and landmark.

In his long career Burnham witnessed a revolution in buying habits. "A half a century ago," he recalled in 1948, "people bought bulk goods which have since been replaced by small, sanitary packages of prepared foods. Time was when oatmeal and rolled oats were the popular cereals and about the only ones." At age 87,

he tired of the pace and his grocery, still old-fashioned in spirit and decor, though up-to-date in its stock, closed in 1959 to make way for the nearby Super Finast market's parking lot. He died in 1962 at age 90.

Customers still talk of how they were greeted by Burnham's clerks, who took them on their rounds of the store, added up their bills by hand, and delivered their purchases. Merle Chapin Beeney, a longtime resident, cherishes fond memories of Burnham's from her schooldays. "We school children got a liberal education by shopping on the way home. On entering the north door there stood the huge Hobart coffee grinder. The fruits were all beautifully arranged and piled into pyramids along the south wall. The sawdust on the floor lent an old-time flavor. Burnham's was an institution – unique and eclectic. It had most everything we needed. Pumpkins and apples on the front steps in the fall, flowers and plants in the spring and summer.

When M.J. Burnham opened his grocery in 1898, West Hartford was a village of about 3,000 people. That there was a curb or even sidewalks on South Main Street was credited to his leadership in the Village Improvement Society. The store, which occupied the same location at 19 South Main St. throughout its 61-year tenure, was lit by kerosene lamps and horse-drawn delivery buggies lined the curb.

The first general store in town was Buckland's (below). In 1856 Leonard Buckland, considered the founder of general retailing here, bought Nathan Burr's hardware store, which had opened in 1840 on the site of the present library. He moved it across Goodman Green to the southwest corner of Farmington and South Main and turned it into a grocery. The corner location was taken over about 1880 by Allen B. Judd, the town's first druggist, whose candy counter was a popular after-school retreat for youngsters like the customer at right.

West Hartford Center expanded in the 1930s from South Main Street onto Farmington Avenue (right rear) and around the corner onto LaSalle Road. Houses in background are taller than the one-story stores along west side of LaSalle Road.

The feeling that came over us as we crossed the threshold was almost one of awe. We were in Mr. Burnham's house – for he and Mrs. Burnham lived on the second floor for many years."

The "awe" of the old shopping days has been replaced by the awesomeness of the new. The early community focus of Burnham's has been superseded by a new community center, Westfarms Mall, which is as important in its own way and yet, in retailing terms at least, is its diametric opposite. Here, climate-controlled and secured shopping, acres of parking, and national, name-brand chain stores draw customers from near and far.

While Westfarms is known for some of the highest retail-sales-per-square-foot in the country, it too is a community focal point. Besides shoppers, its clientele ranges from teen-aged "mall rats" who gather after school to the mostly older, "white-sneaker" set who traipse the corridors for their morning constitutionals before the stores open. The Taubman Co. mall management proved to be a good corporate neighbor. That helped pave the way for a major expansion in time for its 25th anniversary, which produced a large

parking garage and a new fashion wing anchored by Nordstrom, the Seattle-based retailer.

And yet, when Connecticut's largest, most upscale shopping mall opened in 1974 on the property of the old Torza golf complex across from the Corbins Corner Shopping Parkade, then a strip plaza of the old school, West Hartford's local merchants feared for their livelihoods. But the town's long-existing shopping areas have evolved with the times and prospered, each with its own distinctiveness and clientele.

Neighborhood Centers

The town's 1925 zoning map, first of its kind in the state, had the Center as a commercial focal point but was spotted with neighborhood shopping centers. Most gradually disappeared from maps as, one by one, they were engulfed by residential construction. A few remained, notably at Bishops Corner, Farmington Avenue at the Boulevard, and Philip Corbin's farm.

The Center's growth started in the late 1920s and spurted in the 1930s. In 1951 the town Plan & Zoning Commission, chaired by engineer Alfred Kaehrle, proposed a bold design for modest expansion with appropriate buffers to prevent businesses from infringing on surrounding residential areas. The plan was quickly shot down by alarmed homeowners on the fringe. The Town Council refused to get involved. Councilman P. Corbin Kohn gave it the kiss of death by labeling the plan "these airy dreams."

At mid-20th century, the department store delivery trucks making the rounds of West Hartford's residential areas were evidence that the area's retailing hub continued to be Hartford. But West Hartford's retail base was growing beyond the original West Hartford Center and Elmwood shopping districts.

Bishops Corner was the first new center. Lord & Taylor opened in 1954 amid great fanfare, anchoring the first of four strip plazas, one on each corner. Bishops Corner proved a monument to Americans' love affair with the auto. Mainly parking lots at the intersection of two busy streets that make it difficult to get from one corner to the other, it has not proved as pedestrian-friendly as other centers have become.

Early settler Philip Corbin's farm was next. The developer's presentation to the Town Council in 1956 was the most extensive yet. Opponents from the Southwest Home Owners Association sat through three evening sessions before they got a chance to speak. Sears, Roebuck & Co. opened its largest store in New England as the anchor in 1961, and the quaintly named Corbins Corner Shopping Parkade was completed in 1962. Among its 31 early stores were D&L, Neisner's, Kennedy's, and Stop & Shop. The enormous parking area and the buffer zone between it and residences – a brick wall and landscaped strip surrounding the center – were unusual for the time.

In 1959, a Colonial-style A&P supermarket was approved for what is now Sunset Triangle at Farmington Avenue and the Boulevard. The 20,000-square-foot store was larger than either of the town's two new First National stores and the Corbins Corner Stop & Shop, and almost as large as the Grand Union on New Britain Avenue in Elmwood.

By then, the town's retail sections were basically delineated. Prospect Plaza, Kane Street Plaza, and Westfarms Mall would come later, and there would be changes along Park Road, Farmington Avenue, and New Park Avenue as well as in existing areas.

Retailing Grows

When S.S. Kresge opened its second West Hartford store in Elmwood in 1957, it included a luncheonette and a much-ballyhooed public-address system over

Dutchland Farms

Longtime residents remember the delicious ice-cream sodas and milkshakes they enjoyed as teenagers at the wind-milled Dutchland Farms dairy bar on the southwest corner of North Main Street and Albany Avenue. Before Dutchland, it had been known as Joe Bishop's Corner. In the 1940s it was "the place" to take a date after a movie or a dance.

In 1950, wheeler-dealer developer William A. Mauser dreamed of building the region's first large-scale, integrated shopping center with New York's Lord & Taylor as the anchor store. He had shown imagination and insistence on quality in the Niles Street apartments, one of the best post-war housing ideas in Hartford, and he was responsible for luxurious apartments on Outlook Avenue here.

A peppery insurance man, Walter Mallory, organized the West Hartford Home Owners' Association in opposition. The Town Council, headed by Joseph M. Freedman, the first to be called "Mayor," gave its approval. Mallory went to court, aided and abetted by the indomitable Beatrice Fox Auerbach, who saw a suburban shopping center as a threat to her downtown G. Fox & Co. department store.

At the end of January 1952, the West Hartford News produced its first extra edition with the headline "Supreme Court OK's Lord & Taylor Zoning." Later, Mallory was gallantly on hand when the store opened with great fanfare. Highways were jammed for miles as 35,000 people converged on Bishops Corner for a look at Bill Mauser's prize. Ten gallons of Lanvin's Arpege perfume, at $20 an ounce, floated down in an aromatic mist over the brightly lit parking lot. Dorothy Shaver, Lord & Taylor's president and by all accounts America's No. 1 career woman at the time, was the star of the opening, making sure that her new store – the first outside metropolitan New York – would be a jewel.

By April 1954, the complex was finished, with a big Allstate Insurance Cos. regional office and ten smaller stores, including a Doubleday Book Shop, Peck & Peck, and S.S. Pierce. Although the names have changed, suburban shopping here had been altered forever.

Lord & Taylor's showplace store, with its glamorous shoe department (right), emerged in 1954 on the site of the former Dutchland Farms dairy bar (inset, below) at Bishops Corner. Dorothy Shaver, the company president, considered it the best example of her theory that a store should be a beautiful place in which to shop.

which daily specials were announced. By 1957, the 329 stores around the town registered more than $57 million in sales. There were 48 food stores, 46 apparel shops, 23 furniture and home appliance stores, 17 drug stores, and 11 automotive shops.

Thirty-years after Sage-Allen & Co. opened its first and largest branch in the Center in 1930, it needed to expand. Edward N. Allen, chairman, threatened to move if the branch was not allowed to add a second floor

with an escalator. He told the Zoning Board of Appeals, "When it had its opening day in 1930, it took in only $250 – a great contrast to some days when the branch stores's one-day volume is as much as $15,000."

Sage's expansion – along with a burst of apartment and home construction, a big spurt in auto sales, and the opening of the Corbins Corner Shopping Parkade – helped retail sales reach new highs in the early 1960s. Leading retailers like Lux, Bond & Green jewelers, the first Casual Corner, and Joseph A. Banks Clothiers followed at intervals, but West Hartford Center remained a retreat from the trendy modern chain stores that today make almost every upscale shopping mecca look the same. Here, a changing lineup of such local stores as Allen Collins, Pfau's Hardware, S.K. Lavery

The Woman's Exchange And the Sewing Circle

The Woman's Exchange, an unusual retail endeavor, moved to West Hartford Center in 1949 after serving women in Hartford for 66 years. It was rooted in the reform movement of the 1870s and '80s when six Hartford Congregational churches hired as city missionary the activist Virginia Thrall Smith, whose husband owned Sunset Farm here. Working to abolish orphan asylums in favor of foster homes and adoptions, she founded the Children's Aid Society (now the Village for Families and Children), the Newington Home for Crippled Children, and the Sister Dora Society, forerunner of the Woman's Exchange.

The Sister Dora Society's purpose was to provide club rooms and educational advantages for women factory workers, who not only attended lectures and musicals but learned to cook and sew. Thus arose the need for the Woman's Exchange, where they could bring their handiwork and receive "fair compensation." More affluent women volunteered as sales clerks so the consignors could take home all but a 10 percent commission of what their products sold for.

The exchange continues to provide an outlet for women's creations, and the consignors are no longer just from Hartford but from every state and from overseas. And the needs are not always financial. Margaret Buck, who wrote the exchange's centennial history, tells of one woman who delivered her work in a chauffeured Cadillac.

In 1984, the story of the early Woman's Exchange repeated itself. Five churches and a synagogue saw the need for a soup kitchen and founded Loaves and Fishes at Hartford's Trinity Episcopal Church. Like its predecessor, the soup kitchen expanded under executive director Alyce F. Hild of Hillsboro Drive and added sewing and cooking courses.

Again the exchange, still with a volunteer sales force, is providing an outlet for the children's outfits and aprons that women studying at Loaves and Fishes sell, receiving "fair compensation" for their work and a means of self-support.

Appliance Co., Lucy Baltzell Shop, Zacher's, Florence Travis, Modern Woman, the English Shop, J&R Pollack, Gillman's, the Acorn Shop, Artichoke, Henry Miller, Greene's Shoes, LaSalle Music, Metzger's, Jack Handlen's Cheese Shop, Hilliard's Candy, Krohner's Bakery, Bookworm, Bennett's Card Shop, and the Toy Chest held sway.

Former Mayor Catherine Cox Reynolds, who helped open the Comina store in West Hartford Center, sees it as "an upscale, cosmopolitan shopping and dining destination for the region – a successful alternative to the mammoth regional malls."

In the face of Westfarms Mall, the West Hartford News led a successful campaign for the Greening of

Casual Corner

Two town residents who foresaw changing lifestyles opened the first Casual Corner store in West Hartford Center in 1950.

Charles E. Carpels, a Sage-Allen & Co. manager, and Stanley W. Vogel, a buyer at Brown-Thomson, both in Hartford, envisioned a major change in merchandising. "The whole concept of sportswear – it seems silly to say this today – was brand new and in its infancy," Carples said upon his partner's death here in 1989. "We worked in department stores and saw people moving from the city to the suburbs. It was only natural that people were dressing more casually."

They also initiated a style of merchandising that would revolutionize the industry. At the time, merchandise was kept in display counters or away from customers who had to ask to see it. "One of our ideas was to put the merchandise where people could touch and feel it."

The pair borrowed $10,000 to stock their 500-square-foot store here. Their first employees were their wives, Florence Carpels and Jean Bonn Vogel. "When we started we had the idea we'd have 10 stores. That's the last time we ever put a number on it," Carples said. Within a year they opened stores in Springfield and Worcester, but the fourth store in Providence waited until 1957. By 1960, they grossed $2 million and Casual Corner was on the retailing map. In 1970, the pair sold their 25 Casual Corner stores to U.S. Shoe Corp. of Cincinnati, and headed up its specialty retailing division in Enfield. The chain had grown to 800 stores nationwide, including Caren Charles and August Max, at Carpels's death in 1990.

Central Theater advertised a double feature and there are no parking meters nor trees on the sidewalks in this view of Farmington Avenue in the 1950s. Double-parked cars, truck blocking a sidewalk, and jay-walking pedestrians are evident.

West Hartford Center. Shade trees and flowers were planted along the streets. The sidewalks were paved with bricks, and faux-gas lamps illuminated the streets. The semi-annual West Hartford Center Days sales were joined by a new tradition, the annual Holiday Stroll, which epitomized the area's role as a community focus.

From Shoes to Chairs

The owner of the Shoe Box, John Tarrant Kenney, ran a popular shoe emporium – one of the earliest stores in the Center, starting in the 1930s. He was also a passionate trout fisherman, who would disappear on opening day and head for the Farmington River in Riverton. In the spring of 1946, despairing of catching anything, he sat on the bank and looked up at the old factory across the stream, which he described as being "in a sorry state of abandon and neglect."

Somehow intrigued, he began a search into the history of its occupant, the Hitchcock Chair Co., which had failed in 1864. This led him, without prior experience and at great risk, to resurrect the enterprise that once was widely known for its stenciled chairs and tables. The Hitchcock Chair Co. thrives in Riverton to this day.

Despite the invasion of malls, discount stores, and national chains elsewhere (Marshall's, Barnes & Noble, and Wild Oats at Bishops Corner; Eastern Mountain Sports, Borders Books & Music, Toys-R-Us, and Office Max near Corbins Corner), the vacancy rate in the Center has never exceeded six percent. For every business that folds, another takes its place.

Though the Center is as vibrant as ever, the nature of retailing has changed. There are no department stores

The Maple Hill

The Maple Hill restaurant was a fixture in West Hartford Center for 30 years. Owner David LeFavour hired women to staff and cook. "Most men won't take the time needed to prepare simple foods well and women are more careful in habits of cleanliness," he said. From start to finish, "we think of ourselves as a home kitchen." The Maple Hill's sale in 1971 to Foodamerica Corp. came as a surprise to shoppers and residents who thought of the personally owned and operated old-timer as "a pleasant retreat from the sizzling pace of short-order eateries," according to the West Hartford News. Its lemon meringue pie was legendary.

The sound of music wafts across Farmington Avenue in West Hartford Center. The June 1975 performance by the Hartford Chamber Orchestra ensemble was one of a series of monthly street concerts presented by the Center Merchants Association.

like Sage-Allen, no Central Theater, no A&P or LaSalle Market, no place to buy such specialties as fabrics or sewing accessories as at S. P. Dunn's. But there are still independent book and hardware stores, photo and lamp stores, specialty shops, jewelers and hair salons – places where owners know their customers by name, and where personal service is the forte.

An al fresco trend has enlivened the Center, as bagel and coffee shops and restaurants set out tables on the

Creative Playtime

Creative Playtime, an eclectic toy shop run by an eccentric owner known to everyone as "Mr. Fuss," was a Center landmark for 39 years. The store was known for its quirky merchandise mix from Shirley Temple dolls to video games. Like an old curiosity shop, it was "the most far-out place in the world," according to a young employee. Isadore B. Fuss would chat with customers to find out what they wanted. He would "run through my treasure chest and then, zingo! I give them what I have." A town resident, he closed the store in 1987 at age 72, selling its contents to two toy collectors in New York and New Jersey.

An Independent Supermarket

For six decades, the Crown Supermarket, first on Albany Avenue in Hartford and since 1968 on Albany Avenue at Bishops Corner, has provided kosher meats and poultry, bakery products, Jewish delicatessen specialties, and fresh produce to local shoppers as well as customers from a 100-mile radius of West Hartford, drawn by its slogan, "the Good Food Store."

Established in 1940 by Sam Smith, Sam Sowalsky, and Jack Sloat, the Crown has been led in the years since by West Hartford residents and relatives Ralph Seltzer and Marvin Kramer, now retired, and Bill Sloat (self-described as "the only old-timer left here"). The family ownership's third generation is represented now by Mark Seltzer.

Voted No. 1 nationally in its size and category as an independently owned grocery by the Progressive Grocer magazine in 1981, the Crown has survived stiff competition from large, corporately owned supermarkets at Bishops Corner by providing kosher goods and personal service in its niche market. The store was among the first food markets to accept credit cards and to offer a take-out, prepared foods counter to busy shoppers.

By 1970 Bishops Corner's four corners were filled with shopping plazas, all developed in little over a decade. Albany Avenue runs horizontally through this aerial view looking southwest, and North Main Street cuts diagonally from top left to lower right. Original Lord & Taylor store and parking garage are at upper right center, Crossroads Plaza and branch post office at lower center.

Burgoyne Park at New Britain Avenue and Quaker Lane South is dotted with autumn's leaves. A neighborhood task force helped develop plans for the town to provide a terrace, benches, picnic table, and landscaping for the enhancement of Elmwood Center.

sidewalk – and one even added an open-air rooftop café. This followed a modification of sidewalk regulations by the Town Council, which earlier had eased off-street parking requirements for such establishments. Peter Brainard, great-grandson of the Aetna chairman and grandson of retailer Henry Miller, and his brother Newton were in the vanguard of the coffeehouse trend here with Peter B's Espresso. Richard Rosenthal, who launched the wildly popular Max restaurant group in downtown Hartford, finally returned to his hometown to open Max's Oyster Bar. Restaurants like Max's, Bricco, the Elbow Room, the Back Porch, and Arugula became regional dining destinations. New ethnic eateries – Thai, Mexican, Chinese, Indian, Japanese and Vietnamese – vie for diners all across town.

Developer Seymour Sard turned the prime old First National property on South Main Street into the Town Centre, a four-story retail and office complex with a parking garage. Retailer Leonard Udolf converted the old Central Theater into a glitzy shopping arcade and office building. Brokerage and real-estate offices are as common as new bagelries and coffee establishments.

Protected by the cluster of town buildings and the zoning limitation on business expansion into residential areas, the Center remains the heart of local commerce.

Elmwood and Park Road have been improved, too.

Town of West Hartford Photo

Renovated shops, offices and restaurants draw midday shoppers and business people to Farmington Avenue, looking west toward marquee of former Central Theater.

With the assistance of neighborhood task forces, the town provided leadership and funds to reinvigorate these business areas, including new sidewalks and plantings.

Chain Stores – Then and Now

Before the days of CVS and Walgreen's, even the pharmacies in town were local – local chains, in some cases.

The busiest corner in town – Farmington at South Main – was taken about 1880 by Allen B. Judd, the town's first druggist. He retired and sold his pharmacy business in 1922.

Joseph M. Dougherty opened a drug store in 1930 across the street at 974 Farmington Ave. He added stores at 135 S. Main, as well as Park Road at Quaker Lane and in Elmwood, before selling out in 1956.

Maxwell E. Rulnick opened a Maxwell Drug Co. store in West Hartford Center in 1946 and his fourth Maxwell's store at Bishops Corner in 1957. Like other local merchants, he was active in town, helping organize the West Hartford Chamber of Commerce, the Cornerstone Club, and the Senior Center. He was usually a contributor of what some

called "action funds" to get a local activity off the ground.

At Sunset Triangle there were two local pharmacies, Bridlepath and Tunxis, across the street from each other. That was before Stop & Shop bought out the former to expand and CVS moved in and undercut the latter.

Among the last holdouts locally were Suburban Pharmacy at Bishops Corner and Martucci Family Pharmacy in Elmwood.

The same is true of food markets. As the chains dominated, local favorites folded. Still prospering at century's end were Crown Market at Bishops Corner and Kingswood Market and Hall's Market on the East Side.

The bulk of the market share locally went to Stop & Shop at Sunset Triangle and Waldbaum's, Adams, and Wild Oats at Bishops Corner – four supermarkets in a town of 61,000.

Tall shade trees, benches, and planters are among amenities of modern-day West Hartford Center. This view is on south side of Farmington Avenue just west of Main Street, with Fleet Bank building in left background.

Local stores such as Hall's Market, Bazilian's, and Bill Lehmann's draw from wide areas. When the Park Road Association sponsored an old-fashioned parade to celebrate the completion of the street's repaving in 1999, thousands of receptive town residents turned out. Spearheaded by Angelo Faenza, Richard F. Patrissi, and Patrick J. Daly, the parade became an annual event.

In 2000, when Giuseppe Toscano originally from Sicily closed Henry's Shoe Repair, the thriving but shoebox-sized LaSalle Road fixture he bought from Henry D'Onofrio in 1970, it marked the end of an era. The cobbler, who wanted to retire "to enjoy life with my wife while we're still able to walk," was the last of a breed in West Hartford Center.

Neighborhood task force helped Park Road business section get a new look and a new entry marker at the Prospect Avenue intersection. In the background, customers enjoy al fresco dining on terrace outside Prospect Cafe.

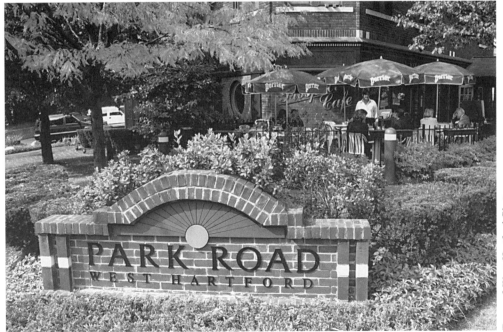

Students pose outside Center School for this photo, taken about 1870. Center School was built in 1865 and in 1872 its second floor became the first high school. It was located at 14 North Main St., on east side just north of Farmington Avenue.

West Hartford Historical Society Photo

72 Learning

Two early school buses arrive, each with a wagon load of children, for the day's classes at the Center School, circa 1907. Opened in 1895, new Center School was shared by high school and elementary grades until 1910, when the high school occupied the entire building and the lower grades moved into the new Whitman School. Center School, later known as the Rutherford Building and used for municipal offices, was razed in the 1970s.

VII. Learning

The evolution of West Hartford's public schools from one-room schoolhouses into the beginning of today's prized school system was foretold by William H. Hall, the town native whose life spanned the spectrum.

By 1910, even though West Hartford's high school enjoyed complete possession of what was called the Center School's North Building at Memorial and Raymond roads, its inadequacy was apparent. Again, Hall had to summon his diplomatic skills and do battle with the politicians. The result was the decision to build a new high school on South Main Street. In 1924, as he laid the cornerstone of the deservedly named William H. Hall High School at the age of 79, he saw his dream fulfilled.

The enrollment of 1,351 students in the town's seven schools in 1915 swelled to 3,257 by 1925, requiring the construction of eight new buildings: Plant, Talcott, and Sedgwick junior highs and Beach Park, Morley, Smith, Elmwood, and Charter Oak elementary schools. Curriculum reform established junior high schools, a 6-3-3 system of grade organization compared with the earlier 8-4. West Hartford was one of the first three towns in the state to establish junior high schools. School playgrounds were introduced in 1916. Another innovation was the establishment in 1918 of kindergartens for children four to six years old.

In the years to follow, the school department became the major component of the town budget. After the post-war baby boom, the number of school children rose so fast, reaching 13,000 at its height, that the Board of Education had to hire nearly

Schooling was mighty different in early schoolhouses as this photo of Center School about 1910 shows.

West Hartford Historical Society Photo

200 new teachers a year and build a new elementary school every other year.

In 1948, ground was broken for Webster Hill School, the first to be built since Sedgwick in 1931. Built on the former Hanson and Sherman farms, it was quickly surrounded by houses, perpetuating the need for still more classrooms. Webster Hill needed an addition three years after opening. It was the first elementary school equipped with a kitchen and dining room for lunch. It had an inner courtyard designed as an outdoor classroom, and a community room and gymnasium facilities for neighborhood use after school hours.

These were among the favorite themes of Edmund H. Thorne, the town's third school superintendent, who served until 1964 when the school building program was completed. Eight elementary and junior high schools were built across town in the 1950s: Bugbee, Duffy, Whiting Lane, King Philip, Braeburn, Wolcott, Norfeldt, and Bridlepath. Aiken opened in 1964. Duffy was the largest grade school and Aiken the smallest. King Philip was the largest school in town when it was built in 1955 to serve nearly 1,000 pupils

as the first elementary and junior high north of Albany Avenue. As the steel girders of the combined school rose, the most rapid residential development in town history was taking place around it, necessitating the construction of Norfeldt and Aiken and the new Hall High.

Brick addition to first Elmwood School opened in 1900 at New Britain Avenue and Woodlawn Street.

West Hartford Historical Society Photo

School Names and Origins

The town's schools reflect the population trends and have taken their names from local officials, educators, scientists, streets, and neighborhoods. They are presented in chronological order of their latest building:

Plant Junior High (1922): Opened in February because of the crowding of the students at the Center high school and the old Seymour (Smith) School, introduced the junior high concept to the town. Named for Alfred E. Plant, longtime secretary of the Town School Committee, who died just prior to the school's opening.

Talcott Junior High (1922): The second junior high, named for James Talcott, Elmwood native and successful New York businessman, member of a family long active in town and school affairs. Built on land contributed from the Talcott estate.

Old Hall High (1924): Named for William H. Hall, the town's grand old man of education, this was the town's high school until Conard opened in 1957. A new Hall opened in 1970. Now the Town Hall.

Beach Park (1926): T. Belknap Beach gave the town a strip of land known as Beach Park, with the stipulation that a school be built on part of it.

Morley (1926): The Fern Street School replaced a three-room portable building. Renamed in 1930 to honor Edward W. Morley, who grew up here, became a much-honored chemistry professor in Ohio and retired in West Hartford, where he built a home and laboratory on Westland Avenue.

Smith (1926): The original eight-room building known as Seymour School opened in 1915 when there were more fields than houses in the vicinity. An eight-room addition opened in 1926. For some years this school was the largest in town, with a peak of 700 children. Its name was changed in 1948 to the Florence E. Smith School in honor of its principal since 1926.

Elmwood (1928): Located at the center of the Elmwood community. Facility began at New Britain Avenue and Woodlawn Street as a two-room school in 1888 with a four-room brick addition in 1900. New school opened following efforts of Charles E. Lord, Elmwood resident and merchant, former Board of Education and Town Council member, and Henry A. Wolcott, board member at the time.

Charter Oak (1930): Successor to the Commons District School, surrounded by oak trees and named after the former park and the famous oak in Hartford that shielded the Connecticut charter. A section cut from the trunk of the tree was preserved in the main corridor.

Sedgwick (1931): Planned as a junior high, also served elementary grades until 1956. Named for William Thompson Sedgwick, town native, internationally known authority on public health and sanitation, and a biology professor at the Massachusetts Institute of Technology from 1883 to 1921.

Webster Hill (1949): First of the post-World War II schools, named for its location on Webster Hill Boulevard. Early principal Leon A. Pierce wrote that it was one of the most modern and well planned schools in New England and "served as a model for others, both domestic and foreign."

Bugbee (1952): The first school on the far west side of town, named for school superintendent Lloyd H. Bugbee, who retired in 1947. Previously, most elementary students who had lived north of Trout Brook had attended Sedgwick School.

Duffy (1954): Rapid growth in the Sedgwick School area prompted construction of a school in the Sedgwick farm tract. Named for Louise Day Duffy, teacher and member of the Board of Education.

Whiting Lane (1954): Named for its location, it replaced the antiquated East School, a seven-room structure built in 1888 that had been deemed a fire hazard. Included in its construction was a gymnasium addition built between Whiting Lane School and Plant Junior High.

King Philip (1955): The first new school north of Albany Avenue, built for both elementary and junior high grades and at the time the largest school in town. It became a junior high for a time only after Aiken opened in 1964. Named for location on King Philip Drive.

Braeburn (1956): Located on Braeburn Road, combining the Scottish words "brae" for the slope adjacent to the field on which the building stands and "burn" for the brook that flows through the adjacent Mooney's Woods to the east.

Conard High (1957): First of two new high schools, named for Frederick U. Conard, School Board chairman.

Wolcott (1957): Opened to ease overcrowding at Elmwood and Duffy. Named for Henry A. Wolcott, former School Board member from whose estate the site was purchased.

Norfeldt (1958): Increased demands for space upon King Philip Elementary led to construction of the school. Eric G. Norfeldt, longtime Hall coach of three major sports and later director of physical education for the school system, died a year before the school opened.

Bridlepath (1959): So called because of its proximity to Bridlepath Road, it was built on land long held by the town as undeveloped recreation area and was the first post-war school in West Hartford to be fully completed by the date required.

Aiken (1964): The last new elementary school to be built and one of the smallest, it was named for Mary Louise Aiken, math teacher and counselor at Sedgwick from 1931 until her death shortly before Aiken opened.

New Hall High (1970): The last public school erected in West Hartford in the 20th century.

Students work in library of old Hall High School beneath the colorful murals painted by local artist Walter O.R. Korder.

Sedgwick School is ready for dedication in 1931 (below). Its architecture was representative of the art deco design of the period. A 1990 addition to the rear of the building (right) retained the look while updating the design.

76 Learning

Significantly, the original Hall High in the Center could no longer accommodate the high school population, and Conard High School was opened in 1957. It was named after Frederick U. Conard, chairman of the Board of Education since 1947, who died in 1954 just after its plans had been approved. He spearheaded the idea of two high schools, each with equal facilities on the south and north sides of town. The implementation required splitting the direction of junior high students, those from Sedgwick and Talcott eventually going to Conard and those from Plant and King Philip to Hall. A new, state-of-the-art Hall High opened in 1970 on the former Laitinen property off North Main Street. Both high schools were substantially renovated and enlarged, Conard in 1998 and Hall in 1999.

No sooner had all the schools been built than an enrollment reversal set in. With the maturing of the town and the aging of its citizens, the school population declined in the 1970s and 1980s. Neighborhood schools, which had become a community expectation as well as a tradition, were closed. Tiny Beach Park was the first, having been declared too small. It was closed in 1973 with little public outcry, as was aging Whitman School in the Center a year later. The decision to close Elmwood School in 1976 was much more controversial, as Elmwood considered the school central to its identity. The community protest that ensued was to be repeated many times across town as beloved neighborhood schools were mothballed or closed.

Each eventually found a new use, however. Beach Park was leased to the Capitol Region Education Council and finally sold to St. Joseph College, which

Lloyd H. Bugbee

West Hartford was a town of 7,500 when Dr. Lloyd H. Bugbee arrived in 1917 as principal of the high school. Five years later he succeeded William H. Hall as school superintendent. Under his quarter-of- a-century administration, 12 new schools were built. He introduced courses in aeronautics, driver education, nature study, and other timely subjects. His curriculum was rated by Columbia University as among the top ten in the country. Dr. Edmund H. Thorne, his successor, credited him with building "a school system with a warm, friendly, cooperative attitude on the part of everyone. He selected people who were very highly qualified." Rabbi Abraham J. Feldman referred to "Bug," as he was generally known, as the "guiding spirit" who made the West Hartford school system one of the finest in the country. Town Manager Rodney L. Loomis remembered him not only for his educational accomplishments but also as "a great fisherman and a strong advocate of good athletic programs." Rumor had it that he occasionally played hookey from administrative duties to go fishing in Trout Brook. One day he rounded a bend and found himself face to face with a group of Hall students similarly engaged. Bugbee retired in 1947, and an elementary school was named after him.

The Conard Connection

When Frederick U. Conard and his wife moved to West Hartford from Stratford in 1937, their four sons were in prep school or college. But the president of Niles-Bement-Pond, which owned Pratt & Whitney Machine Tool Co. and Chandler-Evans, was long involved in youth affairs, from Boy Scouting to the presidency of the Hartford YMCA. He was appointed to the Board of Education in 1946 and served eight critical years as chairman.

A tall, vigorous man of 63, he suffered a fatal heart attack at his Steele Road home in March 1954 – two days after the board had approved plans for a new high school on the south side of town. The board resolved to name the school in his honor, praising his ability to retain "the confidence and respect of citizens of all shades of opinion" during the contentious planning process.

An oil portrait of Conard, by local artist Walter O.R. Korder, was presented to the school by his widow, Julia Hand Conard. It hangs in the library.

One of his sons, John Hand Conard, served as chairman of the Board of Education from 1967 to 1969. He was executive director of the Connecticut Association of School Administrators. Son George was a professor at Lehigh University. Youngest son Mac and his wife ran the Mountain School in Vershire, Vt. The eldest son, attorney Frederick U. Conard Jr., was a former town prosecutor and town Republican chairman and served a term in the state legislature.

A Tale of Two Schools, Separate but Equal

Conard High School

As it turned out, in terms of physical plant Conard is the town's oldest high school, although not generally recognized as such. Upon taking office as the last chairman of the appointed school board in 1947, business executive Frederick U. Conard knew that the town was becoming too large for a single high school. By March 1954, a Citizens Committee on High School Curricula found it "undesirable and uneconomical" to remodel Hall High any further and perennial plans for a large addition were scrapped. It recommended the construction of two new high schools – an idea that worried townspeople who thought divisive the separation of high school students at either end of town.

Following chairman Conard's unexpected death that same month, the board decided to name the new school in the South End in his honor. The swampy, 42-acre property off Berkshire Road was acquired by the town after its owner failed to pay taxes. Local architect Richard D. Butterfield designed what was called a modern, post-war functionalist school, with an emphasis on providing extra space and facilities, such as four language labs and well-equipped faculty work rooms then uncommon in high schools. Even its covered bus pick-up and drop-off area was considered innovative.

The school opened in 1957 as if it always had been there, thanks to transferred staff from Hall who knew many of the 1,137 students. Principal Henry A. Weyland, who had been principal at Hall since 1951, wrote a welcome message in the first edition of the Pow Wow student newspaper: "While no one would call our building lavish, it has within it all the faciliites necessary for a comprehensive high school education."

The Chieftains football team won its first football championship that first year and the inaugural class was ranked at the 99th percentile nationwide in terms of academic achievement upon graduation four years later.

Designed for 1,500 students, within 10 years Conard had 2,000 students and a separate math wing in "temporary" quarters reached by going outside through a corrugated metal tunnel.

In 1998, the school got a $17 million renovation and expansion, four times the cost of the original school. It included a new front entrance of brick, a large library, a new gymnasium, and a new Raymond P. Lachat math wing. And no one was forced to go outside to get to class any more.

New Hall High School

No sooner had Conard opened in 1957 than the Board of Education authorized planning for an equal school in the North End. It was not always clear whether the school was to supplement or replace the Center's Hall High, whose peak enrollment of 1,535 had dropped to 675 with the exodus to Conard. The decision was not made until the mid-1960s, early in the tenure of pioneering Superintendent Charles O. Richter, who introduced some of his innovative ideas into the new school.

Sixteen years after it was conceived and three years later than planned, the "dream facility" opened in 1970 on a 55-acre plot off North Main Street with a view of Avon Mountain. It was divided into two academic houses, Flagg and Rogers, each with its own counselors and housemasters. The school was notable for an absence of study halls as well as for a Media Center featuring a Dial-Select information retrieval system for programmed presentations prepared by teachers, long before computers and the Internet went to school. It also had wide corridors, brilliant colors, flexible space, large group lecture rooms, and teacher work areas.

The school was dedicated following an emotional farewell party in the abandoned Center facility, long to be known as Old Hall High. Student Council president Stephen Saks remarked that at Hall "we learn not just math, English and science, but more importantly, about the real world. For us, Hall is a half-way house."

Reporter Nan Lewis Glass toured the new school with principal Robert E. Dunn and admitted that first impressions of the new Hall "jolted" old Hall grads, herself included. Her article in the West Hartford News began: "The new Hall was conceived and born in controversy at a cost of $9.5 million to replace a traditional high school in the center of town and at the center of many residents' lives since 1924." Once over the jolt, she and other parents were as smitten by both the facility and the teaching techniques as were the students.

As school officials pledged to keep the two schools equal, Hall was renovated in 1999 for $12 million.

Hall High students pause near the balcony during a dance in the old auditorium to observe the "decoration," an effigy of their new crosstown football rivals, the Conard Chieftains.

Conard High School students work in computer lab as part of the most comprehensive selection of electives and advanced placement or college credit courses in the region. Conard and Hall offer advanced courses in 11 subject areas and 27 percent of students are enrolled.

Front of Conard High School has a new look following 1999 renovations that included a larger library at left and a new entrance.

Hartford Times Photo

Marching on Town Hall in 1975, 300 demonstrators protest plans to close Smith School and relocate Morley School.

in 1999 renovated it for its model School for Young Children. Elmwood was renovated in 1979 into the impressive Elmwood Community Center. Plant Junior High School was remodeled in 1986 for senior housing.

Conard Family Photo

Last photograph of Frederick U. Conard was used by artist Walter O.R. Korder for portrait in Conard High library.

Talcott Junior High was sold to become the Coleco Industries headquarters and later head office for Ames Department Stores; the building was idle until 2000, when the town approved its conversion into Trout Brook Commons, a planned residential and retail complex. Whitman was transformed into the town's police and court facility. Old Hall High became the new Town Hall. Bridlepath School is now the Solomon Schechter School, a Jewish day school. The old St. Agnes Home, which the School Board renovated into an Education Center in 1973, was razed in the 1990s to make way for residential development.

Although an aging population occasionally shifted limited resources to other priorities, an influx of new, young families with heightened educational

School Superintendents

William H. Hall, 1897-1922

Lloyd H. Bugbee, 1922-1947

Edmund H. Thorne, 1947-1964

Charles O. Richter, 1964-1973

Paul R. Burch, 1973-1980

Peter D. Relic, 1980-1987

Lloyd Calvert, 1987-1990

John J. Battles, 1990-1995

David P. Sklarz, 1995-

Town of West Hartford Photo

Duffy School students compete in the hurdles event during 1996 field day activities, a tradition at local elementary schools marking the final days of the academic year. Youngsters in all grade levels receive ribbons for participating in relay races, high jump, broad jump, ball throw, and the like.

Elementary School Days

Before computers were in every school, early techies learned the ins and outs of tape casettes. At work here in Braeburn School library in 1973 are (from left) Jeff Niehaus, Lucy Kondratenko, Rex Kochanski, and Carolyn McKenna. Waiting with cassette at right is George Flynn.

Hartford Times Photo

Hartford Times Photo

Police Officer Arnold Bockus discusses drug abuse problems before Webster Hill School class in 1974. In front are Robert Denton (left) and Louis Auger. The effort is part of the police department's community relations program.

Celebrate!West Hartford **81**

Town of West Hartford Photo

Growing enrollments prompted reopening of renovated Smith School to great excitement in 1996 after having been closed for two decades. First day of school brought together parents, teachers, and students.

expectations maintained the town's emphasis on good schools. Special education classes, all-day kindergarten, after-school programs, smaller class sizes, and family resource centers were among the innovations that West Hartford schools undertook in the latter decades of the 20th century to keep ahead of the times. In the 1990s, West Hartford launched magnet-school initiatives: Smith School emphasized

Dr. Robert E. Dunn, principal of Hall High School from 1961 to 1990, came out of retirement for this photo beside the sculpture at the main entrance to the school.

math and science, Norfeldt offered a classical program, and Charter Oak provided an Academy of Global Studies.

Also in the 1990s, as enrollment increased, Aiken and Smith elementary schools reopened after having been leased to the Capital Region Education Council for other purposes.

In 1997, two public-spirited former school parents, Heather Congdon and Dougie Trumble, spearheaded the creation of The Foundation for West Hartford Public Schools, a non-profit organization that raises funds for the enhancing educational projects that go above and beyond school board budgets. Teachers apply for and receive modest grants for extras that they might have paid for out of their own pockets – a piece of equipment that can make a good program even better or to finance a new initiative. In its first three years, the foundation funded $67,000 worth of school projects. As a result, Sedgwick students compose music on computers, Charter Oak's grow and harvest vegetable gardens, Webster Hill's operate a weather station, and Conard students create computer-aided slide shows with a digital camera and scanner. After

Elected Board of Education Chairs

Robert M. Toppin, 1957-1959
Willis G. Parsons Jr., 1959-1965
Edward Mosehauer, 1965-1967
John H. Conard, 1967-1969
Dayson D. DeCourcy, 1969-1971
Madeline S. McKernan, 1971-1973
Elizabeth K. Steven, 1974-1976
Dr. Walter Markham, 1976-1977
James Deephouse, 1977-1979
John E. Davison, 1979-1983
Alyce F. Hild, 1983-1983
Beverly Greenberg, 1983-1986
Arline Brick, 1986-1989
Dr. Raymond J. Krist, 1989-1990
Patricia Genser, 1990-1991
John W. Lemega, 1991-1993
Arline Brick, 1993-1995
Nancy Rion, 1995-1997
Joseph F. DeLucco, 1997-1999
Thomas S. Fiorentino, 1999-

Project Concern

In an historic vote in April 1966, the Board of Education adopted "Project Concern" to bus inner-city children to West Hartford elementary schools to improve their educational opportunity. It was the first suburban school system to do so. Superintendent Charles O. Richter, the principal motivator, advocated it as "a lever to pull Hartford out of poverty." At the time, West Hartford schools had only 25 non-white students, while the majority of students in Hartford were black or Hispanic.

The decision did not come easily. For seven hours, the board debated the proposal at a meeting at Conard High School, with 1,200 townspeople in attendance. The West Hartford News called it "the most passionate meeting" ever.

Community reaction was mixed, but there was strong political leadership from board members Norma Schatz, Edward Mosehauer, David E.A. Carson, and others. Federal funding was available, and a group of parents offered to see that all went smoothly, The objectors, led by Albert J. Marks and Oswald E. D'Arche, circulated an opposing petition to the Town Council, signed by 4,287 residents. It was misdirected, because the council is not allowed to overrule Board of Education decisions.

The program started with the 1966 summer school, when the schools opened their doors to 250 youngsters from Hartford. CBS-TV dispatched Walter Cronkite to do a story for the evening news. All went smoothly, and soon other towns followed West Hartford's lead.

During the 1970s, Hartford paid with federal and grant funds for about 350 Hartford students to attend school annually in West Hartford. The numbers fell through the 1980s and the 1990s until there were only 44 Hartford students in the town's school system in 1997. In the interim, West Hartford's school population had become much more diverse on its own because of changing demographics. African Americans, Hispanics, and Asians made up about 10 percent of the local citizenry in the late 1990s and more than double that percentage in the school system. At one time, many attended Whiting Lane Elementary School, which recently completed a $6 million addition. Its principal called it "a little United Nations," with upwards of 20 languages spoken in pupils' homes.

four years, the foundation had $120,000 more set aside for an endowment to perpetuate itself, similar to the vehicles that alumni, parents, and benefactors use to support private institutions.

West Hartford schools have received many awards, individually and collectively. Over the years, Connecticut magazine ranked its schools best over-all in its size group in the state. The arts and music program has been a particular strength throughout the system. The school district has been cited for the large proportion of students participating in advanced placement courses. More than 90 percent of high school graduates continue their education, about 80 percent of them in four-year colleges.

The schools have not been just for youths. The town has long been a leader in continuing education. When the Adult School started in 1922, it had a nucleus of three classes located in the first Elmwood School. It grew at a rate of about 10 percent a year until the mid-1970s, when growth tapered off. Now, 6,200 adults take 622 different courses from the traditional to data processing.

In addition to the public schools, West Hartford has a number of independent schools and schools affiliated with religious institutions, as well as several institutions of higher education. Among them:

Kingswood-Oxford School

The very model of an English public school headmaster, George Nicholson founded Kingswood School (now Kingswood-Oxford) in 1916 in a small house on Farmington Avenue in Hartford. The son of a Wesleyan Methodist minister, he had been educated at Kingswood School in Bath, England. In 1918, the growing school moved into the Mark Twain House and in 1922 to Outlook Avenue in West Hartford. Here, 85 students and 11 masters enjoyed a 20-acre campus donated by the Rev. Melancthon W. Jacobus, head of the Hartford Seminary. For the next quarter century, Nicholson presided over the growth of the independent "country day" preparatory school for the teen-aged sons of prominent families throughout Greater Hartford. By the time of his death in 1947, Kingswood had an enrollment of 200 and a faculty of 20.

A strict disciplinarian, the "Duke," as the boys secretly called him, was a symbol of indisputable authority and justice as he strode to and from assembly in his flowing master's gown. He molded Kingswood into a personality, not only his but one reflecting a portion of the community itself. As his pedagogic ideal he combined intellectual training with good citizenship. His philosophy of teaching put the individual first. "God," he said, "never made two boys alike....Unless wise training develops his particular worth, the world will be forever the loser....Wise men say that life is charted in 18 years. The tree will grow as the twig has been bent." He was a strong believer that a good home and good school constituted the best education.

Robert A. Lazear

He was known locally as "Uncle Bob" to generations of students, but as dean of New England headmasters to his peers. Robert A. Lazear of Wyndwood Road, headmaster at Kingswood-Oxford School from 1967 to 1988, "was perhaps the most fatherly, compassionate, and understanding man I have ever known," said longtime school trustee Allen V. Collins. He oversaw transition from an all-boys' school into a coeducational facility. During his tenure, K-O's enrollment doubled and the campus expanded, most notably with construction of the Roberts Center for theater and performing arts. His ability to reach out, including to students who didn't fit in, is credited with transforming the school from a local academy into a regional institution that draws students from 44 towns.

"He transformed the school from a pre-World War II model of education to the kind of innovative education that is current today," said Tyler Tingley, a 1964 graduate who is now principal of Phillips Exeter Academy. Before coming here, the Ohio native and Ohio Wesleyan graduate did graduate work at the University of Connecticut. He became assistant to the president of Hampton Institute in Virginia and was active in the civil rights movement. His favorite pastime was his garden at his summer home on Cuttyhunk Island off the southeastern Massachusetts coast.

He served on the boards of three other area independent schools, plus the University of Hartford, the Hartford Art School, American School for the Deaf, New Britain Museum of American Art, and the Bushnell Memorial.

Aerial view of Kingswood School after it moved to its West Hartford campus in 1922 shows dome-topped Seaverns Hall at left center, academic buildings and early athletic fields. This view looks west toward Trout Brook, hidden in trees running across top of photo below Raymond Road. At upper left is the Boulevard and at right center, entrance to campus from Outlook Avenue. Trout Brook Drive has not yet been built, and houses of the era have detached rear garages.

Kingswood alumni, many of whom returned here after college and pursued various careers, are testimonials to his wisdom. At the entrance to the school is a boulder with this inscription: "Thanks for Beings, Groups, Love, Deeds, Words, Books," a quotation from Walt Whitman. Under the stone lies George R.H. Nicholson.

Oxford School for Girls started in two side-by-side houses on Oxford Street in Hartford's West End in 1909, but soon moved to the west side of Prospect Avenue in West Hartford. Its founder was Mary Martin– "Miss Martin," according to her engraved calling card– who died in 1951. She minimized her own accomplishments, but her epitaph would have been her school and the long list of young women who graduated into community leadership.

Oxford merged with Kingswood in 1969 and became Kingswood-Oxford's middle school. Headmaster Robert A. Lazear was responsible for the amalgamation. An ongoing capital campaign for $25 million aimed to consolidate the schools early in the 21st century on the Kingswood campus.

Today the school enrolls 565. Its Roberts Arts Center and sports facilities serve the wider community as well. As Kingswood-Oxford sloughed off lower grades to concentrate on the high school years, Kingswood ceded some of its land for a private elementary school.

The Junior School held classes on Trout Brook Drive for more than two decades in buildings that later became the Children's Museum of Hartford and the Science Center of Connecticut.

Renbrook School

The mother of four Renbrook School graduates, Grace Ellsworth, said of Florence M. Greene, the headmistress: "She left her imprint on a whole generation of young people and will never be forgotten."

Renbrook was formerly the Junior School, which in turn was founded in 1935 as the Tunxis School. The next year its 39 pupils were gathered in the rambling old Niles G. White house at the corner of Farmington and Outlook avenues. Its new headmaster lasted only one hectic day and Florence Greene, the kindergarten teacher, was asked to fill the breach. She did, for the next 31 years.

Outgrowing the White house, the fledgling private elementary school serving Grades K-8 moved a block west to Trout Brook Drive on three and a half acres acquired from Kingswood School, where Florence Greene's husband taught history. The school grew rapidly and by 1957 its walls were bulging when a once-in-a-lifetime opportunity arose. The Albany Avenue estate of Frederick B. Rentschler, founder of Pratt & Whitney Aircraft, was being offered as a gift to any educational institution that could afford its maintenance. With more courage than financial ability, the Junior School trustees made and won a bid to occupy it. They renamed the school Renbrook.

Mrs. Greene ran her school with an amazing combination of firmness and serenity. A Quaker, she had a talent for putting parents and children at ease. Schooling, she said, is a great privilege, something that never can be finished. Her recipe for the good life: "take some time for play, add generous amounts of friendliness, save a little while to be quietly alone, serve others wherever you are, add a pinch of pain to bear the hard things, and fill to the brim with interesting work. Mix a fresh batch every day."

She retired from Renbrook in 1967, leaving 420 devoted students and a staff of 12. But that was not the end of her career. Two years afterward she accepted the challenge to head the private Watkinson School, then on the brink of closing on Bloomfield Avenue. She told its trustees, "I will act like a lady, think like a man and work like a dog." In two years she rejuvenated a nearly century-old secondary school that had lost its bearings. She died in 1985 at age 83.

The Mount

When Mount St. Joseph Academy moved in 1909 to punctuate the early West Hartford skyline on Hamilton Heights, it already had 56 years of selfless education achievements inspired by the Sisters of Mercy – the moving force behind parochial schooling in the Hartford diocese.

The first Catholic school for girls in Connecticut, the Mount outgrew its early quarters in Hartford next to St. Patrick's Church on Church Street and later on the former Morgan estate opposite the Aetna on Farmington Avenue. Anticipating Hartford's westward growth, the order's mother superior at the time arranged for the purchase in 1902 of a hilltop property off Fern Street in West Hartford. Seven years later, wide-eyed students moved into a massive, red-stone building that looked to them like a medieval castle, high on a hill.

The Mount was primarily a boarding high school until its growing popularity began to crowd its three spacious floors, overflow its impressive chapel, and tax its library. The change in 1937 to a day school released dormitory rooms for classroom space. The pace continued well into the 1960s when more than 650 girls arrived by bus, car, and foot from Catholic, Protestant, and Jewish homes for a well-rounded education offered by 16 sisters and 12 lay teachers. In a day when Dial-Select and closed-circuit TV and filmmaking classes dominated larger high schools, the Mount was still known for its grand marble staircases and its "Blue Parlor Room," designed by Elsie DeWolfe, described in newspaper accounts as the nation's first interior decorator. It was also known for its small classes and students in their trim navy blue uniforms with white collars – the only concession to female fashion being the hemlines that undulated up and down through the volumes of the school yearbook.

In the 1970s, enrollments declined and costs escalated. The Mount closed at the end of the 1978 school year. "We sought to bring out the potential in each girl," said Sister Patricia McKeon, principal at the end and herself an alumna of the school. "There was always a sense of community here."

Meanwhile, Renbrook continued to thrive. A major fund-raising campaign culminated in 1999 with two unprecedented million-dollar gifts from local

Mount St. Joseph Academy was a leading Catholic girls' school until 1978. It is now an assisted-living facility.

benefactors Harry J. and Helen Gray and Dr. Paul and Melinda Sullivan. The school named its new commons hall for both couples.

St. Joseph College and Mount St. Joseph Academy

The Sisters of Mercy moved their Hartford secondary school for girls to Hamilton Heights in West Hartford in 1909. They renamed it Mount St. Joseph Academy and opened with 101 resident students and 30 day students. After an illustrious career in women's high-school education here, "The Mount" closed in 1978. It became first a training center for the Hartford Insurance Group and in 1998 was renovated into an assisted-living facility.

In 1932, the Sisters of Mercy added to the academy Mount St. Joseph College, a junior college for women with 63 students and, a year later, extended the college curriculum through four years. It was the first liberal-arts institution in this area to prepare teachers. From its inception, courses for adults were offered evenings and summers.

In 1936, the college division moved to its own 84-acre campus farther west on the north side of Asylum Avenue, between Steele Road and Trout Brook Drive, where it was renamed St. Joseph College. The campus had been carefully planned by the Olmsted brothers, famous landscape architects, as a complete university complex for the future. The college included space for an exceptional Pre-School (long favored by many local parents of all faiths as a nursery school and now the School for Young Children), a teaching laboratory for the study of early childhood development.

Between 1955 and 1965, St. Joseph College added five residence halls, a student center, a library, and a chapel to its complex of neo-Georgian buildings. It added the Gengras Center for Exceptional Children, and opened a graduate division where both men and women earned master's degrees. It re-established a nursing program in 1975. Under the leadership of Winifred E. Coleman, the first lay person to serve as president, it dedicated the Carol Autorino Center for the Arts and Humanities in 2000. The center connects the buildings on campus into the original design outlined by the Olmsteds. Enrollment in the college's three divisions exceeds 2,500 students.

The Sisters of St. Joseph of Park Road, led by Sister Helen Dowd, run the ecumenical Intensive Education Academy for students who do not succeed in public school in the property formerly occupied by the United

Wearing beanies, Hartford College students gather for classes in a house at 47 Highland St. in 1940.

Hartford College for Women Photo

Synagogues of Greater Hartford at North Main Street and Mohawk Drive.

Northwest Catholic High School

Planned to serve high school students from 17 area parishes, Northwest Catholic opened in 1961 on a 30-acre campus off North Main Street. The one-story structure, designed by local architects Russell Gibson von Dohlen, was built around two inner courts. The opening principal, the Rev. Bradford Colton, headed a staff of eight Dominican sisters and four lay teachers. He was succeeded by the Rev. William O'Keefe, principal from 1968 to 1977.

By the school's gala 25th anniversary weekend in 1986, the administrative structure was changed to include a president, the Rev. Henry C. Frascadore, as well as a principal, Sister Doris Regan. They served a student population of 550 from 26 towns.

A major addition to the school was under way in 2000. School president Michael Griffin announced the naming of a second gymnasium for Walter Stosuy, a mainstay of the school's athletic program since 1963

and football coach from 1963 to 1978 and from 1995 to 1997. The expansion also included the addition of the Mortensen Theater, an art gallery and studio, and the Father Lawrence Bock Seminar Room.

Hartford College for Women

Hartford College for Women began as a junior college in West Hartford in 1939 in a house at 47 Highland St. The college outgrew the converted residence after several decades, moved to a roomier campus along Asylum Avenue in Hartford and, in 1991, became part of the University of Hartford.

During the Depression, Mount Holyoke College had offered a two-year course at the Hartford YWCA for women who could not afford four years at a residential college. After the Mount Holyoke program was discontinued, the need for affordable, non-denominational liberal-arts education for women continued.

The heart and soul of Hartford College was Laura Johnson, a Vermonter who became dean in 1940 and later the college's first president. Under her guidance, the college enabled women of different ages and few resources to continue their education.

The University of Hartford

Two hundred acres on the east side of Bloomfield Avenue, a portion of which is in West Hartford, used to be a farm occupied mainly by grazing cows. Now 4,100 undergraduates and 1,700 graduate students walk what has become the campus of the University of Hartford.

On Feb. 21, 1957, Gov. Abraham A. Ribicoff signed the bill granting a charter to a new higher education institution. Initially, it comprised three existing organizations: the Hartford Art School, founded in 1877 by Mrs. Samuel Colt and Harriet Beecher Stowe; the Hartt School of Music, and Hillyer College, created by the YMCA. It was the brainchild of a small group of community leaders, most from West Hartford, who were spearheaded by Bice Clemow. Among them were Alfred C. Fuller, the original Fuller Brush Man; John G. Lee, director of research at United Aircraft; Mrs. T. Merrill Prentice, Atwood Collins II, and Rep. George Schwolsky. The founders envisioned the university's purpose to "provide programs for youth and adults of the Central Connecticut area, designed to develop economic competence, social responsibility, intellectual curiosity, and a sense of spiritual values."

The first two buildings to be completed were Hillyer Hall and Auerbach Auditorium. Between 1959 and 1967 there followed residence halls, the Fuller Music Center, a Visual Arts Center for the Hartford Art School, the Gengras Student Union, the Physical Education Center, and the Barney School of Business & Public Administration. Physical growth escalated in 1971 with the completion of five major structures, including the Mortensen Library, two new residence halls, the Ward School of Technology, and the University Commons. Later came the 780-seat Lincoln Theater. The momentum launched by president Archibald Woodruff, a scholar and land-use/tax expert, continued under high-profile president Stephen J. Trachtenberg, who was appointed in 1977. The university made the transition from a group of commuter colleges into a regional university. Construction of the Village Apartments in 1984 provided housing for 1,000 more residents.

Solomon Schechter Day School

From classrooms in the basement of Emanuel Synagogue to a renovated and expanded former public school building on a park-like setting overlooking the town skating rink, aquatics center, and golf course. That's the rags-to-riches odyssey of the Solomon Schechter Day School of Greater Hartford.

The school opened in 1971 in the Mohegan Drive synagogue with two basement classrooms and 32 children in kindergarten, first and second grades. Pressed for space, it moved across town in 1984 after the 30-year-old Bridlepath School was mothballed by the Board of Education. Supported by parents and benefactors, the private school eventually bought the property and completed a multi-million-dollar renovation and expansion into an educational and architectural showplace in 2001. About 300 pupils are enrolled in kindergarten through Grade 8.

The sprawling, one-story school has an airy new front entrance and a new two-story wing for middle school classes and amenities such as a state-of-the-art library, computer room, science labs, and music and art rooms. A focal point is a Beit Tephillah, or "house of prayer" – a chapel-like room with twelve windows representing the twelve tribes of Israel and columns with lights representing the candles of a menorah. It opens onto an outdoor courtyard.

The school, which was in the midst of a curriculum update for its religious and general studies, received accreditation in 2000 from the Connecticut Association of Independent Schools. Carl Mandell, whose daughter attended Schechter, became principal in 1997 after a 28-year career as a principal and administrator in the Hartford public schools.

The Helen & Harry J. Gray University Center in 1988 completed 30 years of remarkable growth. It also gave a permanent home to the Museum of American Political Life, showcasing the vast collection of political memorabilia amassed by town resident J. Doyle DeWitt, former Travelers chairman and UofH trustee.

During the presidency of Walter Harrison, an impressive magnet school serving 350 elementary pupils from West Hartford, Hartford and five nearby towns opened in 2001 on the UofH campus near the site of the former Watkinson School.

Life-size whale replica greets visitors to Science Center of Connecticut facility on Trout Brook Drive.

University of Connecticut Branch

Based in Storrs, the University of Connecticut became a permanent part of the West Hartford community in 1962 with the construction of a new building on Asylum Avenue west of Trout Brook Drive for its law school. In 1967 and 1970 respectively, the university's School of Social Work and the regional undergraduate program moved from separate mansions in Hartford's West End to a new building adjacent to the law school. As a result of rapid growth, the law school relocated in 1984 to the former home of the Hartford Seminary in Hartford. The law school building became available for an enlarged library, offices, and classrooms for the School of Business Administration, and other operations, such as the Cooperative Extension Service and the Institute of Public Service International.

The West Hartford campus at one time offered a full undergraduate experience to its two-year student body, most of whom "branchferred" to Storrs to finish their degrees. Now with more than 2,000 graduate and undergraduate students, the Greater Hartford regional campus recently joined with Waterbury and Torrington as part of a tri-campus initiative designed to increase the number of course offerings and to implement a series of four-year undergraduate programs. At the same time, the School of Social Work looked ahead to offering a doctoral degree.

Children's Museum of Hartford/ Science Center of Connecticut

When Jane B. Cheney received an honorary doctorate from the University of Hartford in 1972, President Archibald Woodruff said: "She has an extraordinary ability to explain the sciences of the earth, the heavens, the ocean, and the creatures that inhabit them. Her simple but eloquent teaching makes clear the poetic beauty that lies behind the stark facts of science."

Jane Cheney was the director of the Children's Museum of Hartford, now the Science Center of Connecticut. She was the personification of the little museum on Trout Brook Drive that enlightened thousands of youngsters about the mysteries of nature. A Quaker from New York City, she began teaching at the institution in 1931 and ultimately served as director for 22 years, by far its longest tenure. After moving from Hartford to the old Junior School property here in 1957, the museum added a number of programs to attract school groups. Especially popular was the Summer Science Academy. Mrs. Cheney was a vibrant, tireless woman who ran her domain on a shoestring, unconcerned with revenues and budgets. She often took groups of youngsters on overnight camping excursions to the Burnt Hill Reservoir on the hill off Farmington Avenue opposite Reservoir No. 1. She wrote and narrated two TV shows sponsored by Connecticut Public Television, "Alive & About" and "This Is Connecticut." When in 1966 dinosaur tracks were accidentally uncovered in Rocky Hill, she pressed the state to preserve and display them, leading to the creation of Dinosaur State Park. She was also known to children as the "frog lady" for organizing and staging the annual frog jump at the Mark Twain House. In later years she became a senior scientist at the Bermuda Biological Station and conducted workshops there for students.

The museum added the Gengras Planetarium, new touch and technology exhibits, and changed its name to the Science Center of Connecticut to reflect a broader mission.

American School for the Deaf

A native Mississippian, Edmund "Burke" Boatner elevated the American School for the Deaf, the oldest institution for the handicapped in North America, to top rank during his 35 years as its administrative head. Through his wife Maxine Tull Boatner, a teacher of the deaf, he became interested in deaf education after a brief career as a civil engineer. In 1932 the Boatners joined the staff of Gallaudet College in Washington, D.C., and in 1935 came to West Hartford.

Founded in 1817 in Hartford, ASD started as the American Asylum for the Deaf and Dumb, which gave Asylum Avenue its name. It moved from the site of what is now the Hartford Insurance Group to a 98-acre tract on North Main Street in 1922. During the Boatner tenure, the school more than doubled in size to over 450 students, and the campus expanded from one building to an attractive complex of facilities. He started a pre-primary school for children under 5 and the Graham Anthony Vocational Rehabilitation Center, and raised funds for a gym and swimming pool.

An alumnus, David Halberg, eulogized him in these

Noah Webster Memorial Library

No educational service is more widely used than West Hartford's Public Library, which celebrated its 100th anniversary in 1997. At first it was located in the Congregational Church and funded jointly by the state and town with annual donations of $350. The first librarian, Elizabeth Elmer, held the job for 22 years. She was also the church's clerk. In 1901, a branch was opened in Elmwood with Julia Faxon in charge.

As the collection of books and their circulation increased, larger quarters were needed. The Sarah Whitman Chapter, Daughters of the American Revolution, mounted a campaign for a separate building and raised $40,000. In 1917, the Noah Webster Memorial Library was dedicated at 10 North Main St. In 1932, the Elmwood branch was moved into permanent quarters in the original Elmwood elementary school. By then, the main library was overflowing and the present facility at 20 South Main St. was built in 1938.

With the library system again overburdened in the post-war era, a new Elmwood branch was dedicated in 1954 and named for Julia Faxon, its librarian for more than 40 years. The main library was remodeled and expanded in 1962 under Asbury W. Schley, who served as librarian from 1956 to 1979. In 1966 came the Bishops Corner branch with Ruth Giddings in charge.

Denis M. Lorenz was named library director in 1979. He oversaw the library's electronic revolution and moved to make all facilities accessible to the handicapped during a 1987 expansion. The combined circulation of books, magazines, and video tapes exceeds 840,000 annually, and more than 30,000 residents are registered borrowers.

words: "The deaf children loved Dr. Boatner. He was a man with a smile of nature and a soul of love. Most of the deaf who have graduated from ASD know they are indebted to their parents for living but to our friend, Dr. Boatner, for living well."

Lately, the Gallaudet-Clerc Room at ASD has evolved into the most important historical collection of items relating to deaf education in America, according to headmaster Winfield McChord Jr.

The ASD campus is also the home of a Montessori School, where pupils 3 to 12 are taught through the Montessori developmental methods.

First Church of Christ, Congregational, is a handsome landmark facing Goodman Green in West Hartford Center.

David Harrington Photo

VIII. Worshiping

For nearly two centuries, early West Hartford – like the rest of Connecticut – was a theocracy run by the established Congregational Church. In 1818, a state constitutional convention cleared the way for other Christian denominations. In 1843, the General Assembly granted Jews "equal privileges with Christians in forming religious societies." By the 21st century, the town's evolving religious and ethnic diversity had produced 26 churches and eight synagogues. In addition to ministering to the religious needs of their congregations, they have played a vital role of outreach in a town noted for its spirit of caring for the less fortunate. They are presented here in the order of their chronological development locally.

The Congregationalists

Facing Goodman Green at the town's main intersection, the landmark, white-steepled First Church of Christ, Congregational, is the direct descendant of the original parish church that held a monopoly on both religious and secular affairs in the West Division for nearly 200 years. It reached its apex in the mid-20th century under the Rev. Dr. Elden H. Mills, a master minister-showman. Christian Century magazine called it "one of the 12 great churches of America."

The Congregational meeting houses have always occupied a prominent place in the town's center, moving from one corner to another at the crossroads of Farmington Avenue and Main Street as more space was needed. The fourth structure, a Gothic edifice erected in 1882 on the southeast corner, was fondly called "the greystone church" in contrast to its "old white church" predecessor. Stone or not, it was destroyed in 1942 in the town's most spectacular fire. Coincidentally, the Central Theater was showing a film that week that ended with a conflagration. Movie-goers emerged onto Farmington Avenue one cold January night to witness the real thing. Rabbi Abraham Feldman and his Temple Beth Israel congregation, who had built the town's first synagogue on Farmington Avenue just six years earlier, offered to share their facilities with the Congregationalists until their church could be rebuilt. Church parishioners worshiped in the temple rent-free for 22 months at the height of World War II. When

The Rev. Dr. Elden H. Mills

Although early pastors served longer, none served with more impact on the town than the Rev. Dr. Elden H. Mills. When he answered the call to First Church in the late 1930s, the church numbered 700 members. Over the next two decades, it grew to 5,000 – one of the largest Protestant congregations in America. Those who crowded into one of three Easter morning services to hear hundreds of choir voices were equally certain to hear a bold scolding from the pulpit on their ceremonial faith. Reared a Quaker in Indiana, Dr. Mills earned divinity degrees from Hartford and Union theological seminaries.

An aura of drama and spectacle enveloped him wherever he appeared. On the cold night in January 1942 when his greystone church burned beyond redemption and was still smoldering, he stood on the sidewalk planning a more elegant replacement. No member would forget the tender moment when he sang a eulogy to his eldest son who gave his life during World War II. And each time he stood at the back of the nave and intoned the benediction in his deep voice "And now may the Lord bless and keep you...," every spine tingled.

By the summer of 1943 the townspeople, sick and tired of wartime deprivations, decided to hold a Labor Day Fair. Forty-one civic and religious groups came together and chose Elden Mills as chairman. They staged a family day centered at the high school, with folk dancing and singing outside and hobby, flower, and garden shows inside. More than 10,000 showed up for the beginning of what became an annual tradition until the 1970s. In 1954 he performed as "the voice of the past" for the pageant that opened West Hartford's centennial celebration. Dressed in a flowing robe of 17 yards of blue satin and taffeta, he entranced an audience of 10,000 for two successive nights.

Two years later, Elden Mills abruptly resigned. He left town overnight, having succumbed to what some ministers refer to as their "occupational disease." He was divorced and soon married to one of his parishioners. Moving to Martha's Vineyard, he became pastor of the tiny West Tisbury Congregational Church and retired in 1973 at the age of 75.

Choirs lead singing during processional hymn in crowded sanctuary at First Church in the 1950s.

their new, 850-seat sanctuary was dedicated in 1947, plaques in each building commemorated the event.

First Church has always been known for its music, from "Uncle Thomas" Brace in the 19th century, through Gordon W. Stearns in the 1930s and '40s, to Don David McKeever in the late 20th century. Thomas Brace, deacon and choirmaster, was a revered fiddler around the state. He believed that the Bible declared organ music sinful and that only stringed instruments and human voices were proper for religious services. He resigned abruptly in 1867 when the church fathers, over his objections, installed an organ.

Gordon Stearns served not only First Church as organist and choir director but also Temple Beth Israel. Some in its congregation had attended the church's services there and liked the music they heard. He became the temple's director of music for eight years, resigning in 1951 when he was needed fulltime at First Church. He was famed for his 75-voice youth choir, for which there was always a waiting list. "It's quite a thing to see the high school fellows on the football field on Saturday and in the church choir on Sunday," he

once mused. He added a 70-voice junior high choir upon becoming fulltime.

The church allowed women and freed blacks in the early days to vote on church matters. In the mid-20th century, E. Olivia Shelton, president of the Hartford section of the National Council of Negro Women, taught Sunday School for nearly 40 years and was elected a church deacon.

The 1,800-member congregation celebrated its 275th anniversary in 1988. The church's prized John P. Webster Library is a repository of religious volumes used by scholars of all faiths.

Two smaller Congregational churches in town are Covenant and Flagg Road United Church of Christ.

Covenant began as a 38-member church of Swedish immigrants in Hartford in 1889. First called the Swedish Evangelical Zion Church, it joined the Covenant denomination in 1936. Moving to a new church on Westminster Drive opposite Sedgwick School in 1960, it lost some of its ethnic roots and embraced multiculturalism. The 200-member congregation celebrated its centennial here in 1989.

Quaker burial ground dating to late 18th century is located in front of new Friends meeting house built in 1950.

Religious Society of Friends

An early group of Friends (Quakers) had come to the West Division from New York State in 1780. They were the first sect the Congregational Ecclesiastical Society allowed to settle in town. Joined by several local families, they built a meeting house and school in 1799 on Quaker Lane, giving the street its name. In the late 1830s, most of the farmer members of the meeting moved to Connecticut's Western Reserve in Ohio and other western states for better soil. They "laid down" the West Division meeting, which became the East District School, and left money with the town for the upkeep of their cemetery. The Gilbert family, prominent Quakers who owned much of the land south of Farmington Avenue between Quaker Lane and Trout Brook, remained and were leaders in the fight against the West Division separating from Hartford.

It was 1950 before another group of Hartford Friends reclaimed the property. They had been meeting for meditation and discussion at the Hartford Seminary since 1937. Quaker decisions are made by consensus and the decision to build didn't come easily. Only when it was agreed to create a place that would be used on weekdays as well as on Sundays did plans for a meeting house go forward. The building at 144 Quaker Lane South was dedicated in 1950. In addition to hosting a

nursery school, it is used by a variety of community and activist groups. The Friends lent their original meeting house for the first Episcopal services in town in 1843 and again in 1954 when the new meeting house was used Friday evenings by the Beth El congregation as its new temple was being built. Lately, a Mass is held in the main room for worship every Sunday evening by a Catholic gay community called Dignity.

The Episcopalians

Quaker generosity was instrumental in the beginning of the town's third religious group. The Episcopalians were the first denomination to expand into West Hartford after the 1818 state constitutional convention allowed other Christian denominations to worship. The two Episcopal churches in town evolved from Hartford's Christ Church, which was founded in the late 18th century and became a cathedral in the early 20th.

The first Episcopal service took place in the Quaker Meeting House in 1843. Not until 1854 did the Episcopalians number enough to build St. James's Church, a small, Norman-style edifice, on the west side of Goodman Green. That was the year the town was incorporated, and reflected the beginning of religious diversity in West Hartford. St. James's was founded with the blessings of all three of Hartford's established

As parishioners watch, a youngster assists the Rev. Douglas W. Kennedy in g r o u n d - b r e a k i n g ceremony for the new St. James's Episcopal Church at Farmington Avenue and Walden Street in 1961.

Hartford Times Photo

Episcopal institutions: Christ Church, St. John's, and Trinity College, all of which contributed funding and manpower in time of need. For a couple of years during the Depression, St. James's lived under the sheltering wing of St. John's. The vicar serving here from the established church was a young priest named Walter H. Gray, who later became bishop of Connecticut and a leading figure in the national church.

As late as 1947, there was a balance of six cents in the parish bank account and about 75 families were members. That year, the Rev. Douglas W. Kennedy was appointed rector and 100 new families joined the church. In 1949, the Women's Guild staged at the West Hartford Armory its first Antiques Show and Sale, which became the largest of its kind in Connecticut. During

Canon Kennedy's 24-year tenure, the parish built first a parish house and chapel and, by 1962, a stone and brick, Gothic-style church at Farmington Avenue and Walden Street. They were funded by a series of capital campaigns as well as from proceeds of what had become the semi-annual Antiques Show and Sale, a community tradition until 1996. The event, called by parishioners the lifeblood of the church, fell victim to a lack of volunteers and competition from larger shows. "It's been very much part of the life and ministry of this church," the Rev. John L.C. Mitman said upon its passing. He and his predecessors, the Rev. Ronald L. Woodruff and Canon Kennedy, participated in St. James's Sesquicentennial service in 1993.

The church school expanded to more than 500 under

A year after its sesquicentennial was celebrated, St. John's Episcopal Church sanctuary was in shambles following a 1992 fire that caused $7 million in damage. The rebuilt church opened in 1995.

Mary Howe, consultant in Christian education for 32 years. In 1995, the church's 20-member girls' and boys' choirs were invited to sing at the White House during holiday tours. It capped a year in which they performed with the Connecticut Opera and toured England for three weeks as choir in residence at three cathedrals, including Westminster Abbey.

St. John's Episcopal Church moved to 679 Farmington Ave. in 1909 from Hartford, where it had started as an offshoot of Christ Church in 1841. Financier J. Pierpont Morgan had offered to buy the church's downtown property in order to expand the Wadsworth Atheneum. The $70,000 price for the site that became the Atheneum's Morgan Wing paid for construction of the impressive stone Gothic edifice here. In 1918, the Rev.

William Hooper, a former science teacher and firm believer in education, became rector. He helped build the church school program to include adults and more than 1,000 students by 1930. He served on the West Hartford School Board as well. For three years in the early 1930s and for 24 years starting in 1952, Clarence Watters, a nationally known organist, enhanced the church's reputation for music. Along with Episcopal churches nationally, St. John's introduced participation by women in the church's liturgy and sacraments beginning in 1975.

The 700-member church celebrated its 150th anniversary in 1991. A year later and barely a year into the pastorate of the Rev. Joseph Pace, a roaring midnight fire destroyed St. John's sanctuary and severely damaged the rest of the stone structure. It took the town's five fire companies more than five hours to extinguish the flames – so fierce they melted the stained-glass windows and destroyed the organ. The $7 million conflagration ranked as the country's largest that year in a public place. Once again, Temple Beth Israel offered the use of its facilities for the temporarily homeless flock. Parishioners also used the Kingswood-Oxford School auditorium and the St. John's chapel before their triumphant homecoming to a rebuilt sanctuary on Easter Sunday in 1995.

The Baptists

In 1858 a group of Baptists bought land for an American Baptist Church on the northwest corner of Main Street and Farmington Avenue, across from Goodman Green. A tavern was on the property, and its ballroom served as the church's first meeting hall. Many in town gathered on Sunday afternoons to watch the baptismal rite of full immersion held in Trout Brook near what is now the Fern Street bridge. The first pastor, Elisha Cushman, presided over the building of First Baptist Church at a time when the country was on the verge of the Civil War. One Sunday, he preached a sermon sympathetic to the South. The next Sunday, parishioners found that pranksters had draped its spire in a Confederate flag.

The church had a close connection with the Hartford Theological Seminary, which supplied preachers and other help to a church whose longest pastorate had lasted only five years. The Rev. Ellis Gilbert arrived in 1926 and stayed for 17 years. By 1936, the spire became dangerously wobbly and the rest of the church was showing its age, so a new white clapboard building – an exact replica of the old – rose a few blocks north at 90 North Main St. After the move, the Baptists joined with the Congregationalists to establish a summer daily vacation Bible School. In 1992, the 320-member congregation was one of the largest American Baptist churches in the state.

The congregation's outreach meant sharing use of their building with various groups such as Alcoholics Anonymous, The Center for Serenity, and the Grange. A Chinese Baptist Church holds Sunday services at the North Main Street church and a Chinese Bible study group meets there weekly. The congregation also exchanged ministers and shared events with Hartford's Shiloh Baptist Church. On the second floor of the church is the headquarters of the Street Ministry (now Hope Works Inc.), an interfaith counseling group that has counseled hundreds of teenagers since its founding by the Rev. Rick Lanz in 1973.

Farmington Avenue Baptist Church, an Independent Baptist Church, was built in several stages during the 1960s at the corner of Farmington Avenue and Mountain Road. Founded in 1959, it held services in Webster Hill School until a chapel could be built in 1961. A larger chapel was added in 1966. The Rev. Wendell D. Mullen dedicated a 750-seat sanctuary, designed by local architects Golden, Thornton & LaBau, in 1971. The property houses the Hartford Christian Academy, serving kindergarten through Grade 12. Its 122 students come from regional Independent Baptist churches too small to have academies of their own.

Elmwood Community Church

Elmwood's religious history officially began in 1873 when George T. Goodwin organized a Sunday school in the old South District schoolhouse at New Britain Avenue and Main Street. The growing membership subsequently expanded into a chapel built at the corner of New Britain Avenue and Grove Street opposite South Quaker Lane. In 1907, it became a branch of the First Congregational Church in the Center, but in 1921 it was reorganized again as a separate and independent church, called Elmwood Community. Its 188 members represented 14 denominations.

The Rev. James F. English, later to become superintendent of the Connecticut Conference of Congregational churches, was its first pastor. The growing congregation dedicated a larger church on Newington Road in 1927. When the Rev. Charles K. Tracy arrived in 1926, the fledgling church was only five years old and, according to the Metropolitan News, the community "was but a blur on the landscape to those who passed it by on trains." He served twenty years, retiring at age 72. Remembered as one of Elmwood's leading lights, he grew the membership to 600 and involved the church in the community – even creating (and personally maintaining) a two-acre play field for neighborhood boys.

The church carillon has tolled the hours and hymns

"Pillars of the Church" is how this 1926 photo was titled. Leaders of Elmwood Community Church gathered in the excavation site to mark the beginning of their new building on Newington Road.

across the community. When silenced in 1992, neighbors joined church members in funding its replacement. Catholic parishioners from nearby St. Brigid's sent a donation because the carillon had played a Navy hymn for the funeral of a monsignor six years earlier.

The Roman Catholics

The Sisters of St. Joseph was the first Catholic organization to move to West Hartford. In 1887 they purchased land at Park Road and Prospect Avenue. A Victorian house on a gently rolling knoll overlooking cows in their back yard became home for the first group of Sisters. Eventually, other buildings were erected to accommodate the growing community and by the late 1800s, "Parkville" was designated the provincial house for the North American province, one of 13 worldwide. The Sisters taught or served as nurses in local schools and founded St. Francis Hospital in Hartford, according to Sister Mary Kelly, a niece of the Rev. John Kelly. Father Kelly was known for his art collection, which he donated to St. Joseph College and became part of the permanent collection at its new art center.

The Sisters of Mercy, the second Catholic organization in West Hartford, were more visible locally. In 1908 they moved their Hartford secondary school for girls to Hamilton Heights and renamed it Mount St. Joseph Academy. The Mount was a prestigious educational institution – one favored by daughters of many leading West Hartford families – until its closing in 1978.

In 1914 the Sisters built St. Agnes Home, a maternity hospital for unwed mothers and an infant asylum, and St. Mary Home for the elderly on Steele Road. They started St. Joseph College in 1932 at Hamilton Heights and in 1936 moved the institution farther west on Asylum Avenue. After the Sisters relocated St. Agnes to smaller quarters on Mayflower Street in the late 1960s, the town purchased the Steele Road building and part of the property for the Education Center, headquarters of the School Administration, which had outgrown its facility next to Plant Junior High School. In 1987 the school administration moved to the old Town Hall. The former St. Agnes building was razed and the property was subdivided for residential development.

The first Catholic church here was St. Brigid in Elmwood, which began in 1918 as a tiny wooden chapel at New Britain Avenue and Cambridge Street under the patronage of Irish Saint Bridget. Before West Hartford Catholics had a church of their own, they attended services in Hartford and New Britain and, during the construction of the chapel, in the office building of the New Departure Co. The frame mission building was razed in 1950 for a new brick structure of modified Gothic design, seating 650 in a sanctuary paneled in oak to match the carved oak pews. It was dedicated in 1951 under the Rev. William Brewer, pastor since 1947. In 1960 the sixth parish pastor, the Rev. Msgr. Arthur J. Heffernan, renamed the church St. Brigid to comply with the original spelling of the saint's name. He also supervised the completion of a parish school and convent on Mayflower Street.

By 1920 there were enough Catholics of French-Canadian, Italian, and Irish descent in West Hartford to make up a second congregation and an enterprising young priest, the Rev. John F. Callahan, was assigned to start St. Thomas the Apostle parish. It first worshiped in a prefabricated church on the southwest corner of Quaker Lane and the Boulevard. Recognizing the rapid northward and westward growth of his parish, Father Callahan in 1926 bought a large Colonial house on Farmington Avenue at Bishop Road for a rectory and property on Farmington at Dover Road for a basement church, an economy popular at the time. When a choice had to be made whether to complete the upper church or build St. Thomas School on Dover Road, Father Callahan decided that the education of his future parishioners outweighed the inconvenience to his current ones. The result was a school regarded as one of the finest in the Connecticut diocese. The parish grew tenfold in a single generation, and what had been essentially a one-man fund drive for a quarter century finally resulted in the imposing brick church for more than 1,000 parish families.

As the town's population boomed, four more Catholic parishes were established: St. Mark the Evangelist (1942), St. Timothy (1958), St. Peter Claver (1966), and St. Helena (1966).

The latter two were founded when St. Thomas and St. Brigid became unwieldy and split in half to accommodate the population's westward movement. The two churches are among the youngest in the Hartford diocese.

For St. Helena's, a house on Ridgewood Road was

Church of St. Brigid Artwork

St. Brigid, the first Catholic parish in West Hartford, began in 1918 as a small wooden chapel at New Britain Avenue and Cambridge Street. It was sketched here in 1949 before being razed in 1950 for today's Gothic edifice.

purchased for a rectory and five acres of land behind for a church. St. Helena parishioners attended Mass at Duffy School before moving into the parish hall at Echo Lane and Mildred Street. A contemporary structure seating 650 was dedicated in 1969 by the Rev. Joseph G. Murphy, founding pastor who was still serving during its 25th anniversary celebration in 1990. By then, the parish had grown from 600 to 900 families.

St. Peter Claver parishioners worshiped in the Braeburn School gymnasium until their strikingly modern, cedar shingle, stone and glass church rose along Pleasant Street. They nicknamed it "St. Braeburn" when the 1,050-family parish gathered for a 25th anniversary Mass in the school gymnasium in 1990. The design of the low-slung church by local architects Russell Gibson von Dohlen won a national architectural award. Long led by the Rev. John Shugrue, the church is notable for its open feeling, with no railing dividing the altar from the congregation. It is also known for an outstanding choir.

Quality education has always been a hallmark of the Catholic faithful in West Hartford. Besides St. Thomas, the Church of St. Timothy also runs an outstanding parochial school. The highly respected Northwest Catholic High School, opened in 1961 off North Main Street, attracts an ethnically diverse student body.

In 1963 the Passionist Fathers opened Holy Family Monastery on 80 acres off Tunxis Road. Later, they introduced ecumenical retreats and programs.

Hartford Courant Photo

The Rev. James L. McKearney asks a question and gets plenty of answers during children's Mass in front of St. Peter Claver congregation in open, stone-walled sanctuary.

St. Thomas the Apostle Church at 872 Farmington Ave. is the largest Roman Catholic church in town. Its pastor from 1954 to 1974, the Rev. Msgr. Raymond G. LaFontaine, was dean of Hartford County West for the diocese. He retired after his 75th birthday in 1976.

Hartford Times Photo

The Methodists

A Methodist church was formed in 1895 by 20 Swedish immigrants from West Hartford, New Britain, and the western section of Hartford. Its services were originally held in New Britain and its first church in Hartford was known as the Swedish Methodist Congregational Church. The church moved many times and changed names as frequently, eventually building a church in 1921 at Lockwood Terrace and the Boulevard in West Hartford, not far from the home and business of plumbing contractor Oscar Hjerpe. Over the years, he filled every assignment his church could have given, from organist to temperance lecturer, and he was chosen to represent West Hartford at the General Conferences of all Methodist branches in 1938 and 1939. By the 1940s the membership was no longer predominantly Swedish speaking. The Rev. Wallace T. Viets, who did not speak Swedish, was appointed pastor, and the congregation outgrew its Lockwood Terrace building.

In 1957 it purchased its present property at New Britain Avenue and Berkshire Road. The Methodists were without a church for the next 14 years, however. They worshipped first in Wolcott School and then in a new education building and fellowship hall. Allen L. Beavers Jr. chaired the building committee for the 250-seat sanctuary, dedicated in 1971 by the Rev. William C. Carroll. Since 1968 it has been known as the West Hartford United Methodist Church.

The West Hartford Methodist Nursery School was founded in 1965 by Frances DeCourcy, whose husband chaired the Board of Education. The church's month-long pumpkin sale, with pumpkins displayed along the church lawn near an entrance ramp to I-84, is as much a sign of autumn as falling leaves. The fundraiser sends the Youth Fellowship on Appalachian mission projects.

West Hartford News Photo

The Rev. Dr. Wallace G. Fiske outside Universalist Church.

The Rev. Dr. Wallace G. Fiske

The Rev. Dr. Wallace Grant Fiske, who served 26 years in the pulpit of the Universalist Church, was revered as one of the town's most inspiring ministers. A proponent of an enlightened, undogmatic, socially concerned ministry, he was in the forefront of interfaith and inter-racial programs as well as mental health and Planned Parenthood activities.

An affable wit, he used to say that among his duties was being a "good five-cent psychiatrist. A minister should sit in with people always in confidence and never in judgment." Looking back at his career, he observed that the greatest danger was the erosion of character, high values, and personal integrity, yet he was "more sure of the reality of spirituality even among the gross materialism in which we live."

A talented photographer who served as chaplain in Gen. Claire Chennault's Flying Tigers in China and also with the 43rd Division in Korea, Dr. Fiske had a lifelong interest in bicycling and mountain climbing. Shortly after retiring in 1973, he was off on his 10-speed bicycle to Keene, N.H., and back, a distance of more than 200 miles. He was a founder of American Youth Hostels in New England.

Topped by a twelve-sided dome of Spanish tile and with an interior full of symbolism, Temple Beth Israel is considered one of the most beautiful synagogues in America. Built in 1936, it houses the 13th largest Jewish congregation in the country.

The Universalists

Like other religious groups, the Universalist Church moved from Hartford, where it started as an offshoot of dissidents from the Second Congregational Church in 1821. Members sold their second location in 1906 to make way for the Travelers Tower and their third in 1930 for the Hartford Fire Insurance Co. The sales made possible the construction in 1931 of the present church on Fern Street, providing that rare entity – a debt-free church from the start.

Under the Rev. Dr. Wallace G. Fiske, its congregation grew to nearly 1,200 members, requiring an extensive classroom addition and parish hall to be built in 1962. Dr. Fiske encouraged a strong church school and education program, run ever since by the Rev. Jean Cook Brown, minister of religious education.

The Universalists completed a $1.5 million renovation of the church in 1999, the tenth year of the pastorate of the Rev. Stephen Kendrick.

The Jewish Community

Jews were forbidden by state law to worship in Connecticut until 1843, the year when the law was changed and Congregation Beth Israel was organized in Hartford. By 1855, Hartford's Jews numbered 200 and owned thirteen clothing stores and eight dry goods stores. By 1880 when the Jewish community had grown to 1,500, the Jewish middle class was concentrated in the Blue Hills Avenue section of Hartford. The immigration of Jews from Eastern Europe eventually swelled their numbers to 30,000 in the area.

As Jews prospered, they moved west along Farmington Avenue and out Albany and Bloomfield avenues to West Hartford and Bloomfield, settling particularly during the 1950s in the then undeveloped area north of Albany Avenue. In 1936 Congregation Beth Israel moved from Hartford and built the town's first synagogue. Seven more would follow, and today nearly 20 percent of town residents belong to one of the three branches of the Jewish faith, represented by five Orthodox, two Conservative and one Reform synagogues.

Beth Israel has been led by strong rabbis and dedicated laymen like Gershon Fox, founder in 1847 of the business that became Hartford's great G. Fox & Co. department store, and fellow merchant Isidore Wise, who was president of the congregation for half a century. It occupied several Hartford sites before moving from Charter Oak Temple to the impressive, Byzantine temple at 701 Farmington Ave. With its gray limestone exterior and twelve-sided dome of deep

Rabbi Stanley M. Kessler stands before the new Temple Beth El prior to its dedication in 1963. The "floating" roof supported by arches around the circular structure represents the 12 tribes of ancient Israel.

Rabbi Abraham J. Feldman

The much beloved Rabbi Abraham J. Feldman epitomized the Jewish ecumenical tradition. Not content only to build the Jewish community's most beautiful temple and fill it with 1,500 families, he also reached out to Christians for friendship and better understanding. In 1942, after the First Congregational Church in West Hartford Center burned down, Rabbi Feldman and his Beth Israel congregation shared their synagogue for several years until the church could be rebuilt – a gesture offered again in 1992 when St. John's Episcopal Church was consumed by fire.

Civic leader and renowned author and lecturer, Rabbi Feldman was nationally regarded as Reform Judaism's most effective champion.

He formed an ecumenical triumvirate in the Hartford area with Episcopal Bishop Walter Gray and Catholic Archbishop William J. O'Brien. As a member of the Hartford Rotary Club, for 37 years he was called upon to give the annual Thanksgiving address. A founder and editor of the Connecticut Jewish Ledger, he published hundreds of pamphlets and more than 20 books. At one time he headed the Central Conference of American Rabbis, the country's largest rabbinical organization. When he died in 1977 at the age of 84, more than 900 mourners attended his funeral at the temple, which he served for 52 years.

orange Spanish tile, the building is one of the most beautiful temples in America. The interior, full of symbolic significance, is a repository of liturgical heirlooms. By 1950, when the Alfred Meyer Silberman Chapel and an auditorium were added, the first Jewish congregation in the state had become the 13th largest in the United States.

Longtime rabbis Abraham J. Feldman and Harold Silver were leading lights in the broader community as they were in the Jewish faith. In 1997, Rabbi Stephen Fuchs became only the temple's fourth rabbi in 79 years. He had served the largest Jewish congregation in Nashville, Tenn., where he was spokesman for the Jewish community, and continues that role here. Also in 1997, the congregation undertook the rare process of writing by hand a new Torah – a first in the Hartford area. The Torah, written in Hebrew and comprising 62 parchment panels stitched together, is read during weekly services and kept in the synagogue's Ark. With 1,500 member families, Beth Israel is the largest Reform temple in New England and one of the oldest in the country.

In 1953 former West Hartford members of Hartford's Emanuel Synagogue met at the Isidore Savin home to discuss forming a new Conservative congregation here. Led by officers Arthur D. Weinstein, Lewis Chernoff, Dr. Gerald Pitegoff, Albert Kaplan, and Harry H. Kleinman, the group purchased 10 acres of land from

Congregation Agudas Achim leaders gathered at ground-breaking for their new synagogue at 1244 North Main St. in 1967. From left are David S. Cohn, master of ceremonies; Harold Veroff, congregation president; David Weinbaum, building chairman; Rabbi Abraham N. AvRutick; Barney Wachtel, oldest member, and Earl Horwitz, the architect.

Hartford Times Photo

nurseryman Peter Cascio to build a religious school and synagogue at 2626 Albany Ave. Stanley M. Kessler, a 30-year-old from Lincoln, Neb., became its first rabbi. Led for 45 years by Rabbi Kessler, Beth El Temple eventually became the largest Conservative congregation in Connecticut. As it neared its 50th anniversary, Beth El undertook a major fund-raising campaign to renovate and enlarge its sanctuary and school facility under the leadership of Rabbi James Rosen, who succeeded Rabbi Kessler.

Emanuel Synagogue started in Hartford, where it grew to more than 1,000 family members, about half from West Hartford. In 1955, the congregation purchased 10 acres at 160 Mohegan Drive for a religious school and future synagogue. Attorney Milton Nahum, congregation president, said the move obviated the need for a substantial addition to the Hartford synagogue on Woodland Street. The school and auditorium were built in 1956 and the sanctuary in 1971.

The religious school at Emanuel is named after Rabbi Morris Silverman, who became the second rabbi of the synagogue in 1923 and led what became for a time the area's largest Conservative synagogue until his retirement in 1961. The nationally known author of many books on Judaism, he wrote *Hartford Jews 1659-1970*, published by the Connecticut Historical Society. The

book, annotating the Jewish contribution to Greater Hartford, was the first of its kind in the country. Rabbi Silverman served more than 25 years on the state Civil Rights Commission, including several years as its chair, and made a round-the-world tour as its emissary.

The first local Orthodox congregation, Beth David Synagogue at 20 Dover Road, was started in 1943 by Rose Rosenstein and Gabriel Levine. For the first year, High Holy Days were observed in the American Legion hall on Memorial Road. The vestry, first of three new buildings at Farmington Avenue and Dover Road, was dedicated in 1954 under Rabbi William Cohen. Rabbi Yitzchok Adler has led the congregation since 1995.

In 1998 United Synagogues of Greater Hartford moved into its new home, a house at 205 Mohawk Drive. The congregation was formed in the early 1960s when five small synagogues in Hartford merged and erected a star-shaped building at 840 North Main St. The congregation moved out in 1996 because its membership had dwindled from 180 families to 45, said Robert Cohen, congregation president. The newly renovated building, shaped in the Star of David, became the home of the Intensive Education Academy.

Other Orthodox congregations are Congregation Agudas Achim at 1244 North Main St., which was an old Hartford congregation, and the newer Young Israel of Hartford at 1137 Trout Brook Drive and Young Israel of West Hartford at 2240 Albany Ave.

The Jewish faithful emphasize education, civic service, and philanthropy. In addition to the Hebrew Academy and Solomon Schechter day schools, Jews are strong supporters of the public schools. West Hartford's Greenberg family endowed a Center for Judaic Studies at the University of Hartford.

The Jewish Community Center of Greater Hartford, located on Bloomfield Avenue in West Hartford, opened in 1962. Melvin W. Title was its first president and membership soon reached 7,832 from 1,760 families. Its educational, cultural, and gymnasium facilities make it a center for both Jews and non-Jews.

The Lutherans

Another religious group, Lutherans from Germany, Sweden, and northern Europe, settled here early in the 20th century. Among their numbers were Bengt M.W. Hanson, who started the Hanson-Whitney Machine Tool Co. in 1920, the Liljedahl brothers and other builders with mechanical aptitudes, and the owners of the Viking Bakery.

The Mission Board of the Evangelical Lutheran Church canvassed the community in 1943 and found sufficient interest to invite the Rev. Martin C. Duchow, then a pastor in Albany, N.Y., to establish a Lutheran congregation in a house it purchased at 74 Westland Ave. When neighbors objected, he found a better location – a 12-room house at Boulevard and South Main Street. In 1951 the congregation built a basement church with a simple, freestanding entrance overhead and, six years later, had raised enough money to complete the church superstructure. The Rev. Mr. Duchow, who served for 30 years until 1974, served as a trustee of the Open Hearth mission and as Protestant chaplain for the West Hartford Police Department. He also helped organize the local chapter of the American Association of Retired Persons.

With a membership of about 600, the church building was renovated and expanded in 1990 under the Rev. Carl J. Anton and the Rev. Robert J. Mikulastik. Those of German heritage stayed here to worship and the Swedes favored Emanuel Lutheran Church in Hartford.

The Presbyterians

Westminster Presbyterian Church was organized in 1950 with 58 members as an offshoot of the First Presbyterian Church of Hartford. During its first year, services were held in the basement of First Church of Christ, Congregational, as well as in the Buena Vista golf clubhouse and the auditorium of Sedgwick Junior High School.

In 1951 the congregation moved to a block-long, three-acre estate at 2080 Boulevard and met in a big white mansion. After erecting a church, it quickly grew to 325 members. The Rev. Gurdon T. Scoville from Pennsylvania, pastor for the first 20 years, brought to town lots of energy and a splendid Spring Strawberry Festival. He instituted strong programs for the mentally and physically disabled. He participated in the Selma civil rights march with Rabbi Stanley M. Kessler of Beth El Temple. The Rev. Ross Ludemann arrived in 1983, retiring 15 years later with a renewed church, a growing congregation, and a thriving music program.

The Boulevard facility has been expanded several times. During its 50th anniversary weekend in 2000, ground was broken for a multi-purpose fellowship hall and an intimate chapel.

Jehovah's Witnesses

The Jehovah's Witnesses built a Kingdom Hall on the northwest corner of South Quaker Lane and The Boulevard in 1957. It is run by a body of elders and several ministers, one of whom is chosen to preside. In 2000 the congregation had outgrown its facility and was seeking more space for its Sunday services, Thursday evening ministry school, and public talks on Biblical subjects the rest of the week. Plans were to build a new hall along Still Road on the West Hartford-Bloomfield town line.

With literature printed in 300 languages, the Witnesses reach out to a diverse communithy. The West Hartford church appeals particularly to Russian, Bosnian, Polish, Portuguese, French, and Vietnamese newcomers.

IX. Making an Impact

As a residential community known for its quality of life, West Hartford has always attracted the movers and shakers of the Hartford region. Though some have been active in town affairs and others only resided here, all have helped give the town a particular cachet through their prominence in business and industry, the professions, the arts, the hospitals, non-profit institutions, and philanthropy.

For most of the 20th century the chief executives of Hartford's insurance companies were a small, elite group who served as directors on one or more corporate boards, were actively involved in local and state politics, and gave generous support to many charities. Arthur J.

Lumsden, longtime head of the Greater Hartford Chamber of Commerce and a town resident, referred to them as "the bishops" because of their dominance over policy making. Very little was done without their concurrence.

One "bishop" was town resident Morgan Brainard, CEO of Aetna Life & Casualty from 1922 to 1955, who in the middle of the Great Depression decided to build a new home office on Farmington Avenue in Hartford. It was the largest colonial-style building ever constructed. His common sense and calmness under crisis carried the Aetna through the hard times without laying off a single employee.

Hartford's Catalyst Convenes 'The Bishops'

For 25 years, from 1956 until his retirement in 1981, Arthur J. Lumsden of Oakridge Lane headed the Greater Hartford Chamber of Commerce. From his first day on the job he was a whirlwind in motion, a messiah for socially responsible urban development. The Chamber, he believed, should be an "agitator," not merely a retail promoter. Within six years, Chamber membership expanded from a few hundred to 2,000 and its annual budget went from $40,000 to $300,000. While he conceived of the plans and actions, he used his directors and hundreds of committee members to implement them. The chief executives of the 20 largest companies became known, in his phrase, as "the bishops."

His first project was Constitution Plaza, a $60-million complex financed mainly by the Travelers Insurance Cos. that opened in 1964 and was hailed as a model of urban renewal. Others included the building of three new bridges across the Connecticut River, the commercial development of the Windsor Street area, and the Hartford Civic Center, financed by Aetna Life & Casualty.

He saw the Chamber's role as going far beyond the economic sphere. Social action, he insisted, was

not incompatible with making a profit. In 1962 he founded the Community Renewal Team, the first program of its kind. He also supported the arts and formed in 1970 the Greater Hartford Arts Council.

Convinced that the future well-being of Hartford and its suburbs depended on a regional approach, he helped create regional agencies for housing, education, planning, and governing. Dissatisfied with band-aid solutions to social problems, he turned to James Rouse, developer of new towns in Reston, Va., and Columbia, Md. As a result, in 1969 the "bishops" organized Greater Hartford Process Inc. to build a new community in Coventry. When the bold but secret scheme was revealed, it stirred up intense opposition from Hartford's minorities, who interpreted it as an effort to move the poor and unemployed out of the city. The planned "new town" was scuttled in 1977.

Despite the failure of Hartford Process, Lumsden could take pride that the trend-setting Chamber, with a budget of nearly $3 million and 50 employees, had become the biggest in the country. He was the best-known Chamber executive and for two years president of the American Chamber of Commerce. He died in 1988 of lung cancer.

Other "bishops" were Aetna chairmen Olcott D. Smith and John H. Filer. Smith, a former Day, Berry & Howard attorney who represented the town in the General Assembly in 1941 and had been an assistant prosecutor in the town court, chaired Aetna from 1963 to 1977. He involved Aetna in Hartford's urban renewal, an effort intensified by Filer. Aetna helped build the Hartford Civic Center and the city's tallest building, CityPlace. Some date the end of "Mother Aetna," as it traditionally was known, with the day in 1984 when Filer announced his retirement. Filer was credited with making Aetna a national leader in corporate responsibility.

Another "bishop" was Frazar B. Wilde, under whose leadership Connecticut General (now CIGNA) became the third largest stockholder-owned insurer in the country. In the 1960s he teamed with developer James Rouse to develop the planned city of Columbia, Md. He was responsible for moving the company's home office to a suburban campus in Bloomfield and erecting in 1957 a modern structure with glass walls that was praised as "the office of the future." Modest yet outspoken, thoughtful and wry, he once told an interviewer, "I've always been a freak Yankee, full of ideas, an absolute maverick."

Wilde took a keen interest in the affairs of West Hartford. So did other insurance executives like Millard Bartels of the Travelers and Thomas W. Russell of CIGNA, both of whom served as town councilmen.

David E.A. Carson, former president of Middlesex Mutual Assurance Co. and more recently chairman of Peoples Bank, was a member of the West Hartford Board of Education.

Judge Thomas D. Gill, a brother of the writer Brendan Gill, was a pioneer in the area of social welfare. For 35 years, from 1942 until his retirement in 1976, he presided over the Juvenile Court of Connecticut. For another eight years he served as a senior judge and referee. As chairman of the Child Study Home Commission, Gill was the spearhead for creating High Meadows, the state-operated home for emotionally disturbed children in North Haven. He was president of the YMCA of Greater Hartford and in 1962 received the Greater Hartford Chamber of Commerce's Charter Oak Leadership Medal.

Other Business Movers & Shakers

A sampling of town residents who had wide influence in the 20th century:

Edward B. Bates, head of Connecticut Mutual.

Morrison H. Beach, CEO of Travelers Insurance Cos.

Lyman P. Brainerd, president and chairman of Hartford Steam Boiler & Inspection Insurance Co.

Walter F. Connolly Jr., president of Connecticut Bank & Trust Co.

George A. David, CEO of United Technologies.

Pomeroy Day, banking and insurance executive.

Attorney Ralph W. Elliott.

James F. English Jr., CEO of Connecticut Bank & Trust Co. and president of Trinity College.

Robert S. Furek, CEO of Heublein Inc. and head of the state-appointed board overseeing Hartford schools.

Arnold C. Greenberg, CEO of Coleco Industries, philanthropist, and chairman of Bushnell Memorial and University of Hartford.

Robert T. Jackson, head of Phoenix Mutual Life Insurance Co.

Charles E. Lord, CEO of Hartford National Bank & Trust Co.

James B. Lyon, lawyer active in numerous non-profit organizations.

W. Erle Martin, CEO of United Technologies.

Robert K. Mooney, retired head of Hartford Despatch Moving & Storage.

Robert L. Newell, CEO of Hartford National Bank & Trust Co.

Leonard J. Patricelli, head of Ten Eighty Corp.

James J. Preble, CEO of former United Bank & Trust Co.

Millard H. Pryor Jr., manufacturer, philanthropist and head of several arts organizations.

Henry R. Roberts, CEO of CIGNA.

Thomas W. Russell, senior executive of Connecticut General Life Insurance Co. (before merger with CIGNA).

Benjamin P. Terry, former president of Society for Savings.

DeRoy C. (Pete) Thomas, president of Hartford Insurance Group.

Wilson Wilde, retired CEO of Hartford Steam Boiler & Inspection Insurance Company.

Roger C. Wilkins, chairman of Travelers Insurance Cos.

Dona D. Young, president of The Phoenix Cos., formerly Phoenix Mutual Life Insurance Co.

Charles C. Cook

Revered as the town's "great compromiser," Charles C. Cook of Highland Street by the age of 43 had made a fortune in construction, especially of government buildings, and retired.

Turning his energies to politics, he first took the spotlight when he opposed and defeated his East Side neighbors who wanted to secede from West Hartford. In the 1895 session the Legislature was asked to annex to Hartford the area bounded by Prospect Avenue, Asylum Avenue, Steele Road, Whiting Lane, and Park Road. The petitioners, mostly wealthy families who had moved west only in the previous 20 years, were having serious problems with their cesspools and were threatened by Hartford's Board of Water Commissioners with higher charges than the residents of Hartford had to pay. The West Enders, mostly farmers, stormed the town meeting in protest. At the height of the argument an erect, sandy-haired young man, a newcomer to the East Side, pushed his way to the front of the old Town Hall and forcibly spoke against hasty action but urged the submission of an opposing petition. With that action the secessionist movement died and Charlie Cook's leadership was born.

But Cook was not content with his victory. He wanted to help his neighbors resolve their difficulties and spearheaded negotiations for an East Side sewer connecting with the Hartford system and for a special fire district with its own equipment. In 1899 he was elected to the Board of Assessors and then to the Legislature in 1901. He became a member of the State Building Commission and for 15 years Cook supervised the building of nearly every state structure, including the State Library.

He continued to chart a constructive course for the town. When a town meeting got snarled in controversy, he would rise from the back and point a peaceful way out. If he didn't make the meeting, it might be delayed until somebody drove down Farmington Avenue to fetch him. His only defeat came at the hands of William H. Hall, who successfully fought for the erection of a new high school on South Main Street.

Nonetheless, Cook was West Hartford's dominant political figure for at least two decades.

E. Clayton Gengras

Clayton Gengras of Prospect Avenue rose from a super automobile salesman and dealer to become a powerful force as the major stockholder of banking and insurance companies and Greater Hartford's premier philanthropist. His life turned the Horatio Alger fable into remarkable reality. A Hartford native, son of an Irish mother and a French-Canadian dentist, he dropped out of high school at age 15 to repair automobiles. Up at dawn every day and the first to arrive at work, the dapper, five-foot-seven dynamo eventually owned several auto dealerships in New England and New York and became head and principal stockholder of Security-Connecticut Insurance Group. He bought the ailing Connecticut Company bus lines and later sold them to the state. But he managed to attend Mass daily and rarely missed dinner with his family.

In 1966 he got the political bug, setting his sights on becoming governor. After a bitter campaign he lost to Gov. John N. Dempsey by more than 114,000 votes, his biggest disappointment. He continued, however, as the Republican party's biggest fund-raiser and contributor. Yet at the same time he crossed party lines to become a close ally of Gov. Ella T. Grasso. His son, E. Clayton Jr., served on the Town Council in 1981-83.

In the twilight of life, Clayt Gengras wanted to leave a legacy to the community that had nurtured him. He made major gifts to numerous institutions: the Gengras Center at the University of Hartford, the planetarium at the Children's Museum/Science Center, the Ambulatory Care Center at St. Francis Hospital, the Center for Exceptional Children at St. Joseph College, and the Institute of Living. Equally important to him were his Catholic faith and the 11 children raised by him and his wife Elizabeth, a West Hartford native. When he died in 1983 at age 74, he was considered West Hartford's wealthiest citizen.

Frederick B. Rentschler

At the age of 37 Frederick Rentschler was a man without a job, having resigned as president of Wright Aeronautical Corporation. "Come hell or high water," he told his brother, "I'm going to stay with aviation." The year was 1925. Hearing that Pratt & Whitney Machine Tool had idle plant and idle capital, he

In 1957 Frederick B. Rentschler's English manor-style mansion off Albany Avenue was made available and became the home of Renbrook School.

journeyed to Hartford and told the management he wanted to make a radial, air-cooled aircraft engine that would surpass anything yet designed. A few days later he got a favorable answer: $250,000 of startup money and the use of the company's space and name. With only six men to work with him, he assembled the first experimental engine. Called the Wasp, it easily passed the qualification test on March 4, 1926. By the end of the year the Navy ordered 200 production engines and in 1930 he erected a large new plant on a big tract of farmland in East Hartford.

Thus began the giant enterprise now called United Technologies Corp. Rentschler created the Hamilton Standard Division to make propellers and brought Sikorsky Aviation into his domain to develop flying boats and helicopters. During World War II the company employed 40,000 and turned out 363,619 engines, one-half of the total U.S. and Allied aircraft power. In 1951 P&W ushered in the jet age with its pioneering J57.

Halfway up Talcott Mountain off Albany Avenue in West Hartford, the aircraft magnate built on rock an English manor-style, stone and wood mansion from which he could gaze down on the city. He died in 1956, and his will directed his heirs to donate the property to an educational institution able to maintain it. West

Hartford's Junior School won the bid and changed its name to Renbrook School.

Dr. Hilda Crosby Standish

At the age of 95 Hilda Standish could look back on a lifetime of crusading for birth control and spreading knowledge of health-related issues, especially to adolescents. Born in Hartford in 1902, she attended Hartford Public High School, graduated from Wellesley, and received her medical degree from Cornell. She spent several years practicing and teaching obstetrics in a missionary hospital in Shanghai, China. In 1935 she became medical director of the Hartford Maternal Health Center, a clinic started by Katharine H. Hepburn and Sally Pease to provide contraceptives, which were illegal in Connecticut at the time. Her involvement, she explained, was based on her conviction that "planned parenthood is an integral part of intelligent present-day living."

Following her marriage to Dr. Myles Standish, Hilda began lecturing young girls in local schools on health. At a time when Connecticut did not mandate health education, she led the way in breaking down the ignorance about growing up. For the next 39 years she managed to balance teaching, family, and social action,

The face of Lillian Marcuson of Mountain Road peered out from the covers of Life, Look, Glamour, Vogue, Bride, Cosmopolitan, and the Ladies Home Journal magazines in the late 1940s and early 1950s. The daughter of the owner of the Viking Bakery became a model for the Eileen and Jerry Ford agency in New York and appeared on 13 magazine covers before returning to West Hartford as Mrs. Joseph Rekas of Meadow Lane.

raising five children, traveling frequently, and serving as a trustee of the Hartford College for Women and Wellesley College. In 1972 the University of Hartford gave her an honorary degree, and Planned Parenthood of Connecticut named its West Hartford branch in her honor. She was among the first inductees into the Connecticut Women's Hall of Fame.

The Suismans

In his quiet and modest way, Edward A. Suisman was a leading Jewish philanthropist, whose mentor was E. Clayton Gengras. "He was my example," Suisman said. "He taught us all how to give." His father, Michael Suisman, emigrated to the United States in 1886 from the Lithuanian part of Russia and in 1899 started a scrap metal business in Hartford. After 1907 it was known as Suisman & Blumenthal. In partnership with his brother Sam, he made Suisman & Blumenthal the leading scrap dealer in New England. Much of their business was done with Pratt & Whitney Aircraft and Eddie became good friends with two future company presidents, William Gwinn and H. Mansfield Horner.

Making money was for him only incidental, though certainly essential, to his desire to help the Jewish community in West Hartford, where he lived from 1927 on. At that time many Jews – first and second generation families who traditionally clung together and cared for

one another – were moving into the north end of town. The number of charities and individuals aided by the Suismans amounted to hundreds. Eddie Suisman chaired one annual or capital campaign after another for such organizations as the Hebrew Home for the Aged and the Jewish Community Center. The Suisman Foundation, founded in 1943, gave more than 125 scholarships and loans to teachers and college-bound students. Another local giant in fund-raising, Frank O.H. Williams, once remarked: "They'll give to anything. I ought to know. I asked them for everything under the sun."

Not surprisingly, Eddie was asked to become a trustee of many non-profit institutions. He was the first Jew to serve on the board of Hartford Hospital. He was a trustee of the University of Connecticut for 15 years. For over 25 years he influenced the Hartford Jewish Federation. For his contributions to education he received an honorary degree from Trinity College and the coveted Nathan Hale Award from the Yale Club of Hartford.

Besides their business and philanthropy, the Suisman family had another passion: golf. Almost every day they played a round at the Tumble Brook Country Club. Over a span of 25 years Eddie won 16 championships.

His offspring have carried on the family involvement in the community. Michael Suisman in particular has been identified closely with the Bushnell Memorial, which he served as president for several years, and as the dynamo behind the Bushnell's successful fund drives and innovative arts programs for area schools. Janet S. Suisman, former president and major supporter of the Hartford Stage Company, was a sculptor specializing in welded metal, using the scrap metal from the family business. John and Kathy Suisman also are active in civic affairs.

David T. Chase

David T. Chase of High Ridge Road, a Holocaust survivor, started a new life in this country selling pots and pans door to door. Born David Ciesla in 1929 in Poland, he changed his name the day he married Rhoda Cohen of New Britain. He bought his first home in 1955 on King Philip Drive.

Over the next two decades, he built a real-estate empire that changed Hartford's skyline, erecting the Gold Building, One Corporate Center, and One Commercial Plaza. In 1974, he bought WTIC-AM and FM, which his son Arnold, a radio buff and early techie, ran for the family. Chase Enterprises later bought Fox Channel 61, and Arnold became president of Chase Communications. Daughter Cheryl Chase Freedman, an attorney, became executive vice president and general counsel for the family corporation.

Forbes magazine listed David Chase on its roster of the 400 richest Americans. Northeast magazine called him one of the wealthiest men on the planet, one who "mingles with presidents and the pope." Chase Enterprises now controls office buildings, malls, insurance companies, banks, and a marina and massive housing developments in Florida. Lately, it has created the same kind of diverse economic empire in Poland, where the Chases were wiring the country for cable TV. Led by Arnold, the family founded the Gemini Network for broadband internet communications. The company is based in West Hartford.

The family keeps a low profile, although Arnold generated publicity with his Haunted Happenings and Winter Wonderland extravaganzas in the mid-1990s in Hartford's former G.Fox & Co. store. The Halloween venture had its genesis in 1980 in front of Arnold's home, which his wife had decorated to the hilt with holiday accessories. The close-knit family live within minutes of each other off Mountain Road.

Eileen S. Kraus

Eileen S. Kraus of Tunxis Road graduated from some of the area's highest volunteer positions to the top board rooms of Connecticut business.

The former president of the Junior League of Hartford became head of her own consulting firm in volunteer management and chaired the Governor's Council on Voluntary Action in 1978. She also drew up plans for a West Hartford after-school day care program that blossomed into the YWCA's Neighborcare, now with more than 30 locations in Greater Hartford.

Her move into the big-business world came when she laid the foundation for consumer banking at Hartford National Bank. Through bank mergers, she became chairman of Connecticut National in 1992. When it morphed into Shawmut and merged with Fleet in 1996, she became chairman of Connecticut operations for the nation's eighth largest banking company.

She "retired" in 2000 but immediately took on a new role as chairman of ConnectiCare, an HMO company in Farmington. She continued to serve on the executive committee of the Bushnell Center for the Performing Arts and the boards of Kaman Corp. and Stanley Works.

And she expressed interest in venture capital investments. Daughter Janet was co-founder of Circles in Boston, an Internet company involved in venture capital. "Her investors have some interesting ideas," Eileen mused.

Blanche Savin Goldenberg

Contractor Blanche Savin Goldenberg of High Wood Road was the first woman leader in a traditionally male domain – the hard-hat construction industry.

She worked at her father's Balf Company, Savin Company and Capitol Pipe Co. Upon his death in 1978, Savin and Capital were made subsidiaries of the Balf Company. She served as CEO of Balf from 1978 to 1994 when it was sold to a company from Dublin, Ireland. She was chairman of all three boards from 1987 to 1997.

Retiring from the business world, in 1998 she became the first woman chairman of the board of both her alma mater, Loomis-Chaffee School in Windsor, and of the Hartford Foundation for Public Giving in 1999. She has been a regent of the University of Hartford, a board

West Hartford Chamber of Commerce presented its citizen of year award in 1975 to Town Clerk Everett D. (Brub) Dow. With him are his wife, Lucille, and on the right, chamber president Louis M. Salzburg and executive director Robert W. Simmons.

member of the Bushnell Memorial, and a leader in Jewish community affairs.

Outstanding Citizen Awards

The West Hartford Chamber of Commerce often recognizes citizens for extraordinary commitment to the community.

Cited variously as citizen of the year or outstanding citizens: Norman G. Fricke, 1966; Bice Clemow, 1967; Richard W. Sheehan, 1968; Claire M. Knowlton, Gordon Bennett, John F. Robinson, Raymond Simkin, 1969; William P. Rush, Dr. Albert Kleiman, Michael Odlum, Louis M. Salzburg, 1970; Charlotte Kitowski, 1971; Sister Consolata, Jay W. Jackson, Ellsworth S. Grant, 1972; Arthur E. Fay, Robert S. O'Brien, David and Doris Rush, 1973; Robert P. Nichols, Roslyn N. Katz, 1974.

Individual recipients of its Noah Webster Awards: Dr. Robert E. Dunn, Sister M. Paton Ryan, 1989; Lloyd Calvert, John Looby, S. Brita Tate, 1990; James Ellis, Christopher Larsen, 1991; Angelo Faenza, Joseph Essa, 1992; Gordon Bennett, Shirley G. Marsh, Paul O. Roedel Jr., 1993; Robert Donahue, Sam Pasco, 1994; Nan L.

Glass, Richard F. Patrissi, 1995; Mario Giardini, Norman P. Lee, Wendell S. Stephenson, 1996; Richard Crowe, Robert M. Rowlson, Robert Walsh Jr., 1997; Carl Donatelli, Barbara C. Gordon, Madeline S. McKernan, 1998; Sister Helen Dowd, Harold Kraus, Ilze Krisst, 1999, James Capodiece, Eleanor Horn, Haig Shahverdian, 2000; Marisa B. Rodriguez, Heather Congdon, Dougie Trumble, Ki Miller, Ken Hungerford, 2001.

Communicators

As the largest and most influential suburb of Hartford, the town has always been impacted by the Hartford media. It provided the largest circulation and advertising base outside of the city itself for the independent Hartford Courant, the oldest daily newspaper of continuous publication in the United States, and The Hartford Times, a member of the Gannett Group. Through the years, both newspapers competed intensely for news, circulation, and advertising dollars in the town – a situation that made more difficult the role of any local media. The afternoon Times folded in 1976, leaving the morning Courant to become the dominant player in the town, region, and state.

The situation was similar in the broadcast media. WTIC Radio, a 50,000-watt pioneer bearing the Travelers Insurance Cos. call letters and nationally known for innovative programming, was managed through the years by West Hartford residents, first James Clancy and Paul W. Morency and later Leonard J. Patricelli of Glenwood Road and Perry S. Ury of North Steele Road. Bernard Mullins of Mountain Road was succeeded as program manager by Ross Miller of North Quaker Lane. Pat Patricelli spent his entire career with WTIC radio, having joined in 1929 and rising to

Maurice S. Sherman

From 1926 to 1947, Maurice Sherman of Bainbridge Road was the distinguished editor of the Hartford Courant. He was a methodical, meticulous gentleman, who turned out up to three editorials a day, always dictating them to his secretary who typed them as he spoke. Bard McNulty, author of the newspaper's history, observed: "One would hardly guess, watching Sherman at his desk, that this calm, pipe-smoking gentleman in vest and shirtsleeves had the granite of New Hampshire in his character. If the Republican leaders of the state ever thought they had the Courant in their pocket, Sherman, a Republican himself, made it crystal clear that the newspaper he edited would serve as the organ of no party." He became a close friend of Democratic Gov. Wilbur Cross, who called him "my dearest enemy." A trout fisherman, he went on fishing trips with President Herbert Hoover and enjoyed the friendship of Calvin Coolidge.

Soon after taking over as editor from Charles Hopkins Clark, Sherman made the paper less strident and partisan. He even had good things to say about Franklin Roosevelt. He opened up the editorial page to letters from readers, the "People's Forum." In 1944 he succeeded Henry H. Conland as publisher. For many years he served as trustee of the Carnegie Endowment for International Peace. He counted as a major accomplishment his unrelenting campaign to bring about the council-manager form of government in Hartford. Despite the obstacles both political parties threw in his path, the new charter was adopted on Dec. 4, 1946. His death the following June marked the end of an era of journalistic excellence.

Another West Hartford resident, William J. Foote, was managing editor under Sherman for 34 years.

Self-Portrait: Ward E. Duffy.

Ward E. Duffy

Few families had stronger roots in the soil of West Hartford than Ward and Louise Duffy. Ward's father, Frederick, had been a high school teacher in upstate New York but yearned to try his hand at farming. After a long search he fell in love with the land along Whitman Falls, southeast of the colonial home he bought at 208 North Main St. Learning from books and brochures on farm management, Frederick Duffy acquired a herd of Jersey cows and distributed milk across the Capitol Region. Feeling that anyone living in West Hartford should be an active part of it, he served on the first Town Council.

Son Ward had different ideas. Determined to be a newspaperman, he attended Trinity College and the Columbia School of Journalism and joined the Hartford Times in 1921. He rose to the editorship in 1953 and retired in 1960. A careful, no-nonsense editor, he had little patience with writing that was windy, wandering, and obscure. Clarity and accuracy were his bywords. Very much a gentleman of the old school, he was kindly and considerate toward the unfortunate and the underdog. His community interests focused on the YMCA, Hillyer and Hartford colleges (now part of the University of Hartford), and the Foreign Policy Association. But foremost in his concerns was the conservation of natural resources: to the day of his death he maintained an active connection with numerous organizations working for pure water, flood control, protection of woodlands, and the extension of state parks, such as the Connecticut River Watershed Council and the Forest & Park Association.

chairman of the Ten Eighty Corp. Upon his death in 1982, he was eulogized as "a living legend in broadcasting" by station manager Perry S. Ury and "a giant in the communications industry" by Gov. William O'Neill. In 1974, both WTIC-AM and FM were purchased by David T. Chase of High Ridge Road. His son Arnold joined the station as a trainee and founded the New England Weather Service in 1989. Chase Enterprises sold the stations in 1996 to concentrate on their cable TV projects in Poland.

While WTIC dominated the airwaves from early in the century, its early television offshoot, now WFSB-TV Channel 3, is the No. 1-rated station in Connecticut. WVIT-TV Channel 30, the NBC affiliate, built its broadcast headquarters near Corbins Corner in West Hartford – a scene that sometimes shows up in its snowstorm coverage.

Another force in local television is Connecticut Public Television Channel 24, many of whose principals have been West Hartford residents. Alfred Steel Jr. arrived at CPTV as an intern while a student at Trinity. He never left, thriving in a public television career that spanned 32 years and serving as everything from program manager to vice president, earning a national Emmy Award nomination along the way.

The West Hartford News

West Hartford had no weekly newspaper until the late 1920s. First appeared the West Hartford Press,

Francis Murphy

Frank Murphy, who retired as editor and publisher of the Hartford Times in 1963, is best remembered for his dominant role in the creation of Bradley International Airport shortly after the end of World War II. For 20 years he headed the Connecticut Aeronautics Commission. The son of a jackhammer operator for a construction company and the oldest of five children, Frank had to go to work to support his family after one year of high school. In 1908 he was hired by the Times as an errand boy at a weekly salary of $3. He rose steadily to become the head of the state's largest afternoon paper. More than any of his peers, this genial, persuasive man was the conscience of Greater Hartford, lending his support to every good cause.

then the Metropolitan Shopping News, and finally the West Hartford News. The early attempts had rough going and little impact until Bice Clemow launched the News in 1947. Clemow and his partners took over the moribund shopper from Thomas Dawson and made it into a lively suburban weekly. Under his tenure, the newspaper was a crusader – tilting at windmills in some cases, but often successful, as in its fight against the plan to build I-291, a circumferential highway through the West Hartford reservoirs.

The News was often opinionated, even controversial in the Time magazine style in which "Bias" (for Bice) Clemow had launched his career. Time magazine was the connection that brought Christopher Larsen, son of Time Inc. co-founder Roy Larsen and a Harvard graduate, to town in 1967 to become publisher of the News and owner of its commercial printing business. Under his leadership, the News increased its local coverage and circulation and became the flagship of a group of award-winning suburban Hartford weeklies that he acquired or started under the name of Imprint Newspapers. Typographically and editorially, they were of exceptional quality because of his insistence on using the latest technology for graphics and printing and because of his cultivation of a dedicated team of editors and managers. Larsen authorized the creation of a number of prize-winning special sections, including prestigious semi-annual fashion sections and a weekly Goodtimes entertainment supplement that was the first of its kind in the area. He launched a community service department to deal with such emotional subjects as teenage drugs and alcohol and family violence and abuse. Imprint became a champion of alcohol-free graduation parties, an idea adopted by every one of the towns it served. Its 14 weeklies had a circulation of 65,000 at their height before he sold the business in 1989 to ABC/Capital Cities. Although his newspapers were local, Larsen's interests were regional. He took a leadership role in the Hartford Symphony, the Wadsworth Atheneum, Hartford Hospital, and the Connecticut Historical Society.

The news side of the newspaper was enhanced by Richard M. Woodworth, who joined the News as managing editor in 1971. He succeeded Clemow as editor in 1975 and became executive editor of Imprint Newspapers in 1976. During his tenure, the News won

Bice Clemow: The Town's Conscience and Goader

A Montana native who was educated at the University of Washington, Thomas Bice Clemow moved east for a job as press editor of Time magazine. He moved his family to West Hartford in 1939 to become an editor and publisher in his own right. He and several Time staffers, including Francis G. Smith Jr. and Jonathan Kilbourn, boldly launched the Hartford Newsdaily, the only daily newspaper founded in Connecticut during the period. A tabloid formatted like Time and Life, the paper lacked the resources to compete with the dominant Hartford Times and lasted only 100 days.

Clemow was not one to give up easily, however. During World War II he was assistant to Chester Bowles, head of the Office of Price Administration and subsequently a Connecticut governor, congressman, and ambassador to India. Returning to West Hartford in 1947, Clemow and his friends launched the West Hartford News. The editor was soon recognized as the town's conscience, booster, and goader, pushing his favorite causes with wit and invective. He spearheaded the founding of the University of Hartford in 1957, strongly supported the Center business district and better public schools, and editorialized for more effective leadership.

Clemow retired as editor in 1975, but he launched a weekly opinion column, "Box One 06107." A consummate yet at times obscure writer, he delighted in sending readers to the dictionary to ascertain what he meant. Expanding

Richard Noyes Photo

his devotion to public education, he took on many assignments for the Ford Foundation. Often called the dean of Connecticut journalists, he abhorred the custom of elected officials meeting secretly to make decisions on public matters. His work in drafting the state's freedom of information bill and shepherding it through the state legislature into law in 1976 is still recognized by the Connecticut Council on Freedom of Information through an annual Bice Clemow Award.

He was viewed by his peers as a combination of "father figure, dutch uncle, corporate confessor, family counselor, sex therapist, and editorial guru," according to publisher Christopher Larsen. He played a major role in the creation of the Cornerstone Club pool and served on the boards of the Children's Museum, the Noah Webster House, and State-Dime Savings Bank.

Following his death in 2000, the New York Times referred to him as a journalist "who marched to his own drummer." The town often heeded his forthright, frequently iconoclastic observations on local and state affairs, on radio and television as well as in print. He also had other talents. He designed and sewed a handsome inaugural ball gown for Gov. Ella T. Grasso to atone for publicly criticizing her taste in clothing. She wore the gown and called its striking color "bice blue."

the National Newspaper Association's highest award – a first prize for general excellence among weekly newspapers its size in the country. The News was known for special editions covering the 1972 ice storm, the Hartford Civic Center roof collapse, and the Greening of West Hartford Center, as well as hefty extras such as one spearheading West Hartford's celebration of America's Bicentennial in 1976. Its

candidate profiles and endorsements were based on first-hand interviews, and those endorsements were widely followed.

No longer locally owned or with its traditional local presence, the newspaper's circulation has declined. Its office was closed in 1995 and moved by new owners, the Journal Register Co., to Bristol.

In 1997, West Hartford Life, a monthly tabloid

delivered free town-wide, was started by young publisher Christopher White. Mark Jahne, a former West Hartford News managing editor, became its editor. Its mission: to report the good things about community living.

WHC-TV

Local news also comes from West Hartford's Community Access television station. It was started in 1978 through the efforts of then-mayor Anne P. Streeter, Nan Lewis Glass, and Daniel E. Blume. In 1983 Muriel Fleischmann, a former Board of Education member, became executive director and station manager. A public access leader in the region, the station has nurtured many volunteers and interns.

Overseen by a local board of directors, the station started in the basement of the Noah Webster Memorial Library and moved ten times in its first ten years. It broadcast from the old police lock-up room in the basement of the old Town Hall, from a small classroom, and from the town's vault before ending up in a section of the new auditorium stage in the renovated Town Hall.

Funding was an early obstacle. Nan Streeter and Muriel Fleischmann first secured a commitment from the cable company to support the station. Jane Wright's Valentine party was the first of many fund-raising parties. Muriel Fleischmann, recruiting Colin McEnroe

and Pat Seremet, developed an on-cable game show, TV Pursuit, which provided wide town participation in funding and has lasted to this day. Aetna arranged for the station to produce and sell documentary tapes. One of the most successful, produced in 1987 by Muriel Fleischmann and Paul Giguere, was on drunk driving. It was sold to every high school in Connecticut. In 1994, WHC-TV intiated a unique project, "From the State Capitol," videotaping the legislative session and distributing the tapes weekly to outlets throughout the state. After six years, it paved the way for an independent, non-profit "Connecticut Network" associated with WHC-TV, which covers the legislative session 24 hours a day.

The local station televises Town Council and Board of Education meetings, high school graduations, candidates' nights and elections, public forums, and live call-in shows. It is available to local groups for local programs. One monthly program, produced by the West Hartford African American Social and Cultural Organization, was hosted by its president and WHC-TV board member, Dorothy Billington. In 1990, when citizen groups began competing for "equal time" on school district and budgeting issues, the staff led by executive director Cheryl Fine knew the channel had become an imporant communications tool for the town.

Monthly WHC-TV program "Around Town" is televised from the Town Hall studio by camerman Joel Huntington. Harriet Tenney (left) interviews Beth Ryan, who works for the organization Locks of Love. She is about to have her hair cut for wigs for children who have lost their hair to radiation for one reason or another.

WHC-TV Photo

Hall High School Concert Jazz Band played in the East Room at the White House during the 1995 Congressional Ball. Here the students, led by Haig Shahverdian (right), have their pictures taken with President and Mrs. Clinton.

Plant Junior High Symphonic Band, under the baton of Eugene C. Magill, rehearses for a concert before a Music Educators Conference in 1974 at Hartt School of Music. Composer Magill wrote and conducted the works himself.

118 Creating

Hartford Times Photo

Robert Shages blows on sousaphone as 90 members of Conard High School's advanced band leave for Boston. The group was invited in 1968 as one of the region's outstanding bands to perform for faculty and students at Boston University.

X. Creating

Pops and All That Jazz

Arguably West Hartford's best-known and most widely traveled school entity is Hall High School's Jazz Band. Founded by William Stanley, the band is known for its spring Pops and Jazz concerts, has won numerous contests, and has toured Europe several times.

In 2000, under director Haig Shahverdian, the 22 band members won first prize in the "Essentially Ellington" High School Jazz Band Competition and Festival at Lincoln Center in New York. A total of 176 bands entered the competition. Hall also won in 1998, came in third in 1997 and placed second in 1999. Hall was the only school nationally that finished in one of the three top spots four years in a row.

The 20-piece string ensemble I Giovani Solisti began at Conard in 1983 but was expanded by director Edward de Groat to bring together students from both schools, erasing rivalries sparked by sports teams. Its players have traveled to England on biennial exchanges since 1985. In 1992 it was invited to play at New York's Carnegie Hall.

If you wished to see what the arts meant to West Hartford throughout the late 20th century, you had only to try finding a seat near the front for the annual Hall High School Pops & Jazz Concert, which up to 4,000 people attended on several nights each spring. Or to try elbowing your way into a good spot on one of the four evenings when Conard High was putting on its annual Broadway musical. Both extravaganzas indicate the importance of the arts in West Hartford, as reflected in its school system.

It was not always thus. Back in the 1940s, new school superintendent Edmund H. Thorne from Michigan realized the school music program was sorely inadequate. He hired Dr. Frank Groff away from a New Jersey high school to reorganize the music curriculum and coordinate a system-wide program. Within a year, the program had expanded to the point where Dr. Groff had to hire a second music teacher, William Lauer. Within a few years they had a band, a mixed chorus of 250, a girls' glee club of about 60 voices as well as the Hall High Choir with about 75 singers. They started with 25 elementary students in an instrumental program and ended with hundreds. They instituted the Inter-Elementary Orchestra and Choir and, with parents and teachers, formed the West Hartford Cultural Council, bringing in professional artists to expose students to excellence in all the arts. The Inter-El Choir, led by a

specialist in the Hungarian Kodaly technique, was a major force in the 1970s.

Who will ever forget the sight of Sedgwick Junior High School music director and band leader Rodney Wiggin in his white uniform, specially made to fit his

The Noah Webster Statue: An American Epic

The story of the statue of Noah Webster that gazes somberly at South Main Street in front of the Education Center is in a way an epic of American life.

Nowhere else would the ingredients be found: a temperamental, impassioned sculptor, son of a Polish patriot; a community skeptical of artists and monuments; an indifferent Town Council, and a group of enthusiastic young people who knew all about Noah Webster and volunteered to help. No matter that no memorial to West Hartford's most famous citizen had ever been erected; no matter that the sculptor had won first prize at the 1939 World's Fair for his marble portrait of Paderewski.

Korczak Ziolkowski and acolyte work on Noah in 1942.

Korczak Ziolkowski had come to town in the mid-1930s with his wife Dorothy Comstock, a music teacher, and occupied a home and studio on Sedgwick Road. He saw in Noah Webster a real hero and offered to carve a 13-foot statue and donate it to the town. At first he won support. The Town Council donated a plot of land in front of what was then the Town Hall, the Noah Webster Sculptural Commission was formed, and business leader Alfred C. Fuller agreed to be treasurer of the fund drive. The goal was $16,500; the public response was underwhelming. To stir up interest, the artist formed the Noah Webster Fife & Drum Corps, enlisted his wife and mother-in-law and, dressed in a colonial uniform, marched and drummed at fund-raisers. He also mowed more than 700 lawns.

When donations reached $3,700 and stopped, Ziolkowski was disappointed but not discouraged. He would carve that statue if he died in the attempt. He journeyed to Tennessee to buy the

marble, carted the 26-ton block himself to the site, dug the foundation alone, and raised it in place. Gov. Robert A. Hurley dug the first spadeful of soil. On June 21, 1941, the young artist set to work.

His corps of willing volunteers ran errands and canvassed house-to house for dimes and dollars. All that summer the air resounded with the ring of hammers and the clatter of drills. From 7 in the morning until 10 at night, seven days a week, he pounded away, while the townspeople became more critical and the sculptor more controversial. The council wanted Noah sitting down; the artist decided he should stand up.

Everything he did caused trouble. Some thought the head much too big. A minister protested his working on Sundays. When he took off his shirt in the hot sun, there was an outcry. Roughnecks yelled at him: "Hey, you Polack, what do you think you're doing up there?"

Eventually, Ziolkowski had the last word. Without telling anyone, on the book at the statue's side he carved this inscription, a rebuke to the town that had ignored and abused him: "For you I labored, not for my own day, that by the Word men should know brotherhood. My fellow men! You have not understood, since each of you would go his separate way." Asked what he meant, he replied: "I took the words from a letter Noah Webster had written to John Jay."

After military service and with one of his young acolytes as his new wife, the artist left town in 1947 for South Dakota to carve a statue of Chief Crazy Horse on the side of Thunderhead Mountain. At his death, 35 years later, Crazy Horse was still unfinished. But work was continued by his widow and his many children.

Students picket in support of local sculptor Morton Fishman's controversial ecology sculpture in front of office building on North Main Street near Brace Road in 1971. The five-ton, 30-foot-high sculpture eventually was moved to the courtyard of the new Hall High School. It was relocated much later to Manchester.

Hartford Times Photo

outsized frame, marching in Memorial Day parades in front of his sousaphone-heavy Sedgwick band? Or the sounds produced by talented William Stanley, who founded the Hall jazz band and led it on performing tours to Europe? The town has seen evidence everywhere of the exceptional school arts programs directed in recent years by Haig Shahverdian. Many were the participants in the annual art exhibits produced by the fine arts faculty under the supervision of Mary Lou Solomon. Others played roles at Conard in fall plays and spring musicals under the direction of Beverly Jackson and William Lauer.

In addition to theatrical activities in the public schools, private schools have lively drama clubs and there are opportunities for the public to perform. The Mark Twain Masquers, Connecticut's oldest community theater, has been staging plays since 1934, until lately at Kingswood-Oxford's Roberts Arts & Science Center. Its benefactor, Ann T. Roberts, appeared in 27 starring roles with the Masquers and funded the center partly

to provide a stage for the troupe, which was not as active after her death in 1991. The Roberts Foundation, organized to support the local arts scene, was staffed first by Trig Cooley and later Elizabeth Normen. One of its presidents was Janet M. Larsen, the first woman to head the Hartford Stage Company board of directors.

In 1980, former school board member Muriel Fleischmann advocated the idea of an arts center in the renovated but closed Plant Junior High School to house the region's major arts groups. Funded by a planning grant from the Junior League of Hartford, the consortium also involved architects Charles T. Bellingrath and Robert J. von Dohlen, Millard H. Pryor Jr., Diana MacPherson, and Karl Fleischmann. Although ultimately not pursued because of Hartford opposition, the idea led to the Greater Hartford Arts center in an Aetna-owned property on Farmington Avenue in Hartford.

A more recent development is a community theater called the Park Road Playhouse, housed in a renovated milk-truck garage at the site of the old A.C. Petersen Farms restaurant and dairy plant. Founder Howard Hirsch spent his professional career in advertising, but after an emergency heart transplant in 1995, turned his attention to launching a professionally run community theater. It was financed by a $200,000 state arts grant, local fund-raising efforts and a roast of Town Manager Barry M. Feldman, a proponent. Ilze Krisst chaired the board and Patricia Genser, Plato Karafelo, Richard F. Patrissi, Alfred A. Turco, Florence N. Woodiel, and Robert M. Rowlson were leading backers. When it opened in 2001, another board member, Angelo Faenza, head of the Park Road Business Association, predicted it would rejuvenate the neighborhood with arts and restaurants: "It's a magnet – it's going to remake this street."

Arts Institutions

Like the religious denominations, manufacturing industries, and educational institutions before them, some of Hartford arts institutions migrated west, especially in the second half of the 20th century. The migration reflected a community that valued the arts and coincided with the development of West Hartford's renowned public school arts program.

The Hartford Conservatory, organized in 1890 as the Hartford School of Music, has attracted aspiring

Truda Kaschmann

Modern dance came to West Hartford by way of Truda Kaschmann, performer, teacher, and choreographer. Truda and her family, who settled in West Hartford, were early escapees from Hitler's Germany. By 1935, she was teaching in eight different schools. In the West Hartford wartime summer recreational program of 1942, Truda offered a modern dance class, widening the horizons for many women. She was on the faculty of Hartford College for Women from 1940 until her death in 1986. She taught at Miss Porter's School for 33 years and at Trinity College after it became coed. Truda chaired the dance department at the Hartford Conservatory and performed with the Hartford Symphony. She became one of the in-group in Hartford's blossoming artistic community. "Those were golden times for art," it was said of Truda and mid-century Hartford.

'Uncle Moshe' Paranov

With boundless energy and aspiration, Moshe Paranov – performer, director, teacher, and conductor – was probably the town's best-known musician. The son of Russian immigrants, he began playing the violin at age 5 but switched to piano under the influence of his teacher, Julius Hartt, making his professional debut at 15. He co-founded the Hartt School of Music on a shoestring in 1920 and spent the next 51 years building it into a conservatory of national reputation. By the time the Hartt School became a part of the University of Hartford, he was president of the Hartt College and became a vice chancellor of the university.

He conducted the first concert at the Bushnell Memorial, directed several symphony orchestras and formed the Cecilia Club, a womens's singing group, and the Greater Hartford Youth Orchestra. He taught at St. Joseph College and at Kingswood, Loomis, and Avon Old Farms preparatory schools. He conducted about 400 operatic performances for the Hartt Opera-Theater Guild, one of which was *Hansel and Gretel,* the first full-length opera ever to be shown on TV.

Paranov worked passionately to introduce classical music to young people. One of his memorable achievements was the annual Spring Festival at the Bushnell Memorial. Hundreds of singers from seventeen area private schools rehearsed and performed on the imposing Bushnell stage under the direction of "Uncle Moshe." When he died in 1994 at age 98, he had been a central figure in the region's musical life for more than 75 years.

musicians from miles around. In the 1960s, the Conservatory expanded into West Hartford with its dance studio on Kingswood Road. In 1959, a group of dissatisfied faculty from the conservatory formed the West Hartford School of Music on Park Road. It eventually become the Camerata School. Finally it merged and moved back into Hartford in the 1980s, becoming the Hartford Camerata Conservatory.

An upstart competitor to the Conservatory, the Hartt School of Music was organized in 1920 by Julius Hartt and his "top lieutenant," Moshe Paranov. The school grew in size and influence and became very much a part of West Hartford when the Hartt School and the

Hartford Art School joined in 1957 with Hillyer College to form the University of Hartford at a new campus on Bloomfield Avenue.

Theater and the other arts in West Hartford were considerably augmented in 1962 when the Jewish Community Center, led by Murry Shapiro, moved into its new building at Bloomfield Avenue and Simsbury Road. Part of the new complex was a 400-seat theater, built to the specifications of Ann Randall of West Hartford and her arts committee. Ann Randall was a charismatic teacher whose Hartford drama school encouraged considerable local acting talent during the 1940s. After her death in 1954, the Ann Randall Arts Committee continued to bring to the Hartford area some of the best theater, dance, and film in the country. In the 1960s, the committee brought New York theater to the Gilman Theater, named for Ames Department Stores founder Herbert Gilman, before the organization of the Hartford Stage Company. Selma Lobel, Augusta Rubin, Evelyn Gilman, Phyllis Abrahms, Mary Hunter Wolf, Norma Menczer, Ruby Schwolsky, and Shanah Shatz were leaders of the Arts Committee under the staff direction of Muriel Fleischmann and later Joan Cohen.

Many fine artists were connected with the JCC over the years, notably potter Betsy Tanzer, collage artists Margot Rosenthal and Jean Mayo, and watercolorists Barbara Levin and Jane Caplan.

The arts at the Jewish Community Center include Elbert Weinberg's 1981 Holocaust Memorial in front of the center's Bloomfield Avenue entrance.

The town has other fine sculptures. Besides the famous statue of Noah Webster in front of the Education Center, there's a whimsical piece of sculpture in front of West Hartford Art League's Gallery off Buena Vista Road. At the entrance to the American School for the Deaf is a statue of Thomas Gallaudet, founder of the school in 1817, working with his first student, Alice Cogswell. It is a replica of the one made by Daniel Chester French for Gallaudet College in Washington. Herbert B. Fishman created the John Freedman Memorial Sculpture, which stands in the courtyard at Hall High School as a memorial to a senior who was editor of the Hallmarks yearbook and died of a heart ailment. Earlier, Morton Fishman created an ecology sculpture that was moved to Hall in 1971. Carol

From School to Stardom

Tony Award winner James Naughton, who got his start under Conard High School music director William Lauer in the 1960s, has won critical acclaim on stage and in both TV and films. Blessed with singing talent, he made his New York debut in 1971 in an off-Broadway revival of "Long Day's Journey into Night." His mellow baritone voice made him sought after for musical roles. He starred in such films as "The Good Mother" opposite Diane Keaton and "The Glass Menagerie" with Joanne Woodward. For years he has been active in the summer Willliamstown Theatre Festival. His younger brother David is an actor as well.

Hall graduates have gone on to national recognition in the arts, too. Brad Mehldau, described as the premier jazz pianist of his generation, was nominated in 1997 for a Grammy award. He and Hall 1988 classmate Joel Frahm, an internationally known jazz saxaphonist, teamed up for a triumphant homecoming concert in the Town Hall in 1999. Eugenia Zukerman, renowned flautist, author, and commentator on CBS Sunday Morning, has played in orchestras internationally. She grew up as Genie Rich at King Philip and Hall High. Dave Chameides, Hollywood cameraman, directed an episode of "ER." Paul Woodiel is a talented violinist much in demand for Broadway musicals. Josh Cagan, Hall 1990 playwright and director, has written several plays and received awards from the Connecticut Young Playwrights Association. In 2001, he wrote the book for MTV's animated show, "Undergrads."

Steve Campo, Hall '70 grad, promoted drama ventures in his home area. He founded and became director and owner of Hartford's TheaterWorks.

Comedy actor John O'Hurley, a silver-haired, silver-tongued town native, spent 10 years on daytime soap operas and is best known for his role as J. Peterman in NBC's classic sitcom "Seinfeld." Lately he has hosted a remake of the "To Tell the Truth" game show and a syndicated series, "Get Golf With the PGA Tour."

Earlier, Rita Gann Morley of Foxcroft Road, an actress whose career spanned radio, TV, and Broadway, was a familiar face on soap operas including "As the World Turns" and "The Edge of Night." For a time in the 1950s she was so ubiquitous as a spokeswoman for Coty she was dubbed "America's Most Televised Girl." Wilton Graff, whose father owned Graff's Market on Park Road, became a Hollywood actor on stage, screen, and TV.

Davidson's striking work is nationally recognized, and one of Karen Petersen's smooth curved figures in her Sedra series looks comfortably at home near the pond in Elizabeth Park.

Artists

The West Hartford Art League was founded in 1939 by two artists, Rebecca Field and Gertrude H. Patterson, "to bring together the artists and art-loving people in the community to create and foster an interest in all phases of artistic expression and endeavor." Since then, the league has offered art lessons to thousands of aspiring and accomplished artists at the Little Red School House, built in 1878 and once known as the West School, at 87 Mountain Road.

League members honored one of their most memorable teachers, Irving Katzenstein, setting up a fund drive in his name in 1974 to raise money for an exhibition gallery. Katzenstein, who had taught at the Little Red School House for 22 years, was also given a retrospective at the Wadsworth Atheneum's Avery Court the year after he died. His paintings are in the permanent collections of the Atheneum and the New Britain Museum of American Art.

The fund drive was successful and in 1976, the Art League acquired and renovated the Stanley-Woodruff-Allen farmhouse, built about 1750 at 37 Buena Vista Road, saving it from demolition. Bernard Vinick's designs turned it into the Salt Box Gallery, with 200 feet of hanging space.

One of the Art League's local artists and instructors, Ruth Bezanker, first took art classes from her mother, Gertrude Patterson, and helped found the Glastonbury Art Guild. Other leading artists have included Dr. Edward Deming and Dr. Elliott Sweet (both surgeons), Donald LaCroix, May Griswold, N. Ross Parke, Mary

Thomas Gallaudet is shown at work with his first student, Alice Cogswell, in statue at entrance to the American School for the Deaf (above right). At right is Elbert Weinberg's poignant Holocaust Memorial, located in front of the Jewish Community Center.

West Hartford Art League's "portrait" was photographed outside league headquarters in the Little Red School House at 87 Mountain Road for its 40th anniversary in 1974. Artist-instructors David Noyes and Maryellen Shafer flank Louise McAuliffe, board chairman, and A. Richard Harris, president.

Roy, Estelle Coniff, Diane Marinaro, Edwina Jeter, Maryellen Shafer, Dorothy White, and Ruth Lee Silver.

Many other West Hartford artists have excelled. James Goodwin McManus of Ridgebrook Drive, nationally known landscape and portrait artist, helped organize the Connecticut Academy of Fine Arts and taught adult art classes at Hartford Public High School all his life. He was honored in 1954 with a month-long one-man show at the Wadsworth Atheneum, the first time the museum had so honored a native artist.

Alys Harper Pierce Stone was a painter who used Cape Cod for a setting. She also was president of the Garden Club of America in the 1960s. Sally Given created collages. Molly Fowler is known for her weavings and Patricia Kierys for her Victorian Christmas ornaments, 300 of which decorated a tree at the Smithsonian. Needlecrafter Louise McCrady coined the word shirret, combining the arts of shirring and crochet and turning rags into rugs.

Kiki Smith and Annette Le Mieux have exhibited their paintings in well-known New York galleries, as has Ellen Carey her photography.

Musicians

The town has been home to leading musicians. Violinist Paul Rosenblum, early concertmaster of the Hartford Symphony Orchestra, in the 1940s founded the Institute of Music School in Hartford and also taught out of his Asylum Avenue home. Arthur L. Winograd of Stratford Road, founding cellist of the celebrated Juilliard Quartet, conducted the Hartford Symphony for 21 seasons. His wife Betty was a widely admired pianist and teacher, and his son Peter became a professional violinist. Bernard Lurie started in 1951 at age 18 and retired after 50 years with the HSO, 32 years as concertmaster.

Arthur Koret, the area's first native-born cantor, began as cantor in 1952 at Emanuel Synagogue. He

Over the years, a number of talented West Hartfordites have banded together in performing groups to entertain the community as well as school children, senior citizens, shut-ins, charity events, fund-raisers, and the like. Among the longer-running is Strings 'n' Things, led by puppeteer Margot Allison (center). With her in 1975 are Carol Mersereau (standing) and Sue Fisher (seated), who also are members of the Silk and Steel singers. The trio have been performing around the area since the 1960s.

taught at Hartt School, and composed and recorded Jewish sacred music. His "Song of the Synagogue" (1954) was the first long-playing record ever made of chants of Jewish liturgy.

Mezzo-soprano Mignon Dunn of Mountainview Avenue sang more than 30 seasons with the Metropolitan Opera. Her husband, Kurt Klippstatter, was a conductor and teacher at Hartt.

Song writer Fay Whitman Manus was author of the year's top-selling female vocalist record in 1948, "Am I Asking Too Much?" recorded by jazz singer Dinah Washington. She taught writing workshops for West Hartford Continuing Education, is a poet, and runs a small publishing company. Husband Jack Manus, a

composer, wrote scores of songs performed by Frank Sinatra, Billie Holiday, and Sarah Vaughn.

Henley Denmead of Bentwood Road founded the Hartford Chorale in 1972 and is still its artistic director and conductor.

Richard C. Einsel of Sunrise Hill Drive was minister of music for 30 years at Hartford's Asylum Hill Congregational Church, where he and his wife Grace founded the hugely popular Boar's Head Festival, an annual five-performance post-Christmas extravaganza led by West Hartford residents.

Folk music was the legacy of Bill Domler. He was the founder of the Sounding Board Coffee House, a weekly Saturday night folk series held mostly in West

Hartford church basements for more than a quarter-century, and helped create the Connecticut Family Folk Festival in Elizabeth Park. He hosted a folk music radio show for twenty years on the University of Hartford's WWUH-FM. Upon his death in 2001, he was hailed by the Hartford Courant as "first in folk."

Daniel Salazar of Elmhurst Circle, classical guitarist

Hartford Courant Photo

Ed Jones, double bass virtuoso and computer wizard, realized two dreams. He played from 1952 to 1962 with the Count Basie Orchestra and taught himself computer science to land a job with IBM. A football standout at Howard University, he won a tryout with the Green Bay Packers but turned it down because the money wasn't good enough in those days. He also didn't want to risk injuring his hands – his guaranteed meal ticket as a bass player. After serving as a division manager with IBM, he settled in West Hartford and served 22 years at CIGNA, retiring in 1995 as a vice president in computer support technology. In his off-hours here, he was a musical whirlwind in local jazz circles and on periodic international tours. The sound of his bass was "open, booming and spirited, just like Ed himself," said Thom Harris, president of the Greater Hartford Festival of Jazz and editor of New England Jazz News, at Jones's death.

who arranges Spanish music for guitar and orchestra, has played around the world. He founded the annual Guitar Under the Stars series in Hartford's Riverside Park in 1991 while a graduate student at Hartt, where he now teaches.

Teachers and Patrons of the Arts

Many leaders and faculty members of the various art institutions have lived in West Hartford and enriched the town's appreciation of creative achievement. Dorothy and Wilfred Fidlar of Brookline Drive were noted vocal teachers. Royal Dadman, baritone, and Gerald Gelbloom, violinist, taught in their West Hartford homes. Students have studied with Walton Deckelman at his piano studio. Some faculty members have moved on to related fields. Edward Diemente in his retirement became a composer of note. Steve Metcalf is music critic for the Hartford Courant.

George A. Gay, an immigrant from Scotland, amassed one of the most comprehensive collections of etchings in America in his Farmington Avenue home. The man who rose from stock boy to senior partner at Hartford's Brown-Thomson department store was a trustee of the Wadsworth Atheneum. He died in 1940 and following the death of his last heir in 2000, his estate bequeathed $6.2 million each to surprised beneficiaries, the Wadsworth, Hartford Hospital, and Hartford Seminary Foundation.

Untold numbers of residents have been leading patrons of the arts, spearheading and funding activities at the Wadworth Atheneum, Hartford Stage Company, Hartford Symphony, Hartford Ballet, and Connecticut Opera. Micki Savin was an early leader in organized arts consortiums and her daughter, Nancy Savin, became a producer of arts programming for Connecticut Public Television.

The memorable "Five Arts Cookbook" of the 1970s, *Connecticut À La Carte,* was led by West Hartford residents and contained many of their recipes. It was a vivid example of residents' commitment to the Greater Hartford arts scene, which remains strong.

Writers

Perhaps more than in any other field, the town has produced or been home to a number of writers. Noah

Webster, West Hartford's most famous author, would be proud.

Rose Terry Cooke, the town's most noted writer of the 19th century, grew up on the Terry Farm, where the McAuley retirement home is now located. Known as the "pastoral poetess," her only rival was Harriet Beecher Stowe, but John Greenleaf Whittier extolled Rose Terry Cooke as having no equal in her stories of New England and a better ear for the Yankee dialect than the lady on Hartford's Forest Street. She published her first story at the age of 18 and, in the inaugural edition of the Atlantic Monthly in November 1857, hers was the lead article. She wrote sketches and poetry about nature and the family farm in a simple, spontaneous, and humorous manner.

Wallace Stevens, one of the significant and enduring poets of 20th century America, lived on Farmington Avenue near Whiting Lane with his family from 1924 to 1932. Forming lines about "the relations between imagination and the world of reality," the Pulitzer prize-winning poet often walked from his later home just across the city line on Terry Road to the Hartford Insurance Group, where he was a vice president.

Sinclair Lewis, the celebrated and cantankerous novelist, almost settled here. In the fall of 1922 he took a house on Belknap Road with his wife but did not find the atmosphere salubrious. His closest friends were Dr. and Mrs. Thomas H. Hepburn of Bloomfield Avenue, from whom on long walks in the countryside he gleaned material for *Arrowsmith*. His book won a Pulitzer prize, which he refused to accept. He grumbled about the prejudices of the insurance aristocracy and clergy in the city. Hartford, he said, was "just a continuance of Gopher Prairie," proud only of being the wealthiest city of its size. After four months here he left.

Brendan Gill, who grew up on Prospect Avenue, was a leading writer for the New Yorker magazine from 1936 to 1976. He also was skeptical of his hometown, mainly because of perceived snobbery against those of Irish descent. Although occasionally critical in print, he harbored fond memories of his boyhood in the 1920s. West Hartford, he once remarked, provided an idyllic setting: "Prospect Avenue was arched over by mighty elms and much of the year one moved through it as though through a long, deep tunnel. Beyond Walbridge Road stretched a bountiful wilderness and the then-small settlement of West Hartford."

Another native son, Oliver Butterworth of Sunset Farm, wrote several prize-winning children's books. His most popular, *The Enormous Egg,* written in 1956, was translated into six languages. A 23-foot fiberglass statue of Uncle Beazley, the triceratops that emerged from the egg, was fashioned for a 1968 movie of the book and once stood on the Washington, D.C., mall. It

CowParade HQ

The "world headquarters" of CowParade – which since 2000 has organized cow events nationwide to showcase artists' creativity, promote tourism, and benefit charity – is in West Hartford. Local attorney Jerome D. Elbaum is president of CowParade Worldwide Inc., in which former Town Councilman Daniel E. Blume also is involved. The street sculpture shows were started in Chicago in 1999 by a businessman who had seen the first parade in 1998 in Zurich, Switzerland. Lawyers representing Zurich retailers contacted Elbaum, who created a holding company composed of American and Swiss interests.

In announcing New York's wildly successful CowParade with Mayor Rudolph Giuliani in 2000, Elbaum said CowParade "has caught on like wildfire." The basic fiberglass cow sculptures remain the same, but each city's artists are moved by their own interpretation of the cow as an art object. While New York and neighboring Stamford and West Orange milked the cow parade idea, Cincinnati launched the Big Pig Gig. Toronto went for moose, New Orleans for fish, Miami for flamingos, Orlando for lizards, and Buffalo for buffaloes.

Defending cows in a New York Times article, Elbaum was quoted: "These forms like flamingos and hogs will not produce significant or lasting art, because the shapes of the animals are wrong. Flamingos do not have a large surface. A flamingo does not lend itself to art. Cows are benign. They immediately attract art. You speak to artists, serious artists, and they only want to paint cows."

Although his hometown did not join the first copycow parades, Elbaum gave three fiberglass cows to Kingswood-Oxford School students in 2001 to decorate and enter in CowParades of their choice.

The Hepburns

Three generations of the Hepburn family have contributed in different ways.

Dr. Thomas N. Hepburn was the first specialist in urology in Connecticut and a founder of the American Social Hygiene Society, which campaigned to eliminate venereal disease prior to World War I. His wife, Katharine Houghton Hepburn, was a pioneer in the woman's suffrage and birth control movements. In 1910 she was elected president of the Connecticut Woman's Suffrage Association, leading marches, rallies, and demonstrations until the 19th Amendment was passed in 1920. In the 1930s she founded the Planned Parenthood League of Connecticut.

The most famous of the Hepburns' six children was their legendary daughter Katharine, for five decades a film and stage star. Her career in film started in 1932 when she starred in "A Bill of Divorcement." The 40 full-length films she made brought her worldwide fame rivaling that of West Hartford's favorite son, Noah Webster. Another daughter, Marion Hepburn Grant, was a social activist and historian, president of the Junior League of Hartford, and a relentless advocate for change in the hierarchy of the national Congregational Church. Her daughter, Katharine Houghton, has made a mark as an actress and playwright.

Actresses Katharine Hepburn and Katharine Houghton appear together in 1967 publicity photo for "Guess Who's Coming to Dinner."

was eventually moved to the Washington Zoo, where it now grazes among real life elephants.

Jane H. Quigg of Milton Street, a first-grade teacher at Whitman School, wrote eight children's books beloved by the age group with which she was so familiar. William McKellar of Mountain Road began turning out stories for boys in 1954 and didn't stop until he had written 26 books. A more recent children's writer is Susan B. Aller of Prospect Avenue, author of three books.

In 1941 George Malcolm-Smith, a publicist at The Travelers Insurance Cos., made a hit with his comic novel *Slightly Perfect* and followed with five other novels, one of which he called *The Grass Is Always Greener.* Science fiction writer Ben Bova of Sedgwick Road became famous for his imaginative journeys into space. Larry Collins of Mountain Road, a foreign

correspondent in France, pioneered in the 1965 in a new form of historical journalism with the sensational *Is Paris Burning?* Three other best-sellers followed.

Virginia Chase Perkins, who moved to Thomson Road in West Hartford in 1950, wrote several best-selling novels, an English textbook, and a biography of William Phips, a colonial governor of Massachusetts.

Other women have found creative inspiration living in West Hartford. Maxine Tull Boatner, wife of the head of the American School for the Deaf, wrote *Voice of the Deaf,* a biography of Edward M. Gallaudet. Alice DeLana, a former teacher at Miss Porter's School, wrote a well-respected history of the school and co-authored *On Common Ground,* a literary anthology of women writers in Hartford. Mabel Collins Donnelly is an authority on women writers.

Novelist Dominick Dunne, who grew up here and whose father was a physician at St. Francis Hospital, has produced a number of books of fiction.

Arthur Ripley Thompson of Van Buren Avenue, West Hartford's tax collector from 1914 to 1949, wrote several books of poetry and a "fictionalized biography" of a Revolutionary spy. Also an explorer and archaeologist, he chaired the West Hartford Library board.

Marion and Ellsworth Grant of Steele Road authored two histories of the City of Hartford, published by the Connecticut Historical Society. In addition, Ellsworth Grant has written ten corporate histories, underlining his special interest in the development of Connecticut business and manufacturing.

Ridgewood Road residents Nancy and Richard Woodworth formed Wood Pond Press in 1984 to write and publish regional travel guidebooks. Their seven titles, updated in many editions, cover destinations not only around New England but along the East Coast from the Canadian Maritimes to Florida.

Another couple, Barbara Barron-Tieger and Paul Tieger of Beverly Road, published four books about building and sustaining human relationships.

Janice Law Trecker has written suspense fiction and non-fiction. Maria Sassi is known for her poetry. Wordsmith Robert Kyff's syndicated newspaper column, Word Watch, has appeared in book form. Dr. Robert Grant Irving, formerly of Wood Pond Road, wrote *Indian Summer,* which explores the influence of Indian architecture on that of America.

The Rev. Stephen Kendrick authored a definitive book on Sherlock Holmes, *Holy Clues,* while pastor of the Universalist Church of West Hartford.

A 1940 Hall High School graduate, Bernard Bailyn won a Pulitzer prize and the Bancroft Award in 1968 for his historical work, *The Ideological Origins of the American Revolution.*

Eve Soumerai, who taught for eighteen years in the West Hartford school system, produced 30 multi-media tributes to heroic men and women and wrote a book, *Daily Life During the Holocaust.*

Robert E. McEnroe won acclaim for "The Silver Whistle," a comedy that opened on Broadway in 1948 and starred Jose Ferrer. He also wrote the script for the Broadway musical "Donnybrook" in 1961. His son, Colin McEnroe, journalist and radio talk show host, has written a humor book and a novel.

Krishna Sondi started in 1983 in her home a publishing business, Kumarian Press. Her focus is on authors and books on Third World countries.

Dr. Nelson R. Burr

Historians are well represented among the town's literary lights. Nelson R. Burr, the acknowledged authority on West Hartford history, devoted the last decades of his life to researching, lecturing, and writing on his beloved town. Five years with the Historical Records Survey at the Connecticut State Library led to more than 25 years in various duties at the Library of Congress in Washington, D.C. An invitation to deliver an address at the centennial of West Hartford's incorporation in 1954 whetted his appetite to learn more and to tell others about a town he found increasingly fascinating. The Noah Webster Foundation and Historical Society of West Hartford welcomed his interest, and he became one of its most active docents and trustees. Dr. Burr wrote the caption for the historical marker in the Center. In 1976 for the town's celebration of America's Bicentennial, he wrote a West Hartford history, *From Colonial Parish to Modern Suburb,* which he called "an appreciation of the community's character" from its inception to the middle 1920s. In 1987, in cooperation with Gregory E. Andrews, he identified 39 historic buildings and sites, many of which have been marked with commemorative signs or plaques.

Stars over Hall-ywood

A milestone in the life of Hall High School occurred in 1978 when the school was used as the location for a Hollywood movie. About 350 students served as extras, appearing individually and in crowd scenes, in "Promises in the Dark," a Warner Brothers production that opened a year later to generally good reviews in the national media.

"Promises" told the story of a suburban cheerleader's death after a long battle with cancer and its impact on her physician, played by actress Marsha Mason, who used a home at 664 Farmington Ave. as her office. The Hall football team and cheerleading squad, Coach Frank Robinson, Hall's locker room, hallways, and glassed-in catwalk were featured.

The view from Town Hall: windows above main entrance overlook Veterans memorial and Burr Street residential area.

XI. Governing

Chaos or Order?

"For want of a well considered plan of building development each man builds without reference to his neighbor. The result is chaotic."

That perception fired Josiah Woods, West Hartford's original "Mr. Zoner," back in 1923 when he persuaded the town to hire an expert. Brought in from Cleveland was Robert Whitten, a taciturn but prescient man. In six months he had a clear view of the challenges and developed the town's first real planning and zoning map. The plan included three major business areas and 17 neighborhood shopping centers.

He recognized that West Hartford had a distinct and "vigorous" personality but worried that the "open, wholesome, and beautiful residence development" might tempt greedy developers to divide existing lots, crowd houses together, and erect huge apartment houses. With the approval of the state legislature, West Hartford became the first town in the state and one of the first in America to adopt zoning.

Like other towns in Connecticut, West Hartford was first administered by a board of selectmen. The near doubling of residents from 1910 to 1920, the lack of planning and zoning, and fiscal instability brought pressure for a more efficient form of government. It came to a head in 1916 when a bitter quarrel between farmers and suburbanites over the value of land resulted in rejection of the assessment list, so that the town could collect no tax and had to borrow a year's expenses.

A seven-member committee headed by Adolph Sternberg studied the problem and recommended a council-manager setup and a comprehensive zoning plan.

Their adoption in 1919 made West Hartford the first such council-manager government in Connecticut and one of the earliest in New England. Interestingly, the concept was conceived by Richard S. Childs, an industrial executive who lived in nearby Manchester.

Richard H. Custer

"Dick" Custer was the imperturbable, pipe-smoking, thoroughly professional manager of West Hartford from 1962 to 1978. He saw the town reach its population peak of 68,300 and its annual budget approach $50 million. He was hired as Windsor's first town manager in 1947 and served four other communities before coming to West Hartford. He took pride in the fact that his administration here maintained its integrity: "Anybody who enters this field...needs dedication to public service and an understanding and respect that the elected council is boss and makes the policy."

His was not an easy task during a period of growth and change. Not only were his relations with the Town Council sometimes fractious, but he had to deal with the emergence of contentious neighborhood associations and persistent gadflies. The time he had to devote to relations with other levels of government doubled. Three of the major projects he oversaw were the building of the new Hall High School, the construction of I-84 across town, and the Buena Vista recreational complex. He served as president of the Rotary Club of West Hartford and his professional achievements were recognized by his elevation to the presidency of the International City Management Association.

At his retirement dinner he was praised by officials, fellow professionals, and friends. Mayor Anne Streeter noted that managers have to operate in a "no-win situation where if something goes right, it is the council's accomplishment; if things go wrong, the blame is placed on the manager. Unflappable and firmly puffing on his pipe, Dick listened patiently to the raging storms and through it all was able to steer the town in the right direction." Custer's response: "People in West Hartford should feel proud of their community. It is rather an extraordinary place."

Town Managers

Benjamin I. Miller, 1919-1923
Rodney L. Loomis, 1933-1955
Arthur N. Rutherford, 1955-1956
Donald H. Blatt, 1956-1962
Arthur N. Rutherford, January-August 1962
Richard H. Custer, 1962-1978
William N. Brady, 1978-1985
Barry M. Feldman, 1985-

A New Form of Government

The 1919 charter abolished the town meeting system and replaced the decision-making selectmen with a governing body of 15 councilors elected for one-year terms from four districts formed of roughly equal numbers of voters. It also established a variety of boards and commissions – library, sewer, parks, a Board of Relief, and a police and fire commission. The most innovative part of the charter stated that "the Town Council shall appoint a town manager." Benjamin I. Miller was the first town manager in any Connecticut town. By the mid-1930s there still were only 150 towns in the entire country with the council/manager form of government and most of those were in the Midwest.

The comprehensive zoning ordinance of 1923 – the first in the state – established a commission that could create zoning districts and regulate the use of land and buildings. The Town Plan and Zoning Commission could recommend, among other things, the location of roads, size of lots, porch lines, and setbacks. The council was left with the final say, but the TPZ recommendations carry considerable weight.

In 1923, the town got its first police chief, but the almost autonomous club-like fire districts were not united into a fire department until 1937.

In 1925, candidates for town office ran for the first time under party labels. With the exception of four elections, Republicans were in charge for the next 67 years. A revised charter in 1935 reduced the council from nine to seven members, whose terms had already been extended from one year to two, and established the position of council president (mayor), elected by the council from its membership. Another charter change in 1955 added two council members, switched from district to at-large elections, and provided for guaranteed minority-party representation. In 1963, the Board of Education changed from an appointed body to an elected one of seven members serving staggered four-year terms.

When the state mandated collective bargaining for municipal employees, six local unions were formed during the 1960s.

Town Managers

Benjamin I. Miller, a native of Avon, founder of the Avon Library, and a Democratic state representative in 1901, became West Hartford's first town manager in 1919. During his 14 years as manager, the town tripled in population to 24,000 and its grand list increased from $19 million to $65 million.

Upon his retirement in 1933, the council turned to Rodney L. Loomis, town engineer during Miller's regime. When Loomis came here, a single trolley ran along Farmington Avenue; there was no LaSalle Road and there were no stores on Park Road. "I used to walk from my home on Quaker Lane to work," he recalled. "Once – there was about six inches of snow on the ground – a deer bounded out of the woods and crossed my path." The cigar-smoking Loomis faced the tough job of implementing the town's new charter, which gave the manager much more authority and responsibility. He made it clear to the council that he would have "no strings" attached to his job. As manager he also served as director of public works, the police and fire departments, and revenue. "One of the problems in the early days." Loomis recalled, "was to set up high standards. I mean zoning. That was what kept West Hartford good." He retired in 1955 after 35 years as a town employee.

Women Take a Leadership Role

The switch to the council-manager form of government coincided with the culmination of the suffrage movement that resulted in the 19th Amendment giving women the right to vote in 1920. Following the amendment's ratification, the West Hartford League of Women Voters was organized in 1923. Inspired by the example of Ruth M. Dadourian, one of its founders who served as president of the state league, its members have been involved in local

Town Clerks

John Whitman, 1854-1861
Leonard Buckman, 1861-1895
Henry C. Whitman, 1895-1928
Carlyle C. Thompson, 1928-1949
Everett D. Dow, 1949-1976
Helen A. Derick, 1976-1980
Nan L. Glass, 1980-1995
Norma Cronin, 1995-

Everett D. (Brub) Dow

In the 1960s, the town's two political seers were Sam Lavery, who ran the Republican party, and Town Clerk Everett D. Dow, who had his fingers on the pulse of both parties. In 1921, having graduated from the University of Connecticut, he became a reporter and feature writer for the Hartford Courant. His vivid account of the tragic circus fire in Hartford in 1944 was the first wire service report flashed to the nation.

After moving to West Hartford in 1937, his genius for meeting people and making friends drew him inevitably into the political arena. His big opportunity came following a one-year stint on the Town Council. Town Clerk Carlyle C. Thomson had decided not to run again, and Brub Dow was chosen to be the Republican candidate in 1948, a disastrous year for Republicans generally. Harry S. Truman upset Thomas Dewey for president, Abraham Ribicoff was sent to Congress, and Chester Bowles won the governorship. But Brub Dow won the clerk's job handily, 14,718 to 8,935.

The big issue in the town election was whether the town clerk should be paid a salary. Previously, clerks had lived off fees for recording deeds and dog licenses. Brub campaigned for a salary and was supported by the West Hartford News.

Brub served as clerk for 27 years. His office was the unofficial gossip center for officials, reporters, and voters. Newly elected councilors got their baptisms under fire by sitting down with Brub and learning who and what made the town tick. His broad grin and cheery stories were as dazzling as his flamboyant shirts and bow ties. The only things missing in this convivial setting were a stove, cracker barrel, and liquid refreshment, which he often supplied in his home after hours. One reason that the council worked together harmoniously most of the time, despite party differences, was the informal rehash of town business at the Edelweiss Restaurant after every meeting under the spell of Brub's peacemaking geniality.

In 1972, Brub was named Connecticut Town Clerk of the Year.

He was also president of the Town Clerks Association, commander of the Hayes-Velhage American Legion post and a founder of the Historical Society of West Hartford.

and state politics, elections, and educational improvements ever since.

Grace Honiss, vice president of the League of Women Voters, was the first woman elected to the Town Council in 1929. Three years later, Dorothy Lorens, another league officer, was appointed to the School Board. Louise Day Duffy, who helped organize the league, later served on the School Board.

The celebrated 1952 reapportionment court case of Butterworth et al vs. Dempsey et al was league-inspired. The chief instigator was Miriam Butterworth, a longtime activist and proponent of opening the political process, whose varied causes ranged from founding and chairing the Connecticut Caucus of

Ruth McIntire Dadourian

This grand lady, a lifelong champion of progressive legislation for women and children, lived to be 91. Born in Cambridge, she married a mathematics professor at Trinity College. Along with Katharine Houghton Hepburn and other leaders of the Connecticut Woman's Suffrage Association, she helped plan the strategy for passage of the 19th Amendment. In 1926, Ruth became director of the Connecticut League of Women Voters and nine years later its president and lobbyist. An indefatigable activist, she collected and cataloged a vast amount of information on child welfare and labor, public health education, and labor laws.

Louise Day Duffy

Louise Day, a member of West Hartford's first high school class and a Smith College graduate, was persuaded by William H. Hall in 1908 to take a teaching job at the new high school. She left after four years and married Ward Duffy in 1915. Thus began a partnership that united two stalwart and spirited West Hartford families in their dedication to liberal causes. After Pearl Harbor they lived with Mother Duffy at 208 North Main St., and three generations – including the Duffys' five children – worshipped at First Congregational Church.

A lifelong and irrepressible Democrat, her iron will veiled by a persistent and radiant smile, Louise was an organizer of Hall's parent-teacher forum and of the West Hartford League of Women Voters, chairperson of the State Child Welfare Association, a member of the Library Board, and served on the Board of Education from 1938 to 1948. It was no surprise when the town's newest and largest elementary school was dedicated and named in her honor in 1952. At the age of 88, she was able to attend the 20th anniversary of Duffy School, still as cheery and alert as ever and wearing a new dress.

Madeline S. McKernan

Madeline S. McKernan of Rumford Street was raising her family when she ran for the Board of Education in 1969. Her mission: to oppose some of the innovations launched by controversial school superintendent Charles O. Richter. By the time she chaired the board two years later, she had been converted to some of his ways. But in 1973, after costly school renovations and plans for "pools in the schools" had been defeated in referenda, she knew it was time for a change. Never one to shun confrontation, the feisty chairman forced Dr. Richter's resignation and brought in Paul R. Burch, first principal of her Webster Hill neighborhood school, as a calming influence at the helm.

After serving as executive director of the West Hartford Bicentennial Committee, she was hired by the Hartford Insurance Group as director of education resources at its new Hamilton Heights training center. In 1985, she was elected to the Town Council on the Democratic ticket, serving until 1997. As a councilor, she was the one who was liaison to the pension board, library board, the historical society and such. She attended all their meetings and immersed herself in their affairs, providing perspective for both them and the council.

Since 1991, she has been coordinator for the area-wide magnet school opened in 2001 at the University of Hartford – "a part-time position at which she works double time," said a colleague. She switched from St. Brigid to St. Patrick-St. Anthony, the state's oldest Roman Catholic parish in downtown Hartford, for more outreach and diversity. She serves on the parish council, is a lector, teaches religious school, and works in its soup kitchen.

As the 20th century ended, no public figure in West Hartford had been more continuously involved in more varied positions of community leadership than Madeline McKernan.

Election Night returns in 1958 brought jubilation to the faces of Richard P. Smith (left) and his Republican party loyalists. The GOP regained control of the Town Council after the first Democratic takeover and maintained the majority until 1967.

Democrats to serving as the first female chair of the state Public Utilities Control Authority. The court case brought about the state's first constitutional convention since 1818 and gave Connecticut cities and suburbs representation in proportion to their numbers – "one man, one vote." West Hartford gained a senator and increased its representation in the Assembly to three and one-half from the previous two.

By the middle of the 20th century, West Hartford's political climate was changing. Republicans, who had controlled the Town Council since the 1920s, were beginning to lose their majority status. Since World War II, due to rapid growth in the North and South ends of town, Democratic registration had risen steadily. The rise of the Democrats can be told through such leaders as Katherine Quinn, longtime state chairman John Bailey's right hand from the predominantly Catholic South End, the tireless Democratic town chairman Harry H. Kleinman from the predominantly Jewish North End, and old-family New Dealers like John W. Huntington and Catherine C. Reynolds.

Chairman Kleinman began to see his registration

Board of Education chairman Elizabeth K. Steven was among the women who ascended to power in local government circles in the 1970s. Here she chats at a Democratic Election Night celebration with Democratic town chairman Harry H. Kleinman.

Mayor Kevin B. Sullivan leads a line of marchers in a nuclear protest march through West Hartford Center. With him are Bloomfield Mayor David A. Baram; Martha Vinick, head of FREEZE/West Hartford, which sponsored a series of monthly "Freeze Friday" walks in the early 1980s, and Wethersfield Councilman Lucille C. Vaughan.

New Britain Herald Photo

efforts pay off. Attorney Harold F. Keith was elected the first Democratic mayor in 1955, following a referendum that overturned the tax rate. The elimination of district voting in favor of at-large elections enabled Republicans to recapture six of the nine seats in 1959. But the Democratic minority leader, J. William Burns (later head of the state Department of Transportation), correctly predicted in 1963 that "inside ten years the Democrats will be the majority party. The state has become a Democratic state and West Hartford will not remain an isolated island for the GOP."

More troubling for the Republicans was the involvement of some leaders in land deals and zoning changes, such as Bishops Corner and Westfarms Mall. The latter mega-development straddling the West Hartford/Farmington line caused a bitter controversy. First, the council turned down the town portion of the mall and then reversed itself by a close vote in 1966. The approval was challenged in court and finally upheld by the state Supreme Court in 1970. The $40 million project was immensely successful, although West Hartford got most of the traffic headaches and most of the tax revenues went to Farmington.

The Westfarms Mall dealings cost the Republicans heavily. In 1966, a Democratic newcomer, attorney Jay W. Jackson, won a seat in the state Senate. The Republicans were able to hold only two of the town's seats in the House. In the town election of 1967, John W. Huntington, the well-known leonine, pipe-smoking architect, knocked out Republican Richard W. Sheehan as mayor. He credited his victory to "questionable real estate dealings." The losers cleaned house, so to speak, and returned to power in 1969 with Ellsworth S. Grant at the head of the ticket.

In 1968, when the town's population was at its peak, there were 14,671 registered Republicans, 13,068 Democrats and 14,076 Unaffiliated. Thirty years later, the voting registration was 17,141 Democrats, 9,954 Republicans and 13,108 Unaffiliated.

Women continued to move into leadership positions. From 1984 to 1998, Marilyn Cohen served the Democrats as the first female to chair a party locally. Her leadership coincided with a number of Democratic Town Council majorities, the rise of Kevin B. Sullivan as state senator, and the tenure of John F. Droney Jr. as state Democratic chairman.

Legal documents gave Piper Brook Redevelopment Project the go-ahead in 1969. From left are Prentiss L. Peterson, executive director of the Redevelopment Agency; John E. O'Keefe, agency chairman, and Mayor John W. Huntington. The town's largest renewal project included apartments, commercial areas, and single-family homes, such as these on Custer Street (below).

The Mayors

Traditionally, the Town Council elects as mayor the highest vote-getter in the biennial election. The first president of the Town Council to be designated mayor was Joseph M. Freedman in 1947. There have been 15 incumbents since.

Among the mayors, Anne P. Streeter and Kevin B. Sullivan left their council positions due to their election as state senators. Charles R. Matties, a state representative from 1972 to 1980, holds the record for the longest service on the council – a total of 18 years ending in 1995. Matties was the last Republican mayor until 1997, when the Republicans won control of the council for the first time in 14 years.

Clearly, the role of women in politics matured in the last three decades of the 20th century. Four of the last eight mayors have been women, starting with Catherine C. Reynolds in 1973.

Katie Reynolds shares three qualities of politically active women: well-educated, liberated, and spunky. She got her first taste of politics by serving as executive secretary to the non-partisan Citizens Charter Committee in Hartford. After election to the Town Council as the first woman Democrat, Mrs. Reynolds commented that during her "housewife's campaign" women were glad she was running because they thought a councilwoman would be less politically partisan and more likely to get things done.

Celebrate! West Hartford   **137**

West Hartford News Photo

The Town Council office area of the new Town Hall is graced by a grandfather clock, thanks to donations by former mayors and a clock constructed by Philip R. Reynolds, whose hobby is building clocks from kits. With the clockmaker (left of clock) in 1989 are mayor-donors (from left) Charles R. Matties, Richard P. Smith, Harold F. Keith, Ellsworth S. Grant, Catherine C. Reynolds, and Christopher F. Droney.

"Women in politics," she added, "can bring special qualities of compassion and creativity to the job." In the election of 1973, when she became mayor, the four highest vote-getters were women.

Nan Streeter's road to politics was through the League of Women Voters – "the one place where you don't know how many children people have," she once said. In 1979, she was the first woman mayor to head the Capitol Region Council of Governments. She was elected a state senator in 1981.

Sandra F. Klebanoff chaired not only the Town Council but also the Hartford Board of Education. As mayor from 1989-95, she became a relentless booster for regionalism. Head of the Capitol Region Council of Governments, she pushed a welfare-to-work transportation plan that helps inner city residents get to suburban jobs. Recognizing the importance of Riverfront Recapture as a catalyst for Hartford's economic revitalization, she lobbied hard to persuade the Town Council to support the Metropolitan District Commission's plan to finance the maintenance of the new parks on both sides of the Connecticut River. In recognition of her efforts the Hartford Courant chose her as the 1997 recipient of its Regional Leadership Award.

Issues of the 1970s

Town officials during the 1970s wrestled with the perennial issues of schools, taxes, traffic, and zoning. During the mayoral tenure of Catherine C. Reynolds, the council approved the renovation of three elementary schools, Charter Oak, Morley, and Smith, and two junior high schools, King Philip and Sedgwick. It tried to meet the housing needs of the elderly by reactivating the Housing Authority. A plot of land was acquired near the center of Elmwood on Grove Street for 40 state-subsidized rental apartments, which were quickly filled. Despite neighborhood opposition, small, moderate-income townhouse developments also were created along Brace Road near the Center and on Starkel Road at Bishops Corner. The council also passed a group home ordinance, which allowed the town to issue special-use permits to owners of large homes for sheltering supervised groups of handicapped people or youths fleeing difficult domestic situations. In addition, it approved a few homes for the retarded and for the Bridge's shelter for runaway teenagers. Other developments were improvements in handicapped accessibility, an affirmative action plan, diversity training programs for town employees, and establishment of a Human Rights Commission. Later,

Federation Square, the town's first elderly housing project, consists of 99 units built by the West Hartford Housing Authority on Starkel Road at Bishops Corner. Mayor Ellsworth S. Grant presided at the dedication ceremony in 1971. Behind him, facing the audience at right, is Rabbi Abraham J. Feldman.

the town, in cooperation with the West Hartford African American Social and Cultural Organization, instituted annual symposiums and ceremonies to celebrate Martin Luther King Day.

What to Do with Old Hall High?

No newcomer looking at the layout of the present Town Hall, Board of Education, Police Department, and Superior Court can possibly imagine the years of study, debate, twists, and turns involved in its achievement. Arguably, it was the most time-consuming controversy in the Town Council's history.

The tortured process began with the appointment of a Center Resources Committee in 1968, two years before the closing of the original Hall High School and the opening of its successor out North Main Street. The initial idea was to sell the old school site for a prestigious commercial use. A downtown Hartford insurance company expressed some interest. Nothing more happened until 1974 when the Chamber of Commerce

proposed either to expand the overcrowded Town Hall to accommodate the Police Department or to renovate the abandoned high school, which was lying idle on a prime piece of property.

For the next dozen years, the complex issue bounced back and forth, the positions changing depending on the leaders in power. Raze the school or renovate? Build a new town hall or add on to the existing? Renovate Whitman School or build a new police/court facility? Move the Education Center from St. Agnes Home into the main center of government? Finally, after a bond referendum was approved by voters in 1984, the pieces of the puzzle came together: The Town Hall would move to an enlarged and renovated Hall High, which would also have a community center; the Police and Court would occupy an enlarged and renovated Whitman School, and the school administration would settle in the old Town Hall.

Sunday, May 5, 1987, was a red-letter day for town employees, elected officials, and community leaders

Tastes in Wastes

West Hartford's methods of waste disposal have changed over the years. Refuse used to be collected and burned at the Brixton Street incinerator, whose dark smoke belched pollutants into the air, as in photo below, taken in 1972 just before the stack was torn down. Councilman Arthur E. Fay bulldozed Town Manager Richard H. Custer into providing scooters for back yard trash pickup (upper right), a popular town service for years. That reverted to curbside pickup (right center) when the town contracted with a private refuse firm. Town also got out of the leaf pickup business (lower right), now using the private sector.

who for nearly a quarter of a century had studied and debated what to do with old Hall High. That morning, Town Historian Nelson R. Burr, using the council's wooden gavel, knocked three times on the main entrance – an honored medieval custom – and the door opened to the new Town Hall. The next day, 350 employees moved into 110,000 square feet of attractive and spacious offices. The renovation, which cost $5.6 million, refurbished in the town clerk's office the colorful WPA murals of Connecticut history painted by local artist Walter O.R. Korder before World War II in what had been the school library.

The integration of town offices on South Main Street, along with the Library and the Congregational Church facing Goodman Green, has created a cohesive and graceful version of a typical New England town center.

Keeping Up with the Times

In the 1980s and 1990s, town councils met continuing and changing needs as school and town administrations moved into a new municipal center.

Beginning in 1979 and through several votes of residents in the affected areas in the 1980s, West Hartford was among the first in the state to establish historic districts. It also passed an historic properties ordinance to "protect the heritage, aesthetic quality and character of the town…and to provide protection for buildings of historical and architectural significance."

The moves were led by members of the town's Historic District Commission, particularly David Ransom, Gregory E. Andrews, and Richard L. Hughes III. The commission makes an annual award to property owners who maintain the historic and architectural integrity of their properties.

The historic districts are Buena Vista, Boulevard-Raymond Road, and West Hill. Historic properties are designated throughout town from New Britain Avenue, Park Road, North and South Main Streets, and Bishops Corner.

Throughout the period, a recurring theme – as it had been through much of the century – was the natural tension between residential stability and commercial growth. It culminated in the controversial application for a Home Depot on New Park Avenue, eventually approved to add to the tax base and buffered from nearby neighborhoods. Similarly, a controversial plan for the Town Centre retail and office building and parking garage in the Center was approved.

Nan Lewis Glass

"Nan Glass moved from Hartford to West Hartford when she was 11. Now, 57 years later, she is moving back."

So began the lead story in the town news section of the Hartford Courant on Nov. 15, 1997. Her move was front-page news because in the interim, Nan Glass had been a leading player in local politics and community affairs for nearly a quarter-century.

She graduated from Hall High School and the University of Connecticut. After her marriage, she reared four children and began her community involvement "with the usual PTA route." Her father had been photo editor of the Hartford Times, so she was no newcomer to journalism when she applied for a part-time reporter's job with the West Hartford News in 1971. Dissatisfied with merely covering government, she wanted to be in government and ran successfully as a Democrat for Town Council in 1973. She had served two terms and was re-elected to a third, when she resigned from the council to return to the News as managing editor in 1978. Her steady hand and community knowledge served the paper well, as they had the council before. The desire to escape the pressure of weekly deadlines prompted her to seek election as town clerk, a post she won handily in 1979.

Subsequently she was endorsed by both political parties and served as clerk until 1995, when she retired and ran again for Town Council. This time, she led the Democratic ticket and became mayor, deciding against running for re-election in 1997.

Nan Glass was not the traditional "political" politician, but rather a compromiser and facilitator who stood for what was right for the community, however that stance happened to fall. Inside and outside Town Hall, she worked with best friends and colleagues Elizabeth K. Steven and Madeline S. McKernan for the betterment of the town.

After a bad fall down stairs in her Farmington Avenue apartment, she sought a one-floor living space. That prompted her move to a Woodland House condominium high above Hartford, where she took advantage of the city's cultural opportunities. "I'm a regionalist," she said. "West Hartford doesn't exist without Hartford."

But she did not forsake the town she had served so well. Her heart remained here after she moved.

From Flood Control To Beautification

Long-lasting Trout Brook flood control project moved in stages along brook that runs through much of the town. Funded by the federal, state, and local governments, the work neared an end in 1982 (right) in the stretch north of Farmington Avenue and Fern Street. In 1989, pedestrians were enjoying a path along the newly landscaped brook in a park-like setting (below).This section looks east toward the Boulevard bridge.

Neighborhood task forces initiated improvements in what became known as Farmington East and Park Road redevelopment projects. Reconstruction of Park Road, its sidewalks and landscaping in particular contributed to the neighborhood's stability and growth. The town also funded sidewalk and streetscape improvements in the Center and Elmwood, and planted flowers in public spaces all around town.

Modifications to the town's parking ordinance allowed more restaurants to open in the Center. Sidewalk regulations were eased to allow outside dining in what one council leader called "The Restaurant Capital of Central Connecticut."

During the recession of the early 1990s, the town set up a program to help downsized job seekers – some of whom had worked for a single company all their lives – find new employment.

To ease the tax burden, the town "privatized" certain government services, from trash pickup and building maintenance to recreation facilities and user fees. Considerable emphasis has been given Senior Center programs in the Town Hall and Elmwood Community Center, as well as teen and family services through the Bridge.

The town financed continuing school renovations, converted Plant School to senior housing, renovated

Town of West Hartford Photo

West Hartford Historical Society Photo

Richard E. O'Meara Sr. mounts a motorcycle at Goodman Green in West Hartford Center in 1910. Strapped to the lunch box above the gasoline tank is a small white book containing the owner's name and address and registration number of every car in the state.

Patrolman Ed Yescott was part of the Police Department's bicycle patrol. The town was one of the first to implement patrols as part of the community policing thrust of the 1990s to get policemen out of patrol cars and onto the streets.

and expanded the Center and Faxon libraries, sold the old Brace Road firehouse for commercial development, and acquired state-of-the-art fire apparatus.

In an effort to provide affordable housing, the West Hartford Housing Authority – which separated from the town in the 1980s as an independent agency – has offered 40 garden-style units of housing for senior citizens at Elm Grove and 99 at Plant, plus eight units at scattered sites for families. Fellowship Housing at Bishops Corner manages federal and state programs for 214 seniors and people with disabilities. At Starkel

Cemeteries Then and Now

In early times, West Hartford residents buried their dead on church grounds or on the family homestead. In the 20th century, the town took over the responsibility to provide burial facilities. West Hartford has three cemeteries: two ancient ones on North Main Street just north of Farmington Avenue, and Fairview Cemetery, which opened in the 1920s on 50 acres off Whitman Avenue.

The Center Cemetery, less than an acre in size, and the 6.7-acre Old North Cemetery were church burial grounds and have long been closed to new plot purchasers, although each year about three descendants of original owners still find space in their family plots in Old North. In 1990, 30 gravestones there were damaged, including those of Noah

Webster's parents, Noah and Mercy Steele Webster, instigating a restoration movement.

As of the new millennium, 30,000 gravesites in Fairview Cemetery had been sold and there were only about 1,200 left, yet more than 300 new sites were needed each year. The last section of Soldiers Field, where veterans have previously had free burial, was filled. Town officials have been studying solutions, including a mausoleum or smaller crypts. Meanwhile, the town eyed possibilities for expansion and approached Marlene Filer, widow of former Aetna chairman John H. Filer, with an offer to buy an acre of her land that backs up to the cemetery. She declined to sell, but donated the land to the town instead.

Celebrate!West Hartford **143**

Seniors Job Bank

A month after he retired as executive vice president of G. Fox & Co. in 1974, Maurice H. Berins started the West Hartford Seniors Job Bank, a town-sponsored employment agency for retirees who wished to continue working. It was a typically imaginative contribution to society for Moe Berins, who earlier had started the Greater Hartford Arts Festival.

By 2001, the job bank was responsible for more than 20,000 placements, serving more than 11,000 applicants and handling 47,000 job listings.

Patricia Newton, director since its inception, calculates that the retirees the Job Bank has placed in industry (a category that includes everything except handymen and household aides) have earned more than $45 million.

Early officers of Seniors Job Bank included (from left), top, Maurice H. Berins, director Patricia Newton and G. Donald Geckler, and (front), Benita M. Burstein, Betty Stangle, and Lorentz A. Morrow.

Road, Federation Square manages 88 units for seniors and disabled under another federal program. The Christian Activities Council has 11 units for families, mainly single mothers. The West Hartford Interfaith Coalition during the 1990s provided eleven units on scattered sites around town and built 28 apartments on Flagg and Brace Roads and Quaker Lane South.

Community Activists

Every town has its corps of critics and activists. Their concerns range from the significant to the trivial. Most of their complaints are directed at government officials, but the one thing they have in common is the ability to capture attention.

Best known of these was Oswald E. D'Arche, who

Barry M. Feldman: Reinventing Government

West Hartford's government began its journey into the 21st century in 1985. Town Manager Barry M. Feldman arrived after 14 years experience in town management with a bagful of ideas for local government reform, which he began to implement with Town Council support almost immediately.

Now with a tenure exceeded only by that of Rodney L. Loomis, who served from 1933 to 1955, he has led town government into modern times.

His is a "customer-driven" style. He eschews the buzz word "privatization," preferring, as he says, "to make local government competitive by becoming partners with the private sector to provide the best possible service to our customers, the residents and taxpayers of West Hartford."

Among his innovations are competitive bidding for providing traditional government services – including Cornerstone Aquatics Center, Veterans Memorial Rink, trash pickup, public building maintenance, and snow plowing, and an

entrepreneurial culture in town administrative offices.

Those innovations over more than a decade and a half have not come without controversy, but Barry Feldman's persistence and graciousness have won him support in both Democratic and Republican administrations, the business community, and among residents who recognize his achievements and appreciate his practical, "let's-work-out-a-solution" style.

He earned his doctorate in political science at the University of Connecticut in 1998, and teaches government to University of Hartford undergraduates and at the graduate level at UConn.

A self-professed fitness addict, he spends his lunch hour running – often with any colleagues who can keep up with him – on a route that takes him through residential neighborhoods and around the town's recreational facilities. That way he gets to see the "customers" and what they are up to.

ran a plumbing business. His home at 1530 Boulevard was a carefully-groomed showplace beside Trout Brook. His crusades against town budgets, especially teacher salaries, began, it is alleged, when as a young man during the Depression he was on welfare and threw a brick through a window of the Town Hall to protest his inability to find work. His most effective campaigns occurred during the 1950s when he led two tax rate referenda. Ozzie D'Arche spent his own funds for newspaper ads to arouse the taxpayers. The first to overrule the Town Council's setting of a 36-mill rate was carried in 1955 by a 2-1 margin with a 56 percent voter turnout. The second, three years later, won by a smaller margin. In both cases the tax rate was eventually reduced by less than a mill. Since then, the majority of townspeople have consistently supported the budgets.

Other critical voices were the nurseryman Albert Gledhill and Edward J. Madara of Brookmoor Road, who even on his deathbed continued to attack the Town Council. "Ozzie" D'Arche spoke for both of them when he said: "If anyone wants to know who runs this town from now on, you can tell him the people do."

Charlotte Kitowski of Arnoldale Road was an activist with a mission, which she saw realized and which left a permanent imprint on the development of West Hartford. A registered nurse, she first became involved in making government accountable for its actions by speaking out for open housing and against police brutality and the Vietnam War. In 1969, she discovered that the state Department of Transportation was planning to put I-291, an eight-lane superhighway around Hartford, through the middle of the watershed surrounding the MDC reservoirs. With the West

'Stuck – Call Chuck'

For nearly 50 years this slogan was as well-known to local motorists in distress as town resident William Savitt's "Peace of Mind Guaranteed" was to Hartford diamond buyers. It appeared on the five red tow trucks of the Matties Service Station on Farmington Avenue. A native of Hartford, Charles R. Matties opened his station in 1949 after service in the Army. Competition among automobile repair shops was intense, and gasoline price wars were frequent. But the affable owner and his able associate, Olie Ferreira, persevered and attracted a loyal following. Eventually, Matties operated three stations in West Hartford.

Running a successful small business was not enough to keep him busy, however. After moving to the Webster Hill neighborhood, he developed an interest in local affairs and in 1969 ran for the Town Council. More to the point, he walked. To garner support, he knocked on the doors of more than 8,000 homes. His only rival in door-to-door campaigning was Robert W. Barrows, a prominent real estate executive and Democrat, several times a candidate for the council and the state legislature. Easily elected, Chuck Matties expressed surprise that so many voted for "a grease monkey."

In the middle of his second term he was appointed to fill a vacant seat in the state House of Representatives. A conscientious legislator, he said that one of the highlights of his eight years there was winning passage of a bill to provide Vietnam veterans partial tuition benefits for higher education.

In 1981, Chuck returned to the council and became mayor. He immediately found himself in the middle of a turmoil over whether West Hartford should join the Metropolitan District Commission. Since 1930, the town had paid the MDC for water and sewage services but had refused to join and, without representation, now was facing higher fees. Matties felt the time had come for the town to share responsibility with the seven towns in the district. His own party, which controlled the council 5-4, was divided; he needed two Democratic votes to win. A referendum approved his position overwhelmingly, and with bipartisan support West Hartford belatedly joined the Capitol Region's most vital inter-town agency.

Chuck continued to serve on the council until 1995. "Politics," he said, "was my avocation. I never played golf." He cannot begin to count the hours spent in council zoning hearings over 18 years, but he will never forget the last one – about 40 hours on the controversial application for a Home Depot store on New Park Avenue. His vote in favor cost him patronage at his stations.

New stations with convenience stores and expensive environmental mandates on his properties compelled him to retire from business in 1997. "It's sad," he said, "because back when I first began, a person with just a high school education had a chance to get into this business and work his way up the ladder to achieve the American dream."

Sedgwick Middle School Band plays outside Town Hall auditorium during 1994 program celebrating 75th anniversary of West Hartford's council-manager form of government and 140th annivesary of its incorporation.

Hartford News and Town Councilman Lauchlin McLean taking up her cause, she went to war against the DOT and the highway lobby.

Until then, road-building decisions were made virtually without public knowledge or input. Mrs. Kitowski obtained 6,000 signatures on a petition that

Our Town's Mayors

R - Joseph M. Freedman, 1947-1951
R - C. Edwin Carlson, 1951-1955
D - Harold F. Keith, 1955-1959
R - Richard P. Smith, 1959-1961
R - Peter Sullivan, 1961-1963
R - Richard W. Sheehan, 1963-1967
D - John W. Huntington, 1967-1969
R - Ellsworth S. Grant, 1969-1973
D - Catherine C. Reynolds, 1973-1975
R - Anne P. Streeter, 1975-1981
R - Charles R. Matties, 1981-1983
D - Kevin B. Sullivan, 1983-1986
D - Christopher F. Droney, 1986-1989
D - Sandra F. Klebanoff, 1989-1995
D - Nan L. Glass, 1995-1997
R - Robert R. Bouvier, 1997-

Shirley G. Marsh

Even a diagnosis of cancer in 1993 could not slow Shirley G. Marsh, the town's environmental conscience. She remained active on the Town Plan & Zoning Commission, which she served for 14 years, two as chairman, and tended gardens at the Noah Webster House until her death in 1997.

For seven years chairman of the town's Conservation and Environment Commission, she pioneered in guiding development in environmentally sensitive ways. She helped develop an open space index for the town and helped draft the town's first wetlands regulations. "She was a walking encyclopedia – our conscience," said Stanley Johnson, TPZ chairman.

The town took the unusual step of placing a plaque at Spicebush Swamp in her honor. The town doesn't normally install memorials to civic volunteers since there are so many "who serve the town well and with great merit," said Town Manager Barry M. Feldman. "But her contributions deserve special recognition."

Senior town planner Mila Limson called Mrs. Marsh "a very rare individual. In all my years here, I don't think I've ever met anyone as dedicated as Shirley was."

forced the DOT to hold a public hearing. "The politicians pronounced our activity fruitless several times over," she said, but she and her band of highway foes persevered, rounding up pro bono experts to testify that the proposed highway would forever impair the reservoir environment. Her triumph came in 1973 when Gov. Thomas J. Meskill unexpectedly canceled the portion of I-291 between I-91 in Windsor and I-84 in West Hartford.

That did not end her involvement. She continued to oppose highway construction in the state, turning up at hearings and newspaper offices with reams of statistics and articles advocating alternative transportation methods.

Those in State and National Service

U.S. Senators - William A. Purtell, 1953-1957
     Thomas J. Dodd, 1959-1971
U.S. Congressman - Thomas J. Dodd, 1953-1957
U.S. Solicitor General - Seth P. Waxman, 1997 -
U.S. Attorney General - Charles J. McLaughlin, 1937-1938

William A. Purtell

Bill Purtell, the first from West Hartford to serve in the U.S. Senate, was the founder of the Holo-Krome Corp. Easy to know and like, he had mastered the art of salesmanship, a talent that led him into politics.

In 1950, he stumped the state drumming up delegates who would support him in his bid for the Republican party's gubernatorial nomination. The winner of both the nomination and the election was John Lodge, who appointed Purtell to fill a U.S. Senate vacancy. In 1952, he won a full term. Always a mover and shaker, he found the Senate "club" stultifying and did not seek re-election.

The Democrats chose Thomas J. Dodd, the father of current Sen. Christopher Dodd, to replace him. A Congressman from 1953 to 1957, Tom Dodd lived for a while on Concord Street.

Purtell returned to the business world, although he was often in demand as a speaker at political fund-raisers. According to his friend and ally, H. Randall Pease, Jr., "he could give the most rousing speech you ever heard at the drop of a hat."

U.S. District Court Judge -
   J. Joseph Smith, 1941-1961
   M. Joseph Blumenfeld, 1961-1987
   Alfred V. Covello, 1992-
   Christopher F. Droney, 1997-
U.S. Court of Appeals Judge -
   J. Joseph Smith, 1961-1980
   Jon O. Newman, 1978-
U.S. Attorney - Christopher F. Droney, 1990-1997
State Supreme Court Chief Justice - Ellen A. Peters, 1984-1996
Associate Justice - John P. Cotter, 1978-1981
     Ellen A. Peters, 1978-1984
     Alfred V. Covello, 1987-1992
     Peter T. Zarella, 2001-
State Treasurer - Guy B. Holt, 1937-39
     Gerald A. Lamb, 1960-1973
     Joan R. Kemler, 1986-87
     Paul J. Silvester, 1998-2000
Secretary of the State - Henry S. Cohn, 1978-1979
     Miles S. Rapoport, 1995-1998
Speaker of the House - Hiram Hurlbut, 1887-1889
     Harold E. Mitchell, 1943-1945
Senate Majority Leader – Kevin B. Sullivan, 1997-

State Legislators

After it became a town, West Hartford eventually was alloted one representative to the Connecticut General Assembly, but no senator until 1967. Most early representatives served only one two-year term:
Charles Ramsey, 1879-1882
Benjamin S. Bishop, 1883-1884
Leonard Buckland, 1885-1886
Hiram Hurlbut, 1887-1888
Thomas O. Enders, 1889-1892
Frederick C. Rockwell, 1893-1894
Adolph C. Sternberg, 1895-1896
William J. Mansfield, 1897-1898
John O. Enders, 1899-1900
Charles C. Cook, 1901-1902
George F. Scarborough, 1903-1904
Charles A. Griswold, 1905-1906
C. Edward Beach, 1907-1908
William S. Griswold, 1909-1910
Albert V.W. Sherman, 1911-1912
Lucius C. Ryce, 1913-1914

Richard H. Deming, 1915-1916
Carlyle C. Thomson, 1917-1918
Oliver Beckwith, 1919-1920

By the 1921 session, West Hartford's population was large enough to justify two representatives. The norm became to serve more than one term:

Thomas W. Russell, 1921-1922
Huntington Meech, 1921-1924
J. Verner Anderson, 1923-1924
John W. Huling, 1925-1928
Henry A. Wolcott, 1925-28
Clarence W. Seymour, 1929-1930
Frank J. Sparks, 1929-1934
Charles. B. Beach, 1931-1932
Richard Goodwin, 1933-1936
George E. Jones, 1935-1940
Harold E. Mitchell, 1937-1946
Olcott D. Smith, 1941-1942
Wallace E. Campbell, 1943-1946
William H. Dallas, 1947-1948
Kenneth J. Hoffman, 1947-1952
Daniel C. Flynn, 1949-1954
Franklin G. Brown, 1953-1954
Frederick U. Conard Jr., 1955-1956
Reinhart L. Gideon, 1955-1956
Richard W. Sheehan, 1957-1962
George Schwolsky, 1957-1958
Ralph M. Shulansky, 1959-1962
L. Richard Belden, 1963-1966
Nicholas A. Lenge, 1963-1972

In 1967, reapportionment brought about by a court case and the first constitutional convention since 1818 gave West Hartford a senator and three and one-half representatives (the one-half is shared with Farmington).

State Senator:
Jay W. Jackson, 1967- 1972
Nicholas A. Lenge, 1973-1974
David H. Neiditz, 1975-1976
Douglas T. Putnam, 1977-1978
Clifton A. Leonhardt, 1979-1982
Anne P. Streeter, 1981-1986
Kevin B. Sullivan, 1987-

State Representative:
Thomas P. Byrne, 1967-1972
David H. Neiditz, 1967-1974
Owen L. Clark, 1967-1972
Robert W. Barrows, 1969-1970
Clyde Fuller, 1973-1974
Charles R. Matties, 1973-1978
Joan R. Kemler, 1975-1984
Robert D. Shea, 1975-1976
Thomas Clark, 1975-1976

Robert Farr: Affecting People's Lives

Robert Farr has served longer than any other state legislator from West Hartford, but he went to bed on Election Night 2000 thinking he had lost to Democratic challenger Jonathan Harris by 43 votes. The narrow margin required an automatic recount and the following Monday he found he won his 11th term by nine votes. Ironically, it wasn't the first time that Farr was involved in a recount. Several years earlier, the initial count showed he defeated challenger Larry Price by 12 votes and the recount narrowed the margin to eight.

Farr has not only survived but thrived as a member of the minority party representing a heavily Democratic district. "I've been the only Republican getting elected – it's pretty lonely there," he said of the West Hartford delegation.

A practicing lawyer, he began as a town councilor in 1975 and, as the second highest vote-getter, became deputy mayor under Anne P. Streeter.

In 1981 he moved on to the Legislature, where he took special interest in "legislation that affects people's lives." He was instrumental in passage of seat belt laws, much of Connecticut's drunk driving laws, a ban on smoking in public places, and welfare reform. With others in the West Hartford delegation he favored the state income tax, but insisted on the spending caps and fiscal restraints that became law. He has served successively as ranking member of the environment, appropriations, and judiciary committees.

His command of the town's district-by-district voting patterns is legendary on Election Night, and he has been known to predict eventual winners based on early returns. "I'm sort of a political junkie," he explains. "I enjoy following voting outcomes and trends."

West Hartford's longest serving state legislator, Robert Farr (right) got his start on the Town Council. Here he celebrates his initial council victory with his running mates (from left) Ellsworth S. Grant, Anne P. Streeter, Neil R. Danaher Jr., and Dr. Albert H. Kleiman.

John A. Berman, 1977-1978
Dorothy Barnes, 1977-1982
Robert Farr, 1981-
Maureen M. Baronian, 1981-1986
Miles S. Rapoport, 1985-1994
Richard F. Mulready, 1987-1994
Andrew W. Fleischmann, 1995-
Allen Hoffman, 1995-1996
John J. Ritter, 1997-1998
David McCluskey, 1999-

Two Who Moved On

Career government activist Miles S. Rapoport, former Democratic state representative and secretary of the state, lost a bid for U.S. House of Representatives in 1998. Undaunted, he founded DemocracyWorks in 1999. He continued as executive director of the Hartford reform group while becoming president in 2001 of Demos, a two-year-old, national election-reform advocacy group based in New York.

Frank Luntz got his political start working for Robert Farr's council campaign while a student at Hall High School. After advising Rudolph Giuliani's successful mayoral campaign in New York at age 31, the New York Times magazine called him Washington's latest Wunderkind. He was introduced in a speech as one of America's 50 most promising leaders under 40 (Time magazine), as one of the nine most influential Republican minds (USA Today), and as one of the framers of Newt Gingrich's Contract With America.

Kevin Sullivan: Local Boy Makes Good

West Hartford native Kevin B. Sullivan – the first of his family to go to college – has risen from the grass roots to top political ranks in the state. He was first mentioned as a candidate for local office while enrolled at Trinity College, where he was active in civil rights, and upon graduation became more involved in town affairs. As a homeowner on Walkley Road, he joined the East Side neighborhood association and won an upset victory in a Democratic Town Committee primary, becoming district chairman. He soon was appointed to West Hartford's Community Development Block Grant Advisory Committee, where he helped fund neighborhood improvement projects and launched the town's first Neighborhood Block Watch program. He was vice chairman of the town's first appointed Finance Advisory Board and helped lead a successful effort to keep Whiting Lane School from being closed.

In 1981 while finishing studies at UConn Law School, he was elected to the Town Council. He became mayor in 1983 with the first Democratic majority in a decade. In 1986 he was elected to the state Senate, representing West Hartford ever since. Again he rose to the highest ranks, becoming Senate majority leader in 1997 and re-elected in 1999 and 2001.

The career politician has become widely recognized for his work in education, mental health, economic development, tax reform, and services to children and the elderly. As a vice president of Trinity College, he oversees its pioneering public-private neighborhood development initiative and lectures on public policy.

Amusement ride thrills youngsters at Countryfest, typical of town-sponsored events organized by the Department of Leisure Services. This activity was staged for several autumns in the late 1990s around the Town Hall and Education Center.

Boardwalk leads through dense woods in Wolcott Park, a sylvan retreat off New Britain Avenue not far from busy Interstate 84 and shopping areas at Corbins Corner and Westfarms mall.

150 Playing

Few towns have as many and varied recreational facilities as West Hartford. Here, skaters head for the new $500,000 Veterans Memorial Rink on opening day in 1968. Several hundred people turned out for the first open skating session.

XII. Leisure

West Hartford is exceptional in the variety of its recreational facilities and programs. How many towns have four golf courses, two public and two private? Or six reservoirs surrounded by forests accessible for walking and hiking? Or 28 town parks and open-space areas covering 1,200 acres, indoor and outdoor swimming pools, a nature farm, and a hockey arena?

Recreation as we know it boomed with the opening

Town Parks

1931 – Fernridge Park, 30 acres.
1932 – Beachland Park, 30 acres.
1943 – Buena Vista Golf Club, 70 acres.
1943 – Sterling Field, athletic fields.
1953 – Mooney's Woods, 15 acres.
1961 – Rockledge Golf Club.
1962 – Spicebush Swamp.
1965 – Kennedy Memorial Park.
1969 – Eisenhower Park, 17 acres.
1972 – Wolcott Park, 29 acres.
1974 – Westmoor Park, 56 acres.

of Hartford's reservoirs in 1867 at the western edge of town. The reservoir area – today a hilly, sylvan treasure at the town's doorstep – became a favorite spot for picnics, hiking, and horseback riding. After 1894, city-dwellers arrived on the Unionville trolley cars. By 1896, Connecticut magazine touted the area as "one of the most desirable outing spots in the state." The town also benefited from the gift to Hartford in 1894 of the Charles F. Pond estate, which straddles the city-town line and is known as Elizabeth Park. People from near and far also were attracted in the late 19th century to the Charter Oak Park racetrack and later the Luna amusement park.

Golf clubs began in the minds of two young sportsmen, Emerson Taylor and William St. John, who in 1895 deplored the city's lack of a course. Next year marked the start of the Hartford Golf Club, with its course (like part of adjoining Elizabeth Park) located in the West Hartford Common, pasture lands that had been set aside for common purposes. In 1899, the golf club aquired 99 acres north of Asylum Avenue, formerly the Huntington farm, bounded by Whetten,

Rockledge Country Club was purchased by the town in 1961 as a municipal recreation facility. Original clubhouse hugs South Main Street at lower center of 1961 photo. At upper left is Conard High School, but I-84 has yet to appear at top left.

Golfers practice on putting green behind clubhouse at Rockledge. Town built a new club-house in the 1970s and renovated the restaurant section, adding an expansive deck, in 1996.

152 Playing

Horse and carriage waits outside the Hartford Golf Club's original, Victorian-era clubhouse, which occupied the crest of a hill off Whetten Road. A larger clubhouse was opened across Albany Avenue at the end of Norwood Road in 1955.

Rockledge Country Club

When Wilton W. "Mike" Sherman was at Yale, he read of a "gentleman's estate for sale in West Hartford," which was the terminology of 1913. As he visited the 120-acre property on a ridge along South Main Street, he was thinking of the prospects for two farm buildings, a herd of pure guernseys, and four sleek horses. He bought it and ran it thus until after World War I, when a group of sportsmen eyed his farm for a golf course. Their architect turned it down because of the contour of the land and settled on the Miller farm just across the town line in Bloomfield for what is now Tumble Brook Country Club.

That prompted Mike Sherman to rethink the use of his property. He prevailed upon neighbors to back his Webster Hill Country Club until they learned the cost. He decided to go it alone, by 1924 opening a 14-hole course named Rockledge for the terrain of the clubhouse area. The first clubhouse actually was on the east side of Main Street in the former Woolley estate, and the first tee was almost on the street. By 1927, he enlarged the course to 18 holes and a new clubhouse was built in 1933. It rode out the Depression as a nightclub.

Promoter Sherman staged tournaments at Rockledge, bringing in some of the greatest names of golf. His biggest day was in 1932 when the New England Open ended in a tie. Former National Open Champion Paul Runyan won the playoff before the largest golf crowd ever assembled in West Hartford.

Sherman died in 1959 and the town, after a bond-issue vote, bought the clubhouse and 100-plus acres for a municipal golf course in 1961.

Belknap and Sycamore roads. The clubhouse was atop a hill off Whetten Road. The club later bought 216 acres for the present 18-hole course north of Albany Avenue and became one of the largest landowners in town.

Wampanoag Country Club, another 18-hole golf course, was founded in 1924, also in the town's North End. Seven local sportsmen bought the old Cadwell farm and leading architect Donald Ross laid out a course on the site of an Indian battlefield where arrowheads had been plowed up. A grandiose plan for a three-story clubhouse resembling an Italian palace fell victim to the Depression. After 30 years in a white frame farmhouse on North Main Street, a modern clubhouse was erected in 1955 – about the same time the Hartford Golf Club relocated its clubhouse across Albany Avenue to the end of Norwood Road.

The West Hartford Country Club was abandoned in 1935 when its members joined a golf club in Newington. Its nine-hole course lay idle until the town took it over during World War II and renamed it Buena Vista. The town also operates Rockledge Country Club, which was conceived in the early 1920s as the Webster Hill Country Club.

A West Hartford Tennis Club prospered for many years, and by the early 1900s had a clubhouse, now located on Flagg Road.

In the years before World War I came the YMCA, with headquarters in the old Center Schoolhouse and now on North Main Street.

Some of West Hartford's avid tennis players arranged three special townwide tennis tournaments for the town's Bicentennial celebration in 1976. Committee members were (from left), front, Eileen Kraus, Shirley Fry Irvin and James Carroll, and (rear) Tom Walsh, Anita Prete, John Berman, Ralph Chilton, Dr. Bradford Blanchard, and Raymond Goodwin.

Parks and Playgrounds

When the first town charter was adopted in 1919, the Town Council created a parks commission. In 1928 it recommended establishment of a playground program, urging the town to purchase five areas for parks. The commission chose not to set aside "large areas of unused land for special parks as Hartford has." Rather it recommended a plan "to acquire certain smaller sections of land located in different parts of town where the child population is the largest" and to develop these for children's activities and for neighborhood recreational centers.

By 1939, nine parks and playgrounds had been developed, mainly adjacent to schools. Two had tennis courts, almost all had playground equipment and "lawn area for all sorts of games," one had a "swimming hole," and five had baseball diamonds and football fields. There were park supervisors and summer recreational programs, but this wasn't enough to cope with mounting delinquency and vandalism.

Michael Manternach, a gruff, cigar-smoking councilman, decided to do something about what he called "the boy problem." He called together some 40 civic leaders, who expressed "growing concern over the use of leisure time by the boys of West Hartford." Boys, "incidentally, from the better families,"

were hanging out at diners and poolrooms and other places not "conducive to character building." They decided it was the town's duty to "provide our boys a

'A Weekend Town'

"Many West Hartford residents have two distinct roles. By day they are prominent in the business world of Hartford and other communities and in the evening they take up their other duties as West Hartford citizens."

So wrote the West Hartford News in its 1954 Centennial edition. The article added:

"West Hartford also has the air of a 'weekend' community. Most of the heavy food purchasing by the residents is done Friday afternoon through Saturday evening. One of the most notable features of this 'weekend life' which usually draws considerable comment from visitors is the fact that most of the male residents break out in fancy sport-shirts on Saturday morning for their shopping or 'around-the-house' chores. One recent visitor, impressed by the colorful sartorial informality, counted 136 sport shorts of brilliant hues on the north side of Main Street in less than one hour.

"Much of the residential social life is geared to the weekend tempo and it picks up considerably on Friday, continues through Saturday and subsides quickly on Sunday evening."

Ground was broken for Wolcott Park in 1972. Going over plans at the ceremony were (from left) Henry F. Wolcott and Ruth Wolcott, whose family owned the property back to the early 19th century, architect Dean Johnson, and Ernest O. St. Jacques, the town's parks and recreation director.

desirable meeting place under proper supervision in a wholesome environment."

From the group that met in 1939 came the Recreation Commission that Michael Manternach chaired for twelve years. The first director, J.W. Feldman, passed on the reins in 1943 to William Davies, who served 27 years. The commission created many programs sponsored by the town but run by volunteers. Five public swimming pools were built between the 1940s and 1960s. Then public prodding and fund-raising, spearheaded by West Hartford News editor Bice Clemow, resulted in the formation of the non-profit Cornerstone Club. It evolved into today's town-

owned but privately operated Cornerstone Aquatics Center serving more than 6,500 members.

Skating is available on outdoor ponds in winter and almost year-round at the newly renovated Veterans Memorial Rink, which offers more than 445 programs. The town is unusual in that it has two public golf courses: eighteen holes at Rockledge Country Club, which averages close to 60,000 rounds annually, and nine holes at Buena Vista Golf Club, now averaging about 24,000 rounds. Rockledge also has a clubhouse that includes a "view" restaurant leased by the town to a concessionaire – part of a move by the town to privatize appropriate recreation entities. Lately known as

Cornerstone Pool became Cornerstone Aquatics Center after a major upgrading and expansion in 1992, its 30th anniversary.

Life on the Farm

Youngsters frolic in the hay at Westmoor Park, the 56-acre farm with house and barns given to the town in 1961 under the wills of Charles and Leila Clark Hunter. Two naturalists give agricultural and environmental programs among a multitude of activities. Farm residents include the two llamas at left.

Faenza's on Main, under proprietor Angelo Faenza it has become a favorite gathering spot for townspeople as well as golfers.

The community has benefited from gifts of land to our park system. The Beach family's Vine Hill Dairy farmland became Beachland Park in Elmwood. Michael Manternach gave five acres for a skating pond at Buena Vista. The Mooneys donated nine acres of woodland for Mooney's Woods off Mountain Road. The town acquired the land for Spicebush Swamp in 1962. The Wolcott family gave land that became Wolcott Park in 1972. In 1974, Charles and Leila Hunter bequeathed their house, barns, and 52 acres of land on Flagg Road to create the unique Westmoor Park, the latest in West Hartford's park network. At Westmoor, two naturalists teach more than 30,000 visitors a year about nature, the environment and agriculture. A demonstration barn with live animals, a greenhouse, gardens, and nature trails give urban youngsters a taste of the country and rural life.

The town's Leisure Services Department, formerly the Recreation Department, offers a smorgasbord of more than 1,100 instructional programs. Hundreds of volunteers help with these programs.

Under Ernest O. St. Jacques, who ran the Leisure Services Department from 1970 to 1988, and his successor, James Capodiece, maintenance of facilities has kept up with increasing use. The department has developed a separate Enterprise Fund, which diminishes reliance on the General Fund, and has also devised a method of user fees that eases the financial burden on the town, protecting the system from the possible ire of taxpayers and assuring its future.

In 1987, Town Clerk Nan L. Glass conceived the idea of a town-wide celebration called "Celebrate!West Hartford." Now an annual weekend event in early June, it features food, crafts, music, races and games and attracts more than 30,000 people. The town also has a special needs program for children and young adults with mental and physical handicaps through the Department of Leisure Services.

Town Leagues

West Hartford is known for its Boys Baseball League, a local takeoff on the national Little League program. Organized in 1949, the league gives boys aged 8 to 12 the chance to learn and play baseball. The first sponsors were the Civitan, Exchange, Kiwanis, and Lions service clubs, which in addition to financial support provided early leadership. From

Sporting Luminaries

West Hartford is home to – or was the springboard for – several notables in sports.

From the Hartford Golf Club, Henry Redfield was the National Left-Handed Champion at one time. Hazel Martelle Thibault and Dorothy Austin won several early state women's golf titles. Carol S. Patton and Lida Kinnicutt won many. Jim Healey won two state titles in the '50s. Frank Ross, longtime Wampanoag club champion, won two state titles. W.W. (Bill) Whedon, a Spring Lane resident who was Farmington Country Club champ, made two holes in one in a single round of the Insurance City Open, predecessor to the Greater Hartford Open.

Tennis star Shirley Fry Irvin moved here after winning a Wimbledon championship. Ex-Boston Celtics basketball star K.C. Jones moved here to coach basketball.

The town produced two U.S. Olympic competitors in the 1970s. After winning national championships, Karen Schuckman of Newport Avenue participated in gymnastics and Kent Weigle Jr. of John Smith Drive in ice skating.

Michael Burke, a Kingswood-Oxford athletic star, became president of Madison Square Garden in New York as well as of the New York Yankees and New York Knicks.

Peter Savin was owner of the Hartford Knights football team in the 1960s and Burton C. Hoffman was co-owner of the Hartford Capitols basketball team in the 1970s. Attorney Coleman B. Levy is co-owner of the New Britain Rock Cats baseball team today.

Preston Leete Smith, Joseph D. Sargent, Walter Morrison, and Joseph Van Vleck were instrumental in founding Killington, the East's largest ski area. Rod Taylor made a mark in ski racing and opened a ski area in Woodbury.

Daniel E. Doyle Jr., a former Board of Education member and Trinity College coach, became executive director of the Institute for International Sport he founded at the University of Rhode Island.

the original four teams the league has grown to sixteen. When the league was founded, it adopted the rules of the national Little League organization. It soon became apparent that the national rules were too restrictive with an emphasis on winning, so in 1954 the governing board decided to disaffiliate and operate independently. Ken Hungerford spearheaded the program over the years. At least one nationally known athlete, Matt Sinatro, was trained by the town's sports programs. He rose through the ranks of the Boys League to play major league baseball in the 1980s with the Oakland Athletics in the American League championship series against the Boston Red Sox. He later played with the Seattle Mariners and retired as their bullpen coach.

The Boys Baseball League became the model for other town leagues: basketball, soccer, softball, tennis, and hockey, among them. The town offers a teen drop-in center, nature and arts camps, theater and music programs, community gardens, and two senior centers. There are programs for adults as well as both boys and girls.

School Sports

West Hartford has played a leading role in interscholastic sports since 1926, when the Central

Connecticut Interscholastic League of six high schools was founded to compete in basketball, football, soccer, baseball, track, and tennis. Women's sports officially began in 1973 in the CCIL, since reorganized into the Central Connecticut Conference.

The athletic programs at Hall and Conard high schools have consistently ranked among the state's

Baseball's Heyday

The year 1959 was probably the only time everyone in town knew what was going on in the local baseball world.

Crowds gathered in ever-increasing numbers at Sterling Field to watch the Hayes-Velhage Post 96 American Legion baseball team win game after game. Coached by Clayton Johnson, the team – whose personnel came from the entire community, including the private schools – took the state championship and then the regional championship. Hundreds of well-wishers saw them off from Bradley Field for the Little League World Series in Hastings, Neb., where teams from Phoenix, Detroit and Hampton, Va., awaited them. They finished third, but there had never been a sports summer here like it.

Huge crowds followed the Legion team into the regionals the next two years, and Johnson took the team to the World Series in 1961 for the final time. The Legion team made one more trip to the nationals in 1973 under Bob O'Brien.

Hall-Conard Football: All in the Family

When the Hall and Conard high school football teams met in 2000 for the 43rd time, the opening ceremony at Robert S. Chalmers Stadium celebrated the traditional cross-town rivalry known as "The Game" as it entered the new millennium.

It was also a family, small-town affair.

"There's a deep-rooted traditional rivalry between family, friends, and neighbors that this game is a great reflection of," recalled Suzi D'Annolfo, former school athletic director and a member of the program committee. Her son Casey was senior quarterback for Conard during the game.

The ceremonial coin toss starting the game involved longtime coaches Robert McKee and Frank Robinson. McKee, who was football coach at Hall from 1951 to 1957, coached Conard from its opening in 1957 until 1983. Robinson replaced McKee at Hall and coached from 1957 to 1987. His son Frank III, who played quarterback for his father at Hall but came back to town as an assistant coach at Conard, is now Hall's head coach. Conard is under only its second coach, Rob Cersosimo, who played football for Hall under the senior Frank Robinson and married Coach McKee's daughter, Debbie.

The game's commemorative program traced the history of the rivalry from the first game in 1957, headlined "The Tradition Begins." It noted that Conard was the clear favorite, despite being the newer team. "In this initial game of a series that would be fought with pride and spirit over the years, the principal players could hardly think of their opponents as anything but friends. After all, the seniors had been together for two years at Hall, rooting for each other during that time. In a few short months, these friends were on the other side."

Conard won that first game. It also won the millennium game and leads the series, 27 to 14. Three ended in ties.

Conard High School swimmers made history when they competed against Glastonbury High in October 1973 at Cornerstone Pool. The meet was the first of its kind in West Hartford after equal opportunity for girls' sports was mandated by federal law.

Annual Mayor's Award went to Hall High after its football team went undefeated and won the CCIL championship in 1964. At awards ceremony are (from left) jeweler William Savitt, co-captain Kevin Devine, School Superintendent Charles O. Richter, Mayor Richard W. Sheehan, co-captain Kevin Coady, and Coach Frank Robinson.

Celebrate!West Hartford **159**

best. Thousands remember coach Robert McKee, who came to town in 1948 and coached football at both high schools. Frank D'Annolfo became the first coach to win state championships in two sports, soccer and hockey. His wife, Suzie D'Annolfo, in 1979 was the first female director of athletics for the school system. In 1994, she was inducted into the New England Women's Hall of Fame for her contributions to the development and growth of women in sports. Susan McAuliffe Curnias, the first women's gymnastics coach at Hall and first swim coach at Conard, won state championships in two sports and outstanding coach of the year awards in three: gymnastics, cross-country, and track and field. Dave Deacon of Hall was named national soccer coach of the year in 1985 and Jim Solomon of Hall, national tennis coach of the year in 2000. In the Hartford Courant's millennium list of the best high school coaches of the 20th century, Bob McKee of Conard and Frank Robinson of Hall were cited for their football successes. So were Dave Deacon for soccer, Jim Solomon for tennis, and George Beaudry of Conard for wrestling.

And the Best Athlete Is…A Girl

The town's greatest all-around athlete may well be Elizabeth Janangelo of Pebblebrook Drive. In 1997, she became the youngest winner of the Connecticut women's amateur golf title – at age 13, missing by only one year being the youngest state title winner anywhere. She won again in 1998, when she was the youngest ever to play two LPGA tournaments in the same year, and played in the U.S. Women's Open in 2000 – her older brother John was her caddie – before the start of her junior year at Conard High School.

A product of the town-owned Rockledge course, the world-ranked golfer is not a one-sport monolith. She began skiing at 2, won her first golf tourney at 6, and played basketball on the boys' travel team and the Conard junior varsity. At age 12, she led the West Hartford Boys Baseball League in home runs (five) as a pitcher and shortstop. She won two tennis titles and got seven shutouts as a Conard soccer goalie.

She also is a trumpet soloist who plays with the Conard band, jazz band, and orchestra. Says she: "I like playing the trumpet. It's different from sports, and you meet a different group of kids. You can't focus on just one thing."

Community Clubs

Countless other community groups provide social and philanthropic outlets. The Welcome Wagon Newcomers Club welcomed many a newcomer to town, and the Southern Club maintained ties for some. The West Hartford Women's Club celebrated its 50th anniversary in 1991. The Junior Woman's Club has been going strong for years, and the town has at least a dozen garden clubs. The majority of members and leaders of the Junior League of Hartford traditionally have come from West Hartford, and its office, thrift shop, and decorator showhouses are based here. The town has a full complement of service clubs, such as Rotary, Kiwanis, Exchange, Civitan, and Lions, as well

Retired But Not Resigned

In the early 1960s, Winfield I. McNeill retired as a New York executive and chose to relocate in West Hartford because of its many attractions, including the fact that his daughter and her family lived here. Making friends easily and immersing himself in community activities, he one day called on Orwell C. Tousley, then director of the West Hartford YMCA, which had long been known for its youth programs, including the highly popular Indian Guides and Indian Princesses programs. He proposed using the "Y" as a meeting place for an organization of retired men like one he had known in New Jersey.

Tousley liked the idea and McNeill rounded up 37 enthusiastic charter members on Feb. 1, 1966. By the end of that year, the Old Guard had 275 members, most of whom had been town residents for 30 years or more. A third were retirees from insurance companies. More than half had been in the same occupation all their working lives.

To this day, they gather every Tuesday morning to sing, tell "jokes," and hear a speaker. That's not their only purpose: they engage in many volunteer pursuits, such as the Visiting Nurse Association's Meals-on-Wheels, Red Cross Blood Banks, and Salvation Army toy deliveries. Today the Old Guard's membership is close to 400. So popular is the concept that two other clubs, the Regents and the Squires, were subsequently formed and meet in the same place. Their motto: "Retired But Not Resigned."

Women liked the idea, too. They formed the West Hartford Dames.

The old Hall High School auditorium is transformed into a ballroom for the West Hartford Senior Center's Thursday afternoon dances. Dancing is one of the center's more popular activities. The auditorium is now part of the West Hartford Meeting and Conference Center located in the Town Hall.

Singing at Hill-Stead Museum at Christmas 1999 are (from left) Maxine Charette, Julie Slimmon, Joan Warner, Betsy Russell, Lou Eldredge, Lois Grady, Jean McRae, Catherine Reynolds, Judy Kowalsky, and Sally Newell.

The Better Half Notes: Having Fun with Their Audiences

Since 1975 the Better Half Notes, an a capella singing group of West Hartford women, has been performing its light-hearted repertoire for area churches, women's and men's clubs, arts groups, schools, hospitals, and nursing homes. The group practices every Monday afternoon in each other's homes for nine months of the year, memorizing the words and music "so we can have fun with our audiences," according to Jean McRae, director since 1985. Performance times are in December and spring. "Nobody has any idea how many gigs the gals have worked," director McRae said.

Amy Jaffe Barzach (front right) takes a break with backers and users of Jonathan's Dream playground behind Jewish Community Center. Her vision launched a revolution in making playgrounds accessible across the country.

as the Jaycees. There are innumerable clubs and groups devoted to books, current events, gourmet food, card games, music, sports, spiritual life, and more throughout town. It is alleged that one socially minded group formed the IBBT Society, which meets for dinner and cards. The initials connote its main purpose: "in bed before ten."

Such is the attraction of West Hartford that many people tend to remain, even after retirement. Nearly one-third of the residents are over 60 years old. There are numerous convalescent homes and retirement communities like the McAuley, Chatfield, Hebrew Home for the Aged, and Hamilton Heights Place. The Brookview Health Care Facility and The Reservoirs on Farmington Avenue provide health services and rehabilitation. Two senior centers and three private clubs for retired men (and at least one for women) offer an active social life for older people.

Boundless Playgrounds

A year after her infant son's death in 1995 of spinal muscular atrophy, Amy Jaffe Barzach of Forest Hills Lane fulfilled a dream: to create a West Hartford playground that would allow children of all abilities to play together. The Jewish Community Center donated land for the playground behind the center. But little did Amy or her husband Peter realize that their Jonathan's Dream playground would lead to 18 such playgrounds throughout the country.

Amy Barzach now is executive director of Boundless Playgrounds, traveling around the country to provide technical assistance to groups wanting to set up their own playgrounds in the style of Jonathan's Dream. People magazine toured the playground for a story, and its founder was honored in Glamour magazine with a national award called "Women at Their Best."

Pleasant Pastimes

Townspeople enjoy three of the favorite recreational haunts in town. Above left, longtime golf pro Richard Crowe gives putting tips at Rockledge Country Club. At right, bicyclists enjoy a ride through the scenic Metropolitan District Reservoir property. Below, ducks are in the majority but geese get the goodies during family outing at Fernridge Park.

Main Street in Winter: Two Views

Cars are parked along Goodman Green in above view of South Main Street looking north toward Farmington Avenue in 1934. From left, landmarks old and new include Masonic Temple and spire of original First Baptist Church (left), old Town Hall and third meeting house of Congregational Church (left center), and West Hartford Trust Co. bank and fourth stone Congregational Church (right). Lower photo, taken earlier in the 20th century, shows pedestrians trudging out North Main Street through fresh snow in undeveloped area north of the Center.

Trolley jams like this one on Farmington Avenue in the 1920s became a thing of the past as the electric trolleys linking West Hartford and Hartford were discontinued in 1934 with the inauguration of bus service.

XIII. Remembering

For various reasons, a number of familiar town landmarks have disappeared. Another, a theater that might have been, never materialized.

Over the years, the town also has celebrated a number of traditions, ranging from the Memorial Day parades to the Labor Day Fair.

Congregational Church and Town Hall

Erected in 1834, the Third Congregational Meeting House at the northwest corner of Main Street and Farmington Avenue disappeared in March 1957. It took a crane four days to level the stately white structure with its four Greek columns on the porch.

After the Congregationalists moved kitty-corner across the intersection to a stone church on the southeast corner in 1882, the meeting house served as the Town Hall for 54 years. For a while it was occupied by the Boy Scouts and Junior Achievement, but in 1947, a new building code banned wooden buildings for public assembly. Its interior began to deteriorate, and the outside became a pigeon roost. It was finally condemned as unsafe. The site is now partially occupied by a small memorial green next to the former Senior Center.

Charter Oak Park

A race track was established in 1873 at Flatbush and Oakwood Avenues and put West Hartford on the Grand Circuit of harness racing until 1925. Indeed, the biggest entertainment events in town were the almost daily summer trotting races at Charter Oak Park, climaxing in Race Week starting Labor Day.

The track was the brainchild of Burdette A. Loomis, whose backers included Charles M. Pond and Gov. Morgan G. Bulkeley Sr., president of the National Trotting Association. At one time or another, all the leading harness horses and their drivers raced here. West Hartford was known as a "sporting town" in those days. There was heavy betting, and the normal wager of $100 occasionally mushroomed as high as $20,000 on a single race.

William B. Smith's Thomas Jefferson was foaled in 1863 on his early horse breeding farm next to the park. Known as "The Black Whirlwind of the East," he won 41 races during his long career, lived to age 29, and was buried in the infield of the still busy track.

When the state legislature passed an anti-betting law, the park lost its appeal to the gambling public and was eventually sold to the Connecticut Fair Association, which ran state fairs there for a period, reaching the height of popularity in the 1920s. To encourage trolley riding, Luna Park, an amusement park dubbed "West Hartford's Coney Island," was added to the grounds. Even the railroad made a stop near the entrance.

Ironically, a group of investors tried to save the park by bidding for bringing the Hambletonian to West Hartford, but lost by $101 to the town of Goshen, N.Y.

The park's final collapse was due in part to the rise

Ladies watch the menfolk watching something along carnival midway at Luna Park in the early 1900s.

Crowds gather for Sunday outings at Charter Oak Park in the 1920s.

Flyer in 1928 advertises Connecticut State Fair staged during Labor Day Week at Charter Oak Park.

of the Eastern States Exposition in West Springfield. The 112-acre property was foreclosed in 1930. Business leader Alfred E. Honce turned from servicing horses and carriages to dispensing gas at his Charter Oak filling station on the corner of Oakwood Avenue.

In the mid-1930s, the land was offered to the town for a park. After a long political wrangle, the town decided it didn't want it. The site was taken over by the Chandler-Evans Division of Pratt & Whitney in 1940 to meet defense needs in World War II. The colorful

Turreted gate marked entrance to Charter Oak Park.

turreted main entrance, the horse stables, the huge grandstand, and the fairgrounds were soon but memories.

The West Hartford Armory

From 1913 until 1940 the Armory on Farmington Avenue was the headquarters of Troop B Cavalry, formerly the Governor's Horse Guard. Its 100-man company included numerous young men who loved horses, camping, and military discipline. James L. Howard, later a Travelers vice president, was the first captain, Kelso Davis first lieutenant, and Morgan G. Bulkeley Jr., second lieutenant. Other familiar names in the unit were Rawdon W. Myers, Stillman F. Westbrook, Ralph D. Cutler, Roy D. Bassette, Houghton Bulkeley, C. Gilbert Shepard, and Frazar B. Wilde.

The Hartford Courant scoffed at the part-time troopers as "largely a social organization of gilded youths." Relying on members' own resources, mainly the largesse of Howard and former Governor Bulkeley, Troop B acquired the site in 1912 and after the Armory's completion stabled 20 horses there. Hopes for military glory rose when in June 1916, as part of the Connecticut National Guard, they were sent to Nogales, Ariz., to help General Pershing put down the revolt of the swashbuckling Pancho Villa. Instead of glory, they endured heat, boredom, and disease until their return with 87 horses and eight mules, without having fired a single shot. All National Guard units were drafted into the regular Army the following August. Several of its members – especially Bulkeley, Myers, and Westbrook – fought valiantly in France with a machine gun battalion.

In the early 1930s the Armory housed both Troops A and B. But cavalry as a fighting unit was on the verge of extinction, and to add insult to injury the Armory's neighbors complained loudly about the smell. In 1940 the troops were federalized as part of the 208th Coast Artillery AAA regiment. The stables were removed and the tanbark floor of the drill hall replaced with concrete for motorized vehicles.

After being declared surplus in the 1980s, the property was sold to Udolf Properties and renovated for professional office suites.

Hall Closing: 'Such Sweet Sorrow'

When the original Hall High School closed in May 1970, it was cause for an alumni reunion, special ceremonies, dances, and even a parade.

"Parting is such sweet sorrow," proclaimed the sign that welcomed alumni back for the closing weekend. From 1924 to 1957, Hall served as the town's sole high school, giving it a special place in townspeople's hearts.

Dr. Bernard Bailyn, a Hall graduate who had won a Pulitzer Prize for literature in 1968, delivered the major address at the closing ceremony. A parade of classes – some with floats – followed through West Hartford Center. There were two reunion dances. Classes from 1924 to 1954 danced to the music of the Bobby Kaye Orchestra at the West Hartford Armory, while graduates from 1955 to 1969 were entertained by the Legend in the Hall auditorium.

Dr. Robert E. Dunn served as principal from 1962 at the old Hall at 50 South Main St. and from 1970 to 1990 at the new Hall at 975 North Main St. He cited the 2,500 alumni who attended the closing events as a sign of the town's feelings about the old building. "There was a tremendous spirit that built over the years as shown by the very fact that thousands of people would return for that weekend," he said.

Frank Lloyd Wright's Theater

It would have been a distinctive landmark, one nationally hailed by the architectural and theater world, had Frank Lloyd Wright's experimental drama center-in-the-round been built. Wright's blend of contemporary and Grecian motifs would be, he claimed, "a sanctuary for emotion and aspiration." A Broadway producer, Paton Price, wanted to build it in Farmington. "Too far out," people said. Along came local architect James Thomson, who had studied under Wright and whose family owned a five-acre parcel at the northwest corner of Park Road and South Main Street. He offered the property to his mentor and Price. Then all hell broke loose.

Feisty old Col. Clarence C. Scarborough of Sedgwick Road called his neighbors together to form the Sedgwick Road Association and resist any commercial use of the corner. More than 600 people sardined into the Sedgwick School auditorium on April 24, 1950, for an acrimonious Town Plan & Zoning Commission hearing. Price's lawyer presented testimonials from such theatrical stars as Rex Harrison, Helen Hayes, Gregory Peck, and Katherine Cornell. The association's attorney, William Hoppin, denounced the proposal as being "with a veneer of culture spread upon it, a commercial enterprise" that would create "a whale of a traffic jam." At 2 a.m., friend and foe alike went home exhausted.

The battle went on the rest of the year, a seesaw affair involving the TPZ, the Town Council, and the courts. After a second hearing, the TPZ voted 3-2 for a zone change. Now the heat was on the council. More than 700 people jammed Hall High School for the final decision. Four councilmen were in favor but the required fifth vote failed to surface. Price's troops forced a referendum, but the Superior Court, questioning the legality of the town's zoning statutes, granted a temporary injunction. The delays were too much for Price. On Nov. 30, after visiting the great architect, who had even come to town to promote the cause, he admitted defeat.

The new theater went to Dallas, Tex. The corner in dispute became a regional office of the Southern New England Telephone Co.

Early Elmwood

Various approaches to Elmwood are evident in view of Quaker Lane South looking south toward Elmwood Center in 1926 (top), Quaker Lane South from farther north near Trout Brook bridge in 1926 (right), and New Britain Avenue from overpass at New Park Avenue, looking west toward center about 1920 (below).

Historic marker is dedicated in ceremony on Memorial Green in the Center. Among the participants in the 1970 event can be seen Marion H. Grant, Gordon Bennett, and Charles O. Richter.

St. Agnes Home

One of the oldest jokes about West Hartford was that more than 90 percent of the babies born here were illegitimate. That's because most offspring of West Hartford residents were born in hospitals in Hartford, and most of the town's recorded births were to unwed mothers at St. Agnes Home.

In 1914, the Sisters of Mercy built St. Agnes Home on 20 acres adjoining the farmland purchased from the Terry family for St. Mary Home for the aged. St. Agnes was designed to minister to unwed mothers and provide a loving environment for their children. There were sun parlors, roof gardens, and playgrounds. Many of the babies were placed for adoption soon after birth, mainly into Catholic homes; others remained for their first four years. The home also trained scores of children's nurses.

By the 1970s, as the demand for adoption of babies increased and fewer unwed mothers applied, the home's mission had become obsolete. The home moved to smaller quarters on Mayflower Street in Elmwood. In 1973, the four-story brick building on Steele Road was purchased by the town as headquarters for the Board of Education. After the school administration moved into the old Town Hall in 1987, the building was razed to make way for residential development.

The House Nobody Wanted

The Burdett Loomis-Wooley mansion on Prospect Avenue, built in 1874, was considered the town's outstanding Victorian house in the Italian villa style.

Almost a century later, the private Robinson School acquired the property from the estate of Mrs. Wooley for $101,500, but quickly decided the house had to come down. Headmaster John F. Robinson said it couldn't be used for classrooms without exorbitant renovations. "It reminds me of an old Saratoga hotel," he said, "with a hallway as wide as a driveway and ceilings twice as high." Led by local architects Tyler Smith and Jared I. Edwards, a group of preservationists formed to save the house. They lost the battle, but out of the effort emerged the Hartford Architecture Conservancy.

After demolition the school planned to build a one-story classroom behind the Enders home it owned on Highland Street and to landscape the Wooley property as a small park.

Robert Grant Irving, formerly of Wood Pond Road, an

More than 30,000 people lined North Main Street on Memorial Day in 1976 for the Bicentennial Parade, biggest in town history. Here, 3rd Connecticut Regiment Honor Corps fires a salute in front of the escort division led by Mayor Anne P. Streeter at Main and Farmington. After the march, crowds spread through the Center for Kickoff Party fun and festivities.

architectural historian, commented that the loss "spotlights the impending mutilation of the character of the Prospect Avenue neighborhood in much the same manner that Asylum Hill has been destroyed."

The Robinson School soon closed. The property is now owned by Kingswood-Oxford School.

Surviving Landmarks and Traditions

Historically, West Hartford has seized any excuse to get out its marching bands, wave flags, or just gather together to celebrate some event. During colonial times, corn-husking bees and barn-raisings were occasions for feasting and dancing. After the Revolution, the Fourth of July became the most popular time to make noise and be merry.

The festivities continued throughout the 20th century. In 1932, the bicentennial anniversary of George Washington's birth was celebrated here with a pageant and parade. Two years later, 20,000 people jammed the Center for a "Mardi Gras" to celebrate the widening and repairing of Farmington Avenue.

Every Memorial Day, a large number of town organizations – from school bands to Indian Guides – joined to honor the town's veterans with a parade through the Center.

There were an annual Labor Day Fair and an annual

Changes At the Noah Webster House

The deep red house that we know of today as the Noah Webster House and Museum of West Hartford History has undergone many changes over the years. The original four-room house in which Noah Webster was born in 1758 later received a rear lean-to addition and a side porch, as shown in the 1910 photo below. The house was donated to the town in 1962 by the Frederick Hamilton family and a museum wing was added in 1974. Participating in the ground-breaking for the museum wing (above) are (from left) Gordon Bennett, Norman G. Fricke, Mrs. Frederick Hamilton Sr., and Deputy Mayor Arthur E. Fay.

Homecoming Dance for college students at the Town Hall.

The town's annual weekend in June called Celebrate!West Hartford combines an amusement-park atmosphere with local entertainment, food, and an arts and crafts show around the Town Hall.

In 1976, the nation's Bicentennial inspired the biggest town-wide celebration ever. A Bicentennial Committee chaired by Richard M. Woodworth, with Elaine and Jerome Lowengard as co-chairmen, involved hundreds of residents in the planning of activities culminating in six weeks of celebration coordinated by executive director Madeline S. McKernan. Fund-raisers included the minting of Bicentennial coins and Patriot Dinners, which drew more than 1,000 people to private homes for colonial meals. An expanded Memorial Day parade and kickoff party launching the official celebration drew more than 30,000 people along the Main Street parade route from Bishops Corner to the Center, followed by an afternoon and evening of festivities around the Center. Bicentennial highlights included an elaborate Day of Living History at the St. Joseph College campus, guided Walk Through History tours of West Hartford, a Hartford Symphony pops concert, and a costumed Bicentennial Ball with the Lester Lanin orchestra at the West Hartford Armory. The grand finale was a July 4th fireworks exhibition that drew more than 50,000 to Rockledge Country Club. The fireworks company failed to produce, however, and the mighty celebration ended not with a bang but a whimper.

The Noah Webster House

Every morning on his way to work as president of the Whitlock Manufacturing Co., Gordon Bennett used to pass an old, dilapidated house on South Main Street. When finally it caught his attention, he learned that it was the birthplace of Noah Webster and for a long time had been occupied by the Hamilton family.

Realizing it was the town's most notable historic house, he approached Frederick Hamilton, who occupied a larger house on the property. He persuaded the Hamilton family to donate the landmark in front of their home to the town in 1962.

The four-room structure, built in the mid-18th century with an addition in 1787, was restored by a group of citizens who formed the Noah Webster Foundation. The town leased the property to the foundation, and the house was opened to the public in 1968. In 1970, the foundation and the Historical Society of West Hartford merged.

The house is furnished as it might have appeared in 1774, the year Noah departed for Yale College. The furnishings include a desk, two clocks, and 200 pieces of china and glassware – all owned by Webster and his wife Rebecca. In 1974, a museum wing was added behind the house.

For a number of years, the house and grounds were the site in September for the annual Noah Webster birthday party, a festive occasion that drew several thousand people for colonial crafts demonstrations, games, booths, fire truck rides, a book fair, and a spelling bee.

Sarah Whitman Hooker House

The 1976 Bicentennial year sparked the painstaking restoration of the Sarah Whitman Hooker House at 1237 New Britain Ave. The property was donated by restaurateur Brock Saxe to the town. Frances Fransson of Dodge Drive and members of the Sarah Whitman Hooker Chapter, Daughters of the American Revolution, created a foundation to undertake its renovation and reopening. The 1726 mansion house, remodeled in 1806, retains original materials to illustrate two periods of early local architecture. Details of the original construction and decoration can be viewed. It is open for special events.

Celebrations Past and Present

West Hartford's finest march north along South Main Street in annual Memorial Day parade, circa 1930. Here they pass the fourth Congregational meeting house as they near Farmington Avenue.

West Hartford Historical Society Photo

Annual Memorial Day parade has grown, as evidenced by crowds on South Main Street (right), looking north across Farmington Avenue. Daisy Troop 470 is one of scores of local youth and adult organizations that participate. Some of the biggest crowds are those at the annual Celebrate! West Hartford events farther down South Main Street (below).

Town of West Hartford Photos

West Hartford's "skyline" consists of familiar landmarks and an abundance of trees. This view, taken in the 1980s, looks west toward the Center from the roof of Hamilton Heights Place, formerly Mount St. Joseph Academy. Discernible in the Center are the steeple of First Church of Christ, Congregational (behind the Hampshire House condominiums), the Education Center and Town Hall (old Hall High School), and the Farmington Avenue shopping area (right center). Along the mountain are the Buena Vista residential neighborhood and the UConn Health Center at far upper left.

XIV. A Wonderful Town

Today, more people in the nation live in suburbs than in cities or rural areas. Some social scientists and historians find this disturbing and even unhealthy.

For instance, the producers of the documentary film "Between Boston and New York" in 1992 painted a picture of Connecticut as a small state "largely lacking a sense of identity or community, fragmented into regions, isolated in small towns, divided into ethnic and social enclaves, reluctant to confront the enormous demographic changes that have transformed it in the last century."

Does this description fit West Hartford, one of the largest and richest suburbs in the country's wealthiest state? Are we a distinct community with a particular identity? Can we remain independent?

These questions are difficult to answer, but undoubtedly they will be asked again and again at the start of the 21st century. Like the other 168 towns in Connecticut, West Hartford is fiercely proud of its autonomy under the Home Rule Act that gives its officials control over such important matters as education, zoning, and municipal services.

Recent decades have seen a significant change in our population makeup. The percentage of minorities has increased. West Hartford is now home to recent immigrants from Europe, Asia, and Central and South America.

As older residents sell their homes and move into retirement homes or relocate to warmer climates, younger families with children move in. The mix of elderly and young has created a need for a variety of services.

For the older group there are the Dial-A-Ride bus, Meals On Wheels, and the Seniors Job Bank. For former servicemen the Hayes-Velhage American Legion Post and the Hannon-Hatch Veterans of Foreign Wars Post provide havens.

For young people, besides the Leisure Services programs in the schools and parks, there are Hope Works Inc. (formerly the Street Ministry of West

Hartford), a counseling and crisis intervention service, and the Bridge Family Center, which began in 1977 as an informal teen drop-in center and evolved into a multi-service agency counseling youths and families.

One obstacle for newcomers has been a scarcity of affordable housing. The West Hartford Housing Authority, formed in 1942 but now a separate agency of the town, operates 140 units of public housing and a federal rental subsidy program for 575 families. Other housing is provided privately by Fellowship Housing, Federation Square, the Christian Activities Council, and the West Hartford Interfaith Coalition.

The town budget seems inevitably to increase 2 to 3 percent every year in keeping with inflation. The 1999-2000 budget called for total expenditures of nearly $138 million – 86.5 percent of which was raised by property taxes. Of the expenditures, 56 percent went to finance education, 15 percent to public safety, and 12 percent to community maintenance. The remainder covered debt and sundry, general government, and human and cultural services.

As real-estate sales revived at the turn of the 21st century, school enrollment rose, too. Both King Philip and Sedgwick middle schools have about a thousand students, an increase of 500 in the previous five years. A flood of new enrollments in the eleven elementary schools has resulted in reopening some that had been mothballed, and our two high schools have been extensively renovated to meet contemporary needs.

Recycling of bottles, cans, papers, and magazines became state law in 1991, but West Hartford had long before been a model community in curbside refuse collection and street cleaning. How many other towns provide leaf collection in the fall and sweep the streets of winter's sand in the spring? Although old-timers may regret the discontinuance of the town scooters that used to roll into their backyards and empty the garbage cans, residents have become accustomed to the trucks of the private collector and the blue container for recylables.

Annually, the town surveys residents on their feelings about municipal services and budget priorities. Some highlights that are mentioned year after year:

• Public safety (fire and police) rank as the most important services.

• Residents are overwhelmingly satisfied with municipal services.

• "Feeling safe" was considered "the most important factor in determining happiness with a neighborhood."

• Speeding was cited as the number one traffic concern, though 77 percent rated traffic safety as good or better.

• Refuse collection was given high marks.

Another survey conducted by Spectrum Associates in 1997 for the town sheds light on why residents move. Those who move within West Hartford bought new residences because they wanted to change from renting to owning, or they wanted a bigger, better or different-style home. Their main reasons for staying were (a) convenient location, (b) their roots are here, and (c) the quality of the public school system. Those moving into West Hartford chose the town because of (a) its accessibility and proximity to work, (b) the schools, (c) its appearance, (d) safety and low crime, (e) town services, and (f) real-estate values. A small number of those surveyed moved out to other area towns mainly due to a change in their housing needs.

At the start of the new millennium, according to Ronald F. Van Winkle, the town's director of community services, "we are rebuilding our demographic base with new and younger families that will help sustain our population at or near the 60,000 range, a well-educated and prosperous community that will lead the Hartford area in adjusting to significant work-life and home-life changes."

One new development is the increase in computer-driven, home-based enterprises, which the Chamber of Commerce estimates to number about 2,000. A survey showed that well over half of our residents own a computer and have access to the Internet. However, since the town is fully developed, with little vacant land (an average of only 20 homes are built annually), it is unlikely there will be much further growth.

More than 150 years ago, when West Hartford was still a parish belonging to Hartford, the author of *Democracy in America*, Alexis deTocqueville, visited Connecticut and became convinced that the township was fundamental to cultivating democracy, as he said "the life and mainspring of American liberty." It still is.

So let us continue to Celebrate West Hartford!

Town Milestones: A Chronology

1854 – West Hartford incorporated as a town.

1855 – St. James's Episcopal Church dedicated.

1858 – Joseph Bishop's tobacco packing business begins.

1859 – First Baptist Church dedicated.
Selden Hill area annexed from Farmington.

1863 – Town purchases Congregational Church vestry for Town Hall.

1866 – Wyllys Masonic Lodge chartered.

1867 – MDC Reservoir No. 1 opens.
Second Goodwin Pottery, destroyed by fire, rebuilt as three-story pottery.

1872 – New Center School opens at 14 North Main St., with first high school on second floor.

1873 – Charter Oak Park and race track established.

1876 – Elmwood Chapel erected.

1877 – West Hartford district schools consolidated.

1878 – Village Improvement Society organized.

1879 – Trout Brook Ice & Feed Co. started by Edwin H. Arnold.
West Hartford Hose Company organized as first independent fire company..

1881 – Cornelius Vanderbilt builds 27-room mansion on West Hill.

1882 – Free public library opens.
Fourth meeting house of First Congregational Church dedicated.
Third meeting house becomes Town Hall.

1887 – West Hartford Grange organized.

1888 – First Elmwood School opens; addition in 1900.

1889 – Hartford & Wethersfield Horse Railway line extended from Prospect Avenue to Center.

1890 – Beginning of improved roads.

1891 – Whitlock Coil Pipe Co., first large industry, founded.

1893 – Fairview Cemetery established.

1894 – Electric trolley line extended through Center to Unionville.

1895 – Residential development of Buena Vista starts.
East Siders thwarted in attempt to secede from West Hartford.
Center School opens at Memorial and Raymond roads.

1896 – Hartford Golf Club organized in West Hartford.
St. Mary Home opened by Sisters of Mercy.

1897 – Elizabeth Park opens.
Noah Webster Memorial Library founded.

1898 – Myron J. Burnham's grocery store established.

1899 – Allen B. Judd opens first drug store.

1901 – Elmwood branch library opens.

1903 – First municipal rose garden opens in Elizabeth Park.

1906 – Sarah Whitman Hooker Chapter, Daughters of the American Revolution, organized.
Luna amusement park opens as part of Charter Oak Park.

1907 – St. John's Episcopal Church moves to Farmington Avenue.

1908 – West Hartford Businessmen's Association organizes, becoming West Hartford Chamber of Commerce in 1919.

1909 – Mount St. Joseph Academy moves to Hamilton Heights.
East Side Fire District organized.

1910 – Whitman School built.

1911 – Boy Scout Troop 12 organized by First Congregational Church.

1912 – Abbott Ball Co. moves to former Goodwin Pottery site.

1913 – West Hartford Memorial Day Association formed.

1914 – New Departure Co. established.
St. Agnes Home for unwed mothers opens.
Center Fire District organized.

1915 – Quaker Hose Company organized.
Seymour School opens, renamed Smith School in 1946.

1917 – Noah Webster Memorial Library at 10 North Main St. dedicated.

1918 – St. Brigid's chapel opens, first Catholic church in town.

1919 – Town adopts first council-manager form of government in state.
First Police Department organized.
Elmwood Fire District organized.
Oxford School for girls moves to West Hartford.
Spencer Turbine Co. moves to New Park Avenue.

1920 – St. Thomas the Apostle parish organized.
1921 – Swedish Methodist Church erected on Lockwood Terrace.

Hayes-Velhage Post, American Legion, organized.

1922 – Plant and Talcott junior high schools open.

Kingswood School moves to Outlook Avenue.

American School for the Deaf moves to North Main Street.

1924 – William H. Hall High School opens at 50 South Main St.

Wampanoag Country Club founded.

1925 – Brace Road Firehouse erected.
1926 – West Hartford Trust Co., first bank, opens.

St. Thomas the Apostle Church erected on Farmington Avenue.

Beach Park School opens.

Morley School opens.

1927 – Elmwood Community Church dedicated.

Masonic Temple on South Main Street dedicated.

1928 – New Elmwood School opens.
1929 – Wiremold Company moves to Woodlawn Street.
1930 – Charter Oak School opens.

Sage-Allen & Co. store opens in Center.

1931 – Sedgwick School opens.

Metropolitan Shopping News, predecessor of West Hartford News, begins publication.

Universalist Church of West Hartford opens.

Fernridge Park, town's first park, opens.

1932 – Beachland Park opens.
1935 – Junior School, predecessor of Renbrook School, founded.
1936 – New Town Hall opens on South Main Street.

St. Joseph College established on Asylum Avenue.

Holo-Krome builds factory on Newington Road.

Temple Beth Israel moves to Farmington Avenue.

First Baptist Church moves to 90 North Main St.

1937 – West Hartford fire companies consolidated.
1938 – Noah Webster Memorial Library moves to 20 South Main St.

1939 – Recreation Commission establishes town Recreation Department.

Hartford College for Women opens on Highland Street.

West Hartford Art League founded.

1940 – Pratt & Whitney Machine Tool builds plant in old Charter Oak Park.
1941 – Jacobs Manufacturing Co. opens on Newington Road.
1942 – St. Mark the Evangelist parish established.

Labor Day Fair tradition starts.

1943 – Bethany Lutheran Church organized.

Town opens Buena Vista golf course.

Sterling Field opens.

1946 – West Hartford Branch of University of Connecticut opens.
1947 – Dunham-Bush Co. opens on South Street.

West Hartford News evolves out of Metropolitan Shopping News.

Fifth meeting house of First Congregational Church dedicated following 1942 fire.

1948 – Robinson School opens on Highland Street.
1949 – Webster Hill School opens.

Woman's Exchange moves to West Hartford Center.

1950 – Westminster Presbyterian Church established.

Religious Society of Friends dedicates new meeting house.

1951 – Bugbee School opens.

St. Brigid Church dedicated.

1952 – Duffy School opens.
1953 – West Hartford Historical Society founded.

Congregation Beth-El organized.

Mooney's Woods given to town.

1954 – Town celebrates Centennial.

Whiting Lane School opens.

New Faxon branch library opens.

Lord & Taylor and other New York branch stores open at Bishops Corner.

Beth David Synagogue dedicated.

1955 – King Philip School opens.
1956 – Braeburn School opens.

Emanuel Synagogue builds auditorium and school on Mohegan Drive.

1957 – Conard High School opens.

Wolcott School opens.

Children's Museum of Hartford moves to Trout Brook Drive.

Junior School moves to Rentschler estate, renamed Renbrook School.

University of Hartford chartered in West Hartford.

Bethany Lutheran Church dedicated.

Jehovah's Witnesses build Kingdom Hall.

1958 – St. Timothy parish established.

1959 – Bridlepath School opens.

West Hartford School of Music opens.

Farmington Avenue Baptist Church organized.

1960 – Covenant Congregational Church dedicated.

West Hartford Senior Center opens.

1961 – Town acquires Rockledge Country Club.

Northwest Catholic High School opens.

1962 – Corbins Corner Shopping Parkade opens.

Jewish Community Center opens on Bloomfield Avenue.

St. James's Episcopal Church dedicates new church on Farmington Avenue.

1963 – Temple Beth El dedicated.

Holy Family Monastery opens.

1964 – Aiken School opens.

1965 – Kennedy Park opens.

1966 – Bishops Corner branch library opens.

St. Peter Claver parish established.

St. Helena parish established.

Board of Education starts accepting Hartford students under Project Concern.

Old Guard, first retired men's organization, established.

1967 – Auto Club of Hartford moves to Farmington Avenue headquarters.

1969 – East-West Highway (Interstate 84) completed through West Hartford.

Eisenhower Park opens.

1970 – New Hall High School opens; old Hall closed.

Center School/Rutherford Building closed as school, used temporarily for town offices.

1971 – West Hartford Housing Authority dedicates Starkel Road, first elderly housing project.

West Hartford United Methodist Church dedicated.

Emanuel Synagogue sanctuary dedicated.

Solomon Schechter Day School opens in basement of Emanuel Synagogue.

1972 – Culbro creates industrial park off Oakwood Avenue.

Wolcott Park opens.

1973 – West Hartford Street Ministry (Hope Works Inc.) founded.

Piper Brook urban renewal project completed.

Board of Education renovates former St. Agnes Home as Education Center.

East School closed as school administration offices.

Beach Park School is first school to be closed.

1974 – Westfarms Mall opens.

Westmoor Park opens.

Whitman School closes; renovated into Police-Court Facility.

1976 – Elmwood School closes.

Aiken School closes.

West Hartford Art League opens Salt Box Gallery.

Sarah Whitman Hooker House restoration begins.

1977 – Bridge Family Center begins as teen-age drop-in center.

1978 – WHC-TV begins community access television programming.

Mount St. Joseph Academy closes; converted in 1980 into training center for Hartford Insurance Group.

1979 – Elmwood Community Center opens in former Elmwood School.

Town opens Elmgrove Apartments.

Town establishes first historic district along Buena Vista Road.

Bridlepath School closes.

Plant Junior High School closes.

Talcott Junior High School closes.

King Philip Elementary School closes.

1980 – Smith School closes.

1981 – Town joins Metropolitan District Commission.

1983 – Coleco Industries renovates Talcott Junior High School for administrative headquarters.

1984 – McAuley retirement community opens on Steele Road.

Solomon Schechter Day School moves into old Bridlepath School.

Shoppers, pedestrians, and restaurant patrons along Farmington Avenue enjoy today's West Hartford Center street scene.

1986 – Town opens Alfred E. Plant Senior Housing in old Plant Junior High School.

1987 – New Town Hall opens in old Hall High School. Education Center moves to old Town Hall. Noah Webster Memorial Library renovated and expanded.

1989 – Developer Seymour Sard completes Town Centre, largest retail-office complex and parking garage.

1990 – Sedgwick School expands with new addition; Sedgwick and King Philip become middle schools. Aiken School reopens.

1991 – Cornerstone Pool renovated and expanded, becomes Cornerstone Aquatics Center.

1995 – St. John's Episcopal Church rebuilt following 1992 fire.

1996 – Smith School reopens as magnet school. Pratt & Whitney Machine Tool plant is razed for Home Depot and BJ's Warehouse.

Intensive Education Academy opens in former United Synagogues of Great Hartford facility.

Jonathan's Dream playground opens behind Jewish Community Center.

1997 – The Foundation for West Hartford Public Schools established.

West Hartford Life begins monthly publication.

1998 – United Synagogues of Greater Hartford, organized in early 1960s, moves into house at 205 Mohawk Drive.

Hamilton Heights converted into assisted-living facility.

1999 – St. Joseph College renovates Beach Park School for its School for Young Children.

2000 – Veterans Memorial Rink renovated and expanded.

2001 – Park Road Playhouse opens.

2004 – Town marks Sesquicentennial.

Index

184 Index

Acknowledgements

The authors are deeply indebted to a number of public-spirited citizens who contributed ideas and material for this book, but particularly we wish to thank the following:

Margot Allison
Janet Baillit
Gordon Bennett
Dorothy Billington
Robert R. Bouvier
Eleanor Caplan
Timothy Confessore
Heather Congdon

Barbara Cornelius
Sheila Daley
John E. Davison
Robert E. Dunn
Barry M. Feldman
Muriel K. Fleischmann
Linda I. French
William C. French
Ethel Fried
Nan L. Glass
Patricia George
Richard L. Hughes III
Arthur J. Kiely Jr.
Thomas Kilfoil
Elaine King
Ilze Krisst

Christopher Larsen
Carol Lennig
Marsha Lotstein
Richard L. Mahoney
Janice Mathews
Robert McKee
Jean McRae
Madeline S. McKernan
Freeman W. Meyer
Elizabeth Miller
Catherine C. Reynolds
Martha Ritter
Connie Robinson
Edmund T. Smith
Ronald F. Van Winkle
Joseph Waggoner

Special thanks go to Renée B. McCue, public relations specialist for the Town of West Hartford, whose reporting and fact-checking were invaluable.

Special mention, too, is due to the staff of the West Hartford libraries. Their archives of newspaper articles on West Hartford provided considerable information.

Front Endpaper: View of West Hartford looking east-northeast in the 1920s over Hall High School, showing South Main Street, Burr Street, Raymond Road, and several large expanses of new suburban housing on both sides of Farmington Avenue. Landmark at upper center is Hamilton Heights (Mount St. Joseph Academy). Town of West Hartford Photo

Back Endpaper: View of West Hartford looking north-northwest in 2000 over municipal complex, Goodman Green, and West Hartford Center business district. Intersection of Trout Brook Drive and the Boulevard is at lower right. Air Marketing International Ltd. Photo